MULTICULTURAL EDUCATION SERIES

James A. Banks, Series Editor

continued

FACING ACCOUNTABILITY IN EDUCATION

Democracy and Equity at Risk

Christine E. Sleeter

Editor

Teachers College, Columbia University
New York and London

Published by Teachers College Press, 1234 Amsterdam Avenue, New York, NY 10027

Library of Congress Cataloging-in-Publication Data

Facing accountability in education: democracy and equity at risk / edited by Christine E. Sleeter
    p. cm. — (Multicultural education series)
Includes bibliographical references and index.
ISBN-13: 978-0-8077-4780-3 (hardcover)
ISBN-10: 0-8077-4780-7 (hardcover)
ISBN-13: 978-0-8077-4779-7 (pbk.)
ISBN-10: 0-8077-4779-3 (pbk.)
1. Multicultural education—United States. 2. Educational accountability—United States. 3. Educational equalization—United States. I. Sleeter, Christine E., 1948–
LC1099.3.F33 2007
379.1'58—dc22   2007000216
ISBN 13: 978-0-8077-4779-7 (paper)
ISBN 13: 978-0-8077-4780-3 (cloth)

Printed on acid-free paper
Manufactured in the United States of America
14 13 12 11 10 09 08 07   8 7 6 5 4 3 2 1

Contents

Series Foreword

The nation's deepening ethnic texture, interracial tension and conflict, and the increasing percentage of students who speak a first language other than English make multicultural education imperative in the 21st century. The U. S. Census (2000) estimates that people of color made up 28% of the nation's population in 2000 and predicts that they will make up 38% in 2025 and 50% in 2050 (El Nasser, 2004).

American classrooms are experiencing the largest influx of immigrant students since the beginning of the 20th century. About a million immigrants are making the United States their home each year (Martin & Midgley, 1999). Almost four million (3,780,019) legal immigrants settled in the United States between 2000 and 2004. Only 15% came from nations in Europe. Most (66%) came from nations in Asia, from Mexico, and from nations in Latin America, Central America, and the Caribbean (U. S. Department of Homeland Security, 2004). A large but undetermined number of undocumented immigrants also enter the United States each year. The influence of an increasingly ethnically diverse population on U. S. schools, colleges, and universities is and will continue to be enormous.

Schools in the United States are characterized by rich ethnic, cultural, and language diversity. United States schools are more diverse today than they have been since the early 1900s when a flood of immigrants entered the United States from Southern, Central, and Eastern Europe. In the thirty-year period between 1973 and 2004, the percentage of students of color in U. S. public schools increased from 22 to 43%. If current trends continue, students of color might equal or exceed the percentage of White students in U. S. public schools within one or two decades. Students of color already exceed the number of White students in six states: California, Hawaii, Louisiana, Mississippi, New Mexico, and Texas (Dillon, 2006).

Language and religious diversity is also increasing among the U. S. student population. In 2000, about 20% of the school-age population spoke a language at home other than English (U. S. Census Bureau, 2000). Harvard professor Diana L. Eck (2001) calls the United States the "most religiously diverse nation on earth" (p. 4). Islam is now the fastest-growing religion in the U. S. as well as in several European nations such as France and the United

Kingdom (Cesari, 2004). Most teachers now in the classroom and in teacher education programs are likely to have students from diverse ethnic, racial, language, and religious groups in their classrooms during their careers. This is true for both inner-city and suburban teachers.

An important goal of multicultural education is to improve race relations and to help all students acquire the knowledge, attitudes, and skills needed to participate in cross-cultural interactions and in personal, social, and civic action that will help make our nation more democratic and just. Multicultural education is consequently as important for middle-class White suburban students as it is for students of color who live in the inner-city. Multicultural education fosters the public good and the overarching goals of the commonwealth.

The major purpose of the *Multicultural Education Series* is to provide preservice educators, practicing educators, graduate students, scholars, and policy makers with an interrelated and comprehensive set of books that summarizes and analyzes important research, theory, and practice related to the education of ethnic, racial, cultural, and language groups in the United States and the education of mainstream students about diversity. The books in the *Series* provide research, theoretical, and practical knowledge about the behaviors and learning characteristics of students of color, language minority students, and low-income students. They also provide knowledge about ways to improve academic achievement and race relations in educational settings.

The definition of multicultural education in the *Handbook of Research on Multicultural Education* (Banks & Banks, 2004) is used in the *Series*: Multicultural education is "*a field of study designed to increase educational equity for all students that incorporates, for this purpose, content, concepts, principles, theories, and paradigms from history, the social and behavioral sciences, and particularly from ethnic studies and women's studies*" (p. xii). In the *Series,* as in the *Handbook,* multicultural education is considered a "metadiscipline."

The dimensions of multicultural education, developed by Banks (2004b) and described in the *Handbook of Research on Multicultural Education,* provide the conceptual framework for the development of the publications in the *Series.* They are: *content integration, the knowledge construction process, prejudice reduction, an equity pedagogy,* and *an empowering school culture and social structure.* To implement multicultural education effectively, teachers and administrators must attend to each of the five dimensions of multicultural education. They should use content from diverse groups when teaching concepts and skills, help students to understand how knowledge in the various disciplines is constructed, help students to develop positive intergroup attitudes and behaviors, and modify their teaching strategies so that students from different racial, cultural, language, and social-class groups will experience equal educational opportunities. The total environment and culture of the school must also be transformed so that students from diverse groups will experience equal status in the culture and life of the school.

Although the five dimensions of multicultural education are highly interrelated, each requires deliberate attention and focus. Each publication in the series focuses on one or more of the dimensions, although each book deals with all of them to some extent because of the highly interrelated characteristics of the dimensions.

Democracy in nations around the world is threatened by many factors today, including the threat of terrorism, fear, and the widening gap between the rich and the poor. After it invaded Iraq, the United States lost much moral authority in nations around the world. The loss of moral authority has problematized the United States' role as a leader of Western democratic nations.

Democracy and cultural freedom are threatened in U. S. schools as well as in schools around the world. The movement for standards and accountability is one of the most pernicious forces eroding democracy in schools. Since the civil rights movement of the 1960s and 1970s U. S. schools had made significant progress in reforming the curriculum so that it was more inclusive of the cultures and histories of the diverse ethnic and cultural groups in the nation. Schools were being reformed so that they would provide civic equality, recognition (Gutmann, 2004) and cultural democracy (Ramírez & Castañeda, 1974) for diverse groups. As the chapters in this informative and engaging book document, reforming schools so that they reflect cultural democracy and cultural freedom has become more difficult since the rise of the standardization movement and the passage of the No Child Left Behind Act in 2001.

The genesis of this book was a presidential session at the annual conference of the American Educational Research Association (AERA) in 2005 in Montreal when Marilyn Cochran-Smith was president of AERA. The session, which I organized and chaired, focused on "Educating for Democracy and Diversity in an Era of Accountability." Christine E. Sleeter, who gave one of the papers in the session, thought that it would be a good idea if the papers presented in the session were revised and published in book form. This important book is the result of her hard work and commitment to social justice and democracy in schools. To expand the focus on this book, Sleeter invited a number of scholars to contribute to it who did not present at the AERA session. Two of the authors who presented in the session were unable to prepare chapters for this publication.

This book contains incisive and informative essays that present a range of thoughtful perspectives about how schools can navigate the difficult terrain of helping students to succeed in schools and society as they are currently structured and yet develop the knowledge, skills, and commitment to act to make the U. S. and the world more democratic and just communities. Democracies are fragile and rather recent inventions in human history (Dahl, 2000). The public schools are essential for democracy to survive because democrats are made and are not born (Parker, 2003). This significant and timely book contains important insights that can help educators to strengthen democracy in schools and society at a time when it is imperiled around the world.

—*James A. Banks*

REFERENCES

Banks, J. A. (2004a). Introduction: Democratic citizenship education. In J. A. Banks (Ed.), *Diversity and citizenship education: Global perspectives* (pp. 3–15). San Francisco: Jossey-Bass.

Banks, J. A. (2004b). Multicultural education: Historical development, dimensions, and practice. In J. A. Banks & C. A. M. Banks (Eds.), *Handbook of research on multicultural education* (2nd ed., pp. 3–29). San Francisco: Jossey-Bass.

Banks, J. A. , & Banks, C. A. M. (Eds.) (2004). *Handbook of research on multicultural education* (2nd ed.). San Francisco: Jossey-Bass.

Cesari, J. (2004). *When Islam and democracy meet: Muslims in Europe and the United States.* New York: Pelgrave Macmillan.

Dahl, R. A. (2000). *On democracy.* New Haven: Yale University Press.

Dillon, S. (2006, August 27). In schools across U. S., the melting pot overflows. *The New York Times*, vol. CLV [155] (no. 53,684), pp. A7 & 16.

Eck, D. L. (2001). *A new religious America: How a "Christian country" has become the world's most religiously diverse nation.* New York: HarperSanFrancisco.

Gutmann, A. (2004). Unity and diversity in democratic multicultural education: Creative and destructive tensions. In J. A. Banks (Ed.), *Diversity and citizenship education: Global perspectives* (pp. 71–96). San Francisco: Jossey-Bass.

Martin, P., & Midgley, E. (1999). Immigration to the United States. *Population Bulletin, 54* (2), pp. 1–44. Washington, D.C.: Population Reference Bureau.

Parker, W. C. (2003). *Teaching democracy: Unity and diversity in public life.* New York: Teachers College Press.

Ramírez, M., & Castañeda, A. (1974). *Cultural democracy, bicognitive development, and education.* New York: Academic Press.

United States Census Bureau (2000). *Statistical abstract of the United States* (120th ed.). Washington, D. C.: U. S. Government Printing Office.

United States Department of Homeland Security (2004). *Yearbook of immigration statistics, 2004.* Washington, DC: Office of Immigration Statistics, Author. Retrieved September 6, 2006 from www.uscis.gov/graphics/shared/statistics/yearbook/Yearbook2004.pdf

INTRODUCTION

Democracy, Equity, and Accountability

Christine E. Sleeter

California State University Monterey Bay

School reform movements, as products of their political and cultural contexts, have vacillated between emphasizing "excellence" and "equity." As Tyack and Cuban (1995) pointed out, historically reform movements have shifted "from excellence to equality, efficiency to empathy, unity to pluralism—and then back again." They have also reflected broader political pressures that shape contours of school reform movements: "Conservative political climates favored a rhetoric of competition and quality, while liberal eras such as the 1930s and 1960s stressed an ideology of access and equality" (pp. 44–45).

At the same time, there have always been education leaders who maintain that excellence and equity cannot be advanced as competing goals. Fantini (1986), for example, argued passionately that, "Quality in the public schools is achieved when *all learners succeed*, not only those considered most able" (p. 50, emphasis in original). In his view, any school reform that promotes excellence, at the expense of students for whom too little routinely had been expected, is not excellent. Further, he maintained that excellent education for everyone in diverse and democratic societies requires changing how the institution of education works, rather than remediating students to fit the institution.

The current accountability reform movement claims commitment to both goals. Its genesis in the United States is often traced to publication of *A Nation at Risk* in 1983 (National Commission on Excellence in Education), which launched a round of highly visible national discussions that framed the main purpose of schools as regaining U.S. economic competitive advantage internationally. Many reports published during the 1980s argued that U.S. students are increasingly failing to learn the skills and knowledge the United States needs for economic competition, and expressed concerns of the business community: that technological advances and global restructuring were transforming the nature of production and work, and that the United States would need to develop many, many more workers for demands of this new economy. Education standards would need to be raised.

Concurrently, a barrage of highly visible conservative critiques of multiculturalism charged curricular changes and policies that had been instituted in schools and universities as damaging education standards and social cohesion (e.g., Bloom, 1989; Ravitch, 1990; Schlesinger, 1991). They cast multiculturalists as fringe radicals who were undermining fundamental American political and cultural ideals by appealing to the divisiveness of ethnic cheerleading, and argued that multicultural curricula were intellectually weak, damaging minority student achievement by appealing mainly to self-esteem rather than hard work and academic challenge.

In response to the reform reports, in the 1980s states began to construct disciplinary content standards and testing programs, and for a time there were also efforts to establish national curriculum content standards and tests. In 1989, President G. H. W. Bush and the state governors called a summit, held in Charlottesville, Virginia to set goals for improving school. The summit, chaired by then-Governor Bill Clinton of Arkansas, resulted in establishment of the National Education Goals Panel. *Goals 2000: The Educate America Act* and the *Improve America's Schools Act*, passed in 1994, gave impetus to efforts to establish national curriculum standards in math, science, history, and English and other disciplines. National discipline-based groups began writing standards for each discipline. The National Council of Teachers of Mathematics (NCTM) established a set of mathematics standards that have subsequently been used by most states. National standards documents were drafted in other disciplines, but because of philosophical disagreements over what all students should know, attempts to establish national standards waned, and standard-setting was left to the states. To varying degrees, states used national discipline standards documents to inform the writing of their own state content standards. By the mid-1990s, most states had content standards in place, and were designing or beginning to implement statewide systems of testing based on them.

No Child Left Behind, passed by Congress and signed into law in 2001, mandates that states receiving federal funding:

> implement statewide accountability systems covering all public schools and students. These systems must be based on challenging State standards in reading and mathematics, annual testing for all students in grades 3–8, and annual statewide progress objectives ensuring that all groups of students reach proficiency within 12 years. Assessment results and State progress objectives must be broken out by poverty, race, ethnicity, disability, and limited English proficiency to ensure that no group is left behind. (U.S. Department of Education, 2001)

Science was added for testing in 2005. By school year 2013–14, the law requires that all students score at or above the proficient level established by their state. Schools that fail to meet targets not only receive negative publicity and sanctions, but ultimately may be reconstituted or shut down, a consequence beginning to be applied at the time of this writing.

The accountability reform movement, epitomized in the United States by *No Child Left Behind*, has been put forth as promoting both equity and excellence. Concern for equity is reflected in the requirement that student achievement data be disaggregated by "poverty, race, ethnicity, disability, and limited English proficiency to ensure that no group is left behind," and provision of "choices for parents and students." Schools must demonstrate not only that the school as a whole is meeting achievement targets, but also that sub-populations within the school are doing so as well. Concern for excellence is reflected in standard-setting and testing, implementation of "proven" methods of instruction, and the requirement that schools provide "highly qualified" teachers for every classroom (U.S. Department of Education, n.d.). Schools that fail to make Adequate Yearly Progress (AYP) for 2 consecutive years receive funding for professional development, technical support, and transportation for students wishing to transfer. Schools that fail for 3 consecutive years may receive funding for supplemental services like private tutoring. Ultimately, schools that continue not to achieve their AYP may be reconstituted or taken over by the state.

To what extent is convergence of equity and excellence in the current accountability movement substantive, and to what extent is it rhetoric? Debates about this question rage. Some educators focus largely on standards, asking the extent to which standards and standardization both improve education, support equity and democracy (Meier, 2002; Symcox, 2002; Thompson, 2001; Wang & Odell, 2002). While this is an important line of questioning, it can become derailed by debates about whether one is for or against standards. The standards debate hinges on whether one sees standards as a means of ensuring quality by spelling out exactly what everyone should know, or of deepening the capacity of schools to engage students at higher levels intellectually.

Others focus more on testing, asking the extent to which, on the one hand, it serves as a useful lever for improving teaching and learning, especially for students from historically underserved communities (Fuller & Johnson, 2001; Haycock, 2001; Hess, 2006; Palmaffy, 1998; Roderick, Jacob, & Bryk, 2002), or, on the other hand, as a form of punishment for those very same students (e.g., Lipman, 2004; Madaus & Clarke, 2001; Orfield & Kornhaber, 2001; Valenzuela, 2005).

Regardless of where people stand in these debates, most see education as a foundation of democratic life. In diverse societies, it is particularly important that schools serve students from all communities well in order to provide everyone with opportunity, equip everyone for employment, and prepare everyone for democratic participation. At the same time, despite popular beliefs that schools are constructed for these purposes, considerable evidence shows that they actively reproduce a race and class hierarchy instead. As Rogers and Oakes (2005) put it, "Despite our prized cultural legacy of the common public school as a 'great equalizer,' schools also serve the mission of preparing students for their 'rightful' places in an unequal labor market and society" (p. 2187).

To what extent does the current accountability movement support equity? Or, can it better be understood as a mechanism through which historic inequities are reconstituted and solidified? This book assembles the thinking and research of several leading scholars who examine relationships among the accountability movement, educational equity, and democracy.

CONCEPTUALIZING KEY CONCEPTS

Reform movements are usually accompanied by slogans that have sufficient emotional power to draw people in, and sufficient ambiguity to be read through multiple interpretations. So it is with the current reform movement. Democracy, equity, and accountability are three ideals most people support. But these ideals can carry very different meanings which, when left unclarified, often leave people supporting, or thwarting, something other than what they actually value.

Democracy

Around the world, democracy is a popular idea, at least at an abstract level. Many nations are attempting to "teach students democratic ideals and values," often in contexts that "contradict democratic ideals such as justice, equality, and human rights" (Banks, 2004a, pp. 9–10). People generally look to schools to prepare the young for democracy, as reflected in a recent California newspaper editorial: "American children don't learn through osmosis how democracy works and how to make a difference in their communities. Our public schools are, as always, vital to that mission" ("The root of civic culture," 2006, p. B6).

But what does democracy actually mean? In his recent book *First Democracy* (2006), Paul Woodruff, Professor of Ethics and American Society at the University of Texas at Austin, observes:

> Even educated Americans seem to be confused about democracy, seduced by its doubles, and complacent in their ignorance. When I ask my learned colleagues about democracy, they often say it is "majority rule," or they speak vaguely of

putting matters to a vote, as if this made a decision democratic. Sometimes they simply point to the Constitution of the United States, forgetting that this was written by men who feared government by the people and were trying to keep it at bay. (p. 4)

Based on his analysis of ancient Athens, Woodruff posits seven features that are central to the ideal of democracy: freedom from tyranny; the rule of law, applied equally to all citizens; harmony (agreement to adhere collectively to the rule of law while simultaneously accepting differences among people); equality among people for purposes of governance; citizen wisdom that is built on human capacity to "perceive, reason, and judge" (p. 154); active debate for reasoning through uncertainties; and general education designed to equip citizens for such participation. While he notes that no society has ever lived up to all seven features, they constitute ideals to aspire to.

While most people probably agree with these ideals abstractly, people interpret them differently. First is the matter of balancing individuals, communities, and shared common good when it comes to gauging citizen wisdom, equality among people, or what constitutes tyranny. Dewey (1944) addressed the importance of providing for participation of all members "on equal terms" (p. 99), and developing among everyone a sense of "shared common interest" (p. 86) that enables people to engage in "social changes without introducing disorder" (p. 99). Some argue that emphasizing cultural diversity within a nation blunts the rights of individuals and the forging of a common culture by overemphasizing group claims (Hess, 2004; Ravitch, 1990). Others argue that democracy must affirm the right of historically oppressed communities to use cultural expression in its fullest sense to claim citizenship as a precondition to equal participation and forging of common ground (Rosaldo, 1999). Where one stands on the relationship among individual rights, group claims and cultural identities, and shared common interest has implications for the extent to which one will view standardization of schooling and school curricula as a just and democratic means of promoting excellence for everyone.

Second, people who believe in democracy diverge sharply on their perceptions of the relationship between democracy as a governance structure and capitalism as an economic structure. To many, capitalism and democracy go hand in hand. Several years ago, one of my students explained it to me this way: Under a capitalist market economy people vote for what they want by buying things; votes registered in this way are used to determine which what products to produce in what quantity and variety. Similarly, people vote for who they want at the ballot box which, when tallied up, determines who gets elected and subsequently what policies are adopted. In his view, this one-person one-vote structure enables bottom-up decision-making. Pressing for more democracy would include pressing for more free-market capitalism, as they are viewed as two sides of the same coin. One can see this view reflected in U.S. foreign policy measures that attempt to shape nations around the world into U.S.-style democracy, along with free market capitalism.

Conversely, others argue that capitalism is the antithesis of democracy, but unlike democracy, capitalism is rarely named and studied in much depth in school. For example, Perkins (2004) coined the term *corporatocracy* while working as an *economic hit man* promoting U.S. foreign policy and corporate interests. He describes corporatocracy as linking three powerful institutions that are run by a small elite whose members move "easily and often" across institutions: major corporations, government, and major banks (p. 26). Linking these institutions enables an increasingly powerful elite to build a global empire to which most people in the world are subservient (Bigelow & Peterson, 2002). Ordinary citizens shape their conceptions of ideals such as justice, freedom, liberty, and democracy to fit within the contours of corporatocracy, and schools participate in this process of conception shaping.

What it means for schools to serve democracy, then, rests strongly on one's conception of democracy in relationship to pluralism, power, and the economic structure.

Equity

At a rhetorical level, most people favor equity because of the fundamental values of fairness and opportunity the concept suggests. As such, equity can be used to justify positions while skirting diverse points of view on them. Consider the following statement by E.D. Hirsch (1996): "Every child reading at grade level by the end of first or second grade would do more than any other single reform to improve the quality and equity of American schooling" (p. 148). This statement offers a goal virtually no one opposes, namely, that every young child should learn to read at grade level. It also deemphasizes broader consideration of goals of schooling or school reform by rhetorically defining reading achievement scores as the most important indicator of equity. Or, consider this passage from a 2006 newspaper about the new high school edit exam in California:

> As of May, more than 40,000 students in that class had not passed the test. Results from Tuesday's test will likely be released in several weeks. . . granting diplomas to students who have not learned the basics does nothing to create more equity. (Rosenhall, 2006, p. A3)

Equity as used here suggests that all students should have an equal opportunity to succeed and that the route to students' success is strengthening graduation requirements by testing knowledge and skills. Because of No Child Left Behind's attention to closing achievement gaps, embracing equity might imply also embracing No Child Left Behind (NCLB). Conversely, questioning NCLB is often interpreted as offering excuses that accept student failure.

So what does equity mean? To disentangle its meanings, Secada (1989) points out that equity, which has to do with distribution of society's resources, includes two important but different considerations: what one is concerned about the distribution of, and how one decides what constitutes the most fair or desirable distribution. Here lie disagreements that often go unclarified.

Generally, researchers and policy makers examine distribution of at least one of the following when considering equity in education: inputs into schooling (such as financial resources); student access to schools, programs, or significant resources (such as college preparatory curriculum, science labs, or excellent teachers); processes in schools or classrooms (such as which students are praised and which are reprimanded); and outcomes (such as achievement scores or graduation rates). The accountability movement directs most of its attention to outcomes. In the process, it minimizes attention to inputs, access (with the exception of access to "highly qualified" teachers), and processes, leaving these considerations up to states and school districts. To some, this emphasis is appropriate; as U.S. Secretary of Education Margaret Spellings (2005) put it, "what I'm always going to look at is the bottom-line result" (p. 374). Thernstrom and Thernstrom (2003) contend that the racial achievement gap is due mainly to educators' doubts about abilities of African American and Latino children to learn, and that failure to embrace NCLB amounts to continuing to make excuses rather than taking action.

To others, the almost exclusive focus on outcomes—and on outcomes as measured by test scores alone—deflects attention away from conditions that support learning, as well as the deeply impoverished conditions of communities in which many young people live (Berliner, 2006). For example, recent investigations in California have identified factors that systematically reduce access to learning of students who are poor, students of color, and English Language Learners (Gándara, Rumberger, Maxwell-Jolly & Callahan, 2003; Oakes, Blasi, & Rogers, 2004). These include reduction of effective bilingual education programs, and inequitable access to credentialed teachers, teachers with professional training for teaching English learners, forms of assessment that capture what language minority students can do and that help guide classroom instruction, meaningful instructional time when students are in school, sufficient textbooks and other instructional materials that English learners can understand, and functional school facilities.

The focus on outcomes also deemphasizes attention to classroom teaching processes advanced by progressive educators. For example, Banks (2004b) describes equity pedagogy as classroom teaching processes "that facilitate the academic achievement of students from diverse racial, ethnic, and social-class groups" (p. 5). He points out that, from a cultural difference perspective, low-income students and many students of color "are not having academic success because they experience serious cultural conflicts in school. The students have rich cultures and values, but the schools have a culture that conflicts seriously with those of students from ethnic minority groups" (p. 19). Without directly addressing teachers' assumptions and knowledge of culturally diverse students, implicitly schools leave intact a deficiency perspective toward those who historically have not achieved well.

In addition to directing attention to what is distributed, the concept of equity also implies value judgments reflecting how things ought to be. According to Secada (1989), equity does not mean the same thing as equality. *Equality* refers to that which can be counted or measured: test scores, funding formulas, numbers of books in the library, numbers of teachers with teaching credentials, and so forth. *Equity,* on the other hand, refers to judgment about what is most desirable and just: "Educational equity is what gauges how well our educational system lives up to our ideals of justice in the face of changing circumstances and of our evolving notions of justice" (p. 81).

It is here where people who agree passionately that achievement gaps must be addressed, disagree passionately about what that means and should entail. For example, equality might imply specifying that schools should have equal proportions of fully certified teachers. Equity would imply that strong steps be taken to actually ensure that those who have been traditionally under-taught be assigned not just fully certified teachers, but the strongest teachers. As another example, what achievement outcomes are of most value? Test scores are directly measurable; their advocates point out that, "What gets measured gets done" (Spellings, 2005, p. 27). Critics are concerned about a host of measurement-related issues, one of which is that "exclusive focus on test scores ignores the widespread desire for schools that address a broad range of academic and social goals, as reported in public opinion polls" (Guisbond & Neill, 2004). One can also ask: To what extent is what is being taught supportive of equity? Given a long history of controversies over whose perspectives schools teach (Sleeter, 2005; Zimmerman, 2002), and given analyses of whose perspectives dominate and whose are hidden in current content standards (Sleeter & Stillman, 2005), is it equitable to treat debates about curriculum as if they were settled?

Accountability

Like equity, at a rhetorical level few people oppose the idea of schools being accountable—held responsible—for student learning. But people diverge on what accountability means—what schools should report, based on what evidence, how, to whom, and for what purpose. For example, two parent groups in Massachusetts found themselves in conflict while supporting accountability; as one said, "We just want to have a good math program." Yet, they were at odds over public perceptions of what accountability means, and over their own priorities for accountability. While one group wanted to hold the state more accountable for funding schools adequately, the other wanted better evidence of student learning and fiscal responsibility (Black, 2006).

To help distinguish the different meanings of accountability, Darling-Hammond in Chapter 5 of this volume posits 5 types of accountability: political, legal, bureaucratic, professional, and market. Each type suggests using somewhat different evidence, to make somewhat different kinds of decisions, for a somewhat different constituency. For example, plaintiffs in *Williams v. State of California* used data about student access to education resources to hold the state accountable for providing its students with a public education. Test data can be used for market accountability when parents are encouraged to select schools for their children based on test scores. Or, test data can be used to improve professional accountability by identifying whom teachers are teaching well and who they need to teach more effectively. Each type of accountability has strengths and limitations; none is a panacea.

In the United States, states have responded somewhat differently to accountability pressures. For example, California, which had established a system of detailed content standards, testing and accountability targets prior to passage of No Child Left Behind, illustrates top-down, bureaucratic accountability. California requires an extensive test battery given to all students in Grades 2–11, which includes content tests in English/language arts, math, history/social science, and science; and a norm-referenced test in reading, language, mathematics, spelling (Grades 2–8) and science (Grades 9–11). Beginning in 2006, high school graduation is contingent on passing the California High School Exit Examination in language arts and math. Spanish speakers who have been in U.S. schools for less than 1 year or who participate in bilingual programs can take a nationally normed test that measures basic skills in Spanish, but only tests given in English count toward the state's accountability formula.

In Nebraska, by contrast, curriculum and assessment are controlled at the district level, and accountability follows more of a professional model. Nebraska established state-level content standards; districts may either adopt them or develop equally rigorous standards of their own. The state sets a schedule for student assessment; most assessments are chosen and some are developed at the district level, with teacher participation. School districts give a statewide writing assessment, and a combination of additional assessments, including norm-reference tests, criterion reference assessments, and locally developed classroom assessments; districts submit portfolios of assessment practices and procedures for quality review by the state. Emphasis is put on professional accountability in that teachers are directly involved in constructing an accountability system that relates directly to classroom teaching, and ongoing professional development of teachers is part of this system (Jones, 2004).

Thus, accountability need not mean top-down mandated testing. Indeed, one can argue that a top-down flow of authority conflicts with a bottom-up flow inherent in democracy. Accountability and equity raise questions about who should be holding whom accountable for what.

OVERVIEW

The authors of this book raise questions about the current accountability movement, doing so from positions of deep concern for democracy, equity, and particularly the experiences and futures of young people from communities that historically have not been well served by schools and other social institutions. The authors do not speak with one voice; readers will encounter some differences in stances taken toward the accountability movement. But such differences stem from varied experiences with schools, leading to somewhat different interpretations of democracy, equity, and accountability in the context of growing inequalities and erosion of public funding for schools and other public services.

The organization of this book moves from the classroom outward, to a school and program level, a state level, and finally a broader national policy level. In Chapter 1, Christine Sleeter and Jamy Stillman draw on case studies of ten strong and "highly qualified" teachers in diverse or predominantly Latino classrooms to show strategies teachers use to navigate highly prescriptive teaching. In the process, they raise questions about the extent to which accountability pressures actually discourage strong teachers. In Chapter 2, Linda Skrla, Kathryn Bell McKenzie, and James Joseph Scheurich show how visionary school leaders can use accountability systems to support equity and excellence in teaching, and how assessment can be a useful tool for equity if used appropriately. Based on several years of collaborative work with schools, they examine three ways in which accountability and improved teaching can interact to strengthen student learning and result in more equity in achievement. Barbara McCombs in Chapter 3 argues that accountability practices and learner-centered teaching actually need not conflict. After exploring political assumptions underlying the current accountability movement, she shows how a well-conceptualized learner-centered model of instruction supports equity, democracy, and student achievement.

In Chapter 4, drawing on a case study of a high school in the 1930s, Cherry McGee Banks argues that schools exemplifying excellence and equity result from visionary leadership, in which leaders see themselves as accountable to the communities in which they work. Although the case study she reports takes us back about 70 years, it grapples with the same issues facing schools today, showing how value-driven leadership has the capacity to link excellence, equity, and democracy in a real school. Linda Darling-Hammond, in Chapter 5, differentiates among various meanings of accountability, arguing that student learning can be enhanced best when schools concentrate on developing teacher professional capacity, rather than on testing itself. She draws on data from several districts across the United States to tease out responses to accountability that have the best record for improving student learning. In Chapter 6, Robert Linn argues that embodying a shift from norm-referenced to criterion-referenced assessments of learning, standards movement might be viewed as supporting equity because of its emphasis on measuring learning of content rather than drawing comparisons in achievement. However, the process of setting standards and the widely varying definitions of *proficient.* on which state accountability measures rest, imply that measures of accountability be used with far more caution than is currently the case.

The remaining chapters situate the accountability movement within a larger context of race relations and global economic restructuring. In Chapter 7, Jori Hall and Laurence Parker argue that deficit thinking about students of color, though rhetorically challenged by No Child Left Behind, is actually supported through its compensatory formulation. Using critical race theory as an analytical tool, they show how deficit thinking is reflected in NCLB, then explore models of school reform that serve students of color by building on student competencies, linking the school with the community it serves, and building a school culture around achievement rather than compensation for presumed deficiencies. In Chapter 8, David Gillborn uses critical race theory to examine very different impacts of the accountability movement on Black and White students in Britain. He asks three questions about accountability policy: who or what is driving it, who wins and who loses as a result, and what are the effects of policy? Based on his analysis, he links the current accountability to a movement to reassert White dominance. Lois Weiner, in Chapter 9, based on an analysis of neoliberal policies adopted by the World Bank, asks similar questions. She shows how such policies—which inform basic premises underlying No Child Left Behind—press toward dismantling public services globally, particularly in education, in order to expand privatization. Finally, in Chapter 10, drawing on an analysis of accountability measures in varying kinds of schools in Britain, Sally Tomlinson relates accountability policies to a reassertion of competitive meritocracy, again asking who ultimately benefits from accountability policy shifts in education. These last 3 chapters should cause those of us in the United States to think carefully about how similar our own situation might be in relationship to who is driving education reforms, and who actually benefits and loses the most. In his Afterword, James Banks raises several critical questions about the nature of accountability systems in diverse and democratic societies.

Taken together, these chapters raise serious questions about the current accountability movement, whom it benefits, and how accountability might serve to strengthen equity and democracy. The current accountability movement purports to benefit all students and particularly those who have been left behind historically. In some schools and school districts, visionary leaders are using it to do just that. At the same time, the movement was constructed on a logic that rolls back democracy, racial equity, and the public sphere; as a result, it appears to benefit primarily those who are White and native English speakers and a larger movement toward privatization and meritocracy.

CHAPTER 1

Navigating Accountability Pressures

Christine E. Sleeter

California State University Monterey Bay

Jamy Stillman

Barnard College, Columbia University

How do teachers teach with integrity while pressured to raise test scores? On the surface, it might seem that the better teachers teach, the more students will learn. Yet, in the intense pressure to raise test scores, prescribed and controlled teaching conflicts with many teachers' understandings of excellent teaching, particularly in culturally and linguistically diverse contexts (Achinstein & Ogawa, 2006). This chapter examines how 10 teachers of students from historically underserved communities navigate pressure to teach to standards in order to enact their vision of an academically challenging, multicultural, student-centered curriculum. The chapter draws from case studies of elementary and middle school teachers in California to illustrate possibilities and pressures teachers face. In so doing, we raise questions about retaining strong teachers where they are needed most.

RETAINING STRONG TEACHERS: VIEWS FROM THE CLASSROOM

Case studies of teachers who strategically navigate school environments constrained by accountability demands provide practical insights about supporting and retaining teachers in the nation's hardest to staff and most under-resourced schools, even in challenging times. Attracting and retaining qualified teachers for schools that serve students of color, poor students, and English Learners is critically important, especially in light of research that indicates that access to a qualified teacher not only has the single greatest influence on student achievement (Darling-Hammond, 2000; National Commission on Teaching and America's Future, 1996), but that marginalized students are least likely to have this access (Ingersoll, 2001, 2002, 2003; National Commission on Teaching and America's Future, 2003).

Researchers previously attributed culturally and linguistically diverse students' limited access to qualified teachers to a teacher shortage problem, claiming that the rate of new teachers entering the field could not match the rate of teacher retirement. Recent studies, however, characterize the problem as one of inequitable distribution, showing there are more than enough teachers to go around, and naming the high rate of attrition as a major source of disparities (Ingersoll, 2003, 2004; McCreight, 2000). Considerable evidence suggests teachers' decisions to stay in or leave their jobs or the teaching profession altogether commonly result from teachers' degree of satisfaction with their working conditions (Ingersoll, 2003, 2004; Horng, 2005). Increasingly, prescriptive and control-oriented approaches to teaching are causing some new teachers to leave or to be pushed out (Achinstein & Ogawa, 2006).

Nieto's (2003) exploration of "what keeps teachers going" offers several insights as to why some outstanding teachers elect to stay in so-called difficult schools. Though reticent to advance a "recipe" of best practices for teacher success, Nieto delineates several characteristics of resilient veteran teachers: teachers' love and care for students, commitment to democracy and social justice, engagement in the intellectual aspects of teaching, and strong belief in the hope and possibility of public education. These are key elements that sustain teachers "despite everything." Additional studies have also identified engagement in activism and commitment to marginalized youth as critical aspects of urban teacher resilience (Howard, 2003; Lyons, 2004). These qualities matter, and should be supported by working conditions that nurture rather than discourage teachers.

Nevertheless, emphasis on what Cochran-Smith (2004) has called the "emotional, relational, and personal" aspects of teaching can only take us so far. One of the working conditions teachers have consistently named as most intolerable is a lack of autonomy and decision-making power over structures and procedures that impact their day-to-day work (Haberman, 1988; Horng, 2005; Ingersoll, 2003, 2004). With the onslaught of accountability reforms, teachers' control over matters closest to them, such as pedagogy and curriculum content, has diminished because poor test scores commonly lead to increased pressure to teach to the standards and tighter monitoring of teachers' work. Notably, a lack of teacher autonomy is most likely to become an issue in schools that serve historically underserved students since they are the students who most often perform poorly on standardized tests.

We wanted to find out what strong, committed, and well-prepared teachers of historically undeserved students are doing, in the context of accountability pressures. Although we did not begin with a focus on what retains or discourages high quality teachers, our research led us there.

METHODOLOGY

In this chapter, we synthesize two studies of 10 classroom teachers who are committed to working with culturally and linguistically diverse students in California. All of their schools had been designated as underperforming for at least one year during the time of our studies (2002–2005). We include seven teachers from Sleeter's (2005) work and three from Stillman's (2005) work.

Teacher Participants

We both employed purposive sampling. Stillman selected three upper elementary teachers who worked in state-identified underperforming schools. Each had been teaching for at least 3 years, and worked in a school and classroom predominantly comprised of Spanish-speaking English Learners ($\geq 75\%$). All three held California's highest level of certification for teaching English Learners. Sleeter selected seven elementary-middle school teachers who worked in schools serving diverse students; three taught mainly Spanish-speaking English Learners ($\geq 75\%$); four taught classes in which there was no ethnic majority. All seven held California's highest level of certification for teaching either culturally diverse students or English Learners.

Of the 10 teachers collectively, 7 taught in schools in the Monterey-Santa Cruz area, one taught east of the San Francisco Bay, one taught in rural northern California, and one taught in urban southern California. None worked in the same school. The teachers' racial/ethnic backgrounds are Mexican (4), White (4), African American (1), Filipina (1), and Portuguese (1). They taught the following grade levels: first (1), second (2), fourth-sixth (5), and sixth-eighth (2). One was a second-year teacher, five had taught between 4–6 years, and four had over 15 years of experience. Seven had completed a master's degree, and the other three were in the process of doing so, all in equity-oriented university-based teacher education programs.

Data Collection

Both of us gathered data through classroom observations and interviews with the teachers. Stillman conducted two in-depth interviews with each teacher; Sleeter conducted one with each teacher. Stillman completed two,

1-week rounds of classroom observations in each teacher's classroom (approximately 25 hours each). Sleeter completed one to three observations in each teacher's classroom (approximately 8 hours each). We both wrote extensive field notes based on observations. In addition, Stillman facilitated a focus group with teachers from each school site to glean a more comprehensive sense of the school contexts, and interviewed each principal. Sleeter, having had all of her teachers as graduate students, used copies of class papers (with permission), video footage of a course in which several of them were enrolled, and their master's theses. Reflecting feminist methodologies, we also acted as participant-observers in classrooms; after taking field notes, each of us usually remained in the classroom to offer assistance to the teacher. Some of the teachers elected to be referred to by their real names, others preferred pseudonyms.

NAVIGATING STANDARDS

We selected these 10 teachers to study because they were strong teachers who took teaching very seriously, placing their own understanding of their students and what it means to teach well ahead of pressures associated with standards. We wanted to find out how they thought about their work, what strategies they used to navigate the standards, and what issues or supports they experienced in the process.

Teachers' Underlying Beliefs about Students, Teaching, and Standards

As teachers responded to accountability pressures, they were guided by a shared set of intersecting beliefs about their work as teachers and the role that standards and accountability should play in this work. Specifically, teachers saw teaching as a mission, not a job; they shared a critical orientation, viewing schools as sites for transformation; they treated students' cultural and linguistic backgrounds as strengths on which to build learning; and they conceived of "high standards" as college preparedness, while rejecting standardization.

All 10 teachers regarded teaching as more than just a job. Their dedication to students, their families, and the communities where they worked, and their own learning and professional development indicated that, for them, teaching was a way of life and an all-encompassing commitment. Fourth- and fifth-grade bilingual teachers, Isabel and Xitlali, for example, claimed that although they experienced particular challenges in the schools where they worked, they deliberately chose to work in marginalized communities. Isabel, a second-language learner herself, explained, "I know exactly what it is like to start school not knowing a word of English, just being completely mute. . . . I remember thinking, when I grow up I am going to teach, and I'm going to be more patient" (June, 2004). With similar conviction, Xitlali reported that she wanted to work with Mexican English learners because "ELLs and Chicanos are completely falling through the cracks." She continued:

> I needed to focus my attention there and really try to do something for them. And not in a way that's like pity or like I'm going to come save you, but more of, I'm a part of a team that we need to work together. . . for betterment for a community who's been disenfranchised for so long. . . .That's why I'm here and continue to stay. (May, 2004)

In an effort to improve their teaching, most became deeply engaged in the communities where their schools were situated. Although he did not live in the same neighborhood as his students, for instance, Jorge, a fourth- and fifth-grade bilingual teacher, became an activist in the community surrounding his school; he joined the city's coordinating committee and a local grassroots parent organization, and eventually received the city's Volunteer Teacher Award. Middle school dance and Spanish teacher, Gina, likewise set out to learn more about her Mexican students and their community. Though she knew Spanish when she began teaching, she wanted to develop what she called insiders' knowledge in order to teach in a culturally relevant way that did not degrade or tokenize students. This goal led her on an in-depth study of Mexican dance that exposed her to the ethnic, linguistic and regional variation of Mexico, as well as the political relationships that are legacies of European conquest. All 10 teachers were deeply committed to their professional growth, as evidenced by their participation in university courses and numerous learning opportunities specifically designed to improve education for students who have traditionally been denied access to quality educational experiences.

Their unwavering dedication to students and their communities commonly meant that, while they considered the standards to be important, they privileged students' needs over accountability-driven goals when these conflicted. For instance, a second-grade teacher demonstrated her dedication to students through efforts to provide exceptional learning resources. She used her own money to purchase an extensive, multicultural library of children's literature, written by authors from a variety of racial and ethnic backgrounds and including characters that reflected the diverse cultures and languages of her students, to supplement the standards-based language arts program she was required by her district to use.

The teachers also shared a critical orientation, believing in the transformative power of education and its capacity to improve students' lives beyond the classroom. Isabel explained that she became a teacher because:

> I believe that learning is not only power, it's freedom. Yes, I teach my students about the importance of doing well in school so that they can attend college and become our future leaders . . . but I go beyond the importance of education as a way to improve our economic status. . . . [My purpose] is to get them thinking... not for me to give them knowledge but for me to just help them realize how much wealth they house and to put it into action. (June, 2004)

Terri, a sixth-grade language arts and social studies teacher, articulated similar goals: to cultivate students' academic learning as well as prepare them to participate in a democracy. In describing why she involved students in equity-related questions in the classroom, she explained:

> I wanted to bring the issues of democracy and discrimination to the surface in my school environment. . . . I believe, as Freire did, that "as they look at their environment, they will find autonomy to become problem solvers of institutional inequality." (Freire, 1998, p. 128, cited by Pipes, 2002, p. 15)

First-grade bilingual teacher Kathy, likewise, viewed teaching as both a political and ethical act, claiming, "If I refuse to take a position on something I consider to be harmful to children, I am contributing to that harm" (November, 2003).

These critical beliefs understandably impacted the ways in which teachers thought about and responded to the standards and reforms related to high-stakes accountability. In an attempt to empower her students, for example, Xitlali educated them about the demands and consequences of standards-based reform efforts. Referring to the standards as part of "the culture of power," she set out to equip her students with the skills and knowledge necessary for survival in mainstream America. However, she did not feel that mastering skills alone would necessarily lead to students' academic success. She argued that students additionally needed to understand the role that standards and standardized tests play in sustaining dominant power structures.

Notably, teachers' critical perspectives guided their stance toward and work with the standards. In preparation for a unit about Native Americans, for example, fifth-grade teacher Angela explored indigenous perspectives on colonialism, focusing intensively on the Iroquois during the 1600s. When she encountered a clearly different story than that showcased in the state's social studies standards and school's history textbook, both of which took a

European American point of view, she decided to explore this contradiction with her students. Expanding on Standard 5.3 for California's fifth-grade social studies curriculum, which states: "Students describe the cooperation and conflict that existed among the American Indians and between the Indian nations and the new settlers," Angela engaged students in role play activities that provided them with a viewpoint that was conspicuously absent from the textbook.

Teachers' notions about literacy and their language arts instructional approaches likewise revealed their tendencies to look at their work through a critical lens. For example, Xitlali, Isabel, and Jorge shared notions of literacy that were far more robust than those advocated by the standards and standards-based language arts curriculum. They argued that literacy is not simply a set of skills, but also entails students making meaning and formulating connections between the word and their lives—an idea that Freire coined "reading the world." Jorge articulated this concept best when he claimed, "I don't think that somebody who can decode can necessarily function in our society. Literacy is related to agency in our society. So to be literate, you have to be able to make meaning" (June, 2004).

All 10 teachers believed firmly in the value of students' cultural and linguistic backgrounds. Jorge, for example, identified the aspect of the language arts standards that he found most problematic: their exclusive focus on English literacy at the expense of students' primary language:

I believe that my emphasis should be on the acquisition of language.
And if I could be liberated from having to focus on one language, then
I would be empowered to provide language arts education that would
empower students to be the most literate they could be.... For some of
them, that would be in Spanish. (June, 2004)

A fifth-grade teacher created a science unit about the solar system in which she consciously devised ways to link the science standards with students' backgrounds. In one example, she facilitated her students' investigation of how diverse cultural groups have made sense of the solar system; in another, she and the school librarian sent the students on a scavenger hunt for books about the earth and sky that were written by authors from diverse cultural groups. As a member of a local community of dance scholars, Gina's on-going study of Mexican dance was the basis for her curriculum. Reflecting on the links she deliberately made between students' communities and her curriculum, she emphasized how necessary it is to build the curriculum on students' cultural and linguistic knowledge bases. She claimed that "although teachers may not be experts in all of their students' cultures in anthropological-sociological terms, inviting students and families to share their knowledge is essential to students feeling validated in the school curriculum" (Rodriguez, 2002, p. 85).

Most of the teachers rejected standardization while embracing a conception of "high standards" as meaning college preparedness. Most were very clear that their intent was not just to raise test scores, but more importantly to prepare their students for access to higher education. Several claimed that the standards helped raise the bar for students who had historically been denied access to a rigorous curriculum, and helped administrators hold teachers with persistently low expectations more accountable. Several also argued that when they had pedagogical freedom to teach the standards as they saw fit, standards advanced instruction by providing clarity about what students needed to know in order to be successful in the next grade. As a result, teachers claimed to offer their students more explicit instruction than they had previously.

What the teachers objected to was rigid interpretations of the standards, which they often encountered due to their schools' underperforming status. Most notably, teachers expressed considerable frustration about the power of standardized tests to enforce rote interpretations of the standards, which they found to be pedagogically limiting and particularly harmful to marginalized students. One worried that teachers would be negatively impacted since the state test would likely be fact-driven rather than comprehension-driven, a possibility that would disadvantage her students. Others agreed, claiming that increasing student performance hinged on teachers' pedagogical freedom. Xitlali explained:

> I take the standard and then make it mine. I say "Okay, kids need
> to know this, how am I going to teach it in a way that's meaningful,
> humane, they're going to understand it, that includes all of the other
> [instructional] strategies that I believe work with my students?"
> ....The good thing about [the standards] is that they're not prescribed.
> It doesn't say how you should teach the standards. The programs
> do, but the standards don't.... There is some interpretation in there.
> (November, 2004)

Most of the teachers attempted to teach beyond the standards, in order to prepare students for access to higher education. Second-grade teacher Juanita explained that she used the grade-level standards as a guide, but expected and taught more than they require: "The standards say for second graders to be able to write a paragraph or two paragraphs. But why not three paragraphs? Or why not four or five at the end of the year?" (February, 2004). Xitlali likewise went beyond what the standards mandated in accordance with students' "survival and reality." Discussing her impetus for adapting the Houghton-Mifflin language arts program, for example, she claimed that she intended to make the curriculum *more* academically demanding so that her students would be exposed to the rigorous coursework needed to access higher education.

Teachers' Strategies for Navigating Standards and Accountability Pressures

To navigate pressures of standards and accountability and put these beliefs into action, the teachers used several related strategies: prioritizing standards in order to use them strategically; organizing content around meaningful, culturally relevant material; creating college-going cultures in their classrooms; and using social learning and collaborative teaching processes.

Most of the teachers found space to integrate meaningful, culturally relevant content by studying and prioritizing the standards to decide which to emphasize and which to deemphasize or even skip. We call this strategy *using standards strategically*. While the teachers saw standards as useful guides for curriculum planning, they were concerned that there were simply too many standards to cover. Trying to cover all of them would prevent them from engaging students deeply in meaningful learning, so out of necessity they learned to use standards strategically.

Xitlali claimed that she had the standards in her bag "at all times," and that she "worked with them a lot, enough to say that I'm very familiar with them and that I use them to plan my instruction consistently" (November, 2004). She prioritized standards by considering the following questions: "What do [students] really need for the next grade? What do they need for survival? What do I know they need to get into college, and succeed after that?" Similarly, Juanita carefully studied the standards and adopted texts, in order to figure out what is key and what she can skip. She explained that combination of experience, staff development, cues in the text, and her familiarity with college-level work helped her identify which standards were most important. Kathy explained that the standards are a guide, not the curriculum itself: "I certainly look at them and think, okay, have I covered this, how am I thinking about covering it. Some of the standards seem much more important than others, so I try to make sure I cover those" (March, 2004). Standards in subject areas that were outside the purview of testing, such as dance and Spanish, did not have the same constraining effect and did not require the same level of scrutiny, prioritizing, and strategic use.

Only one teacher worked in a school where grade-level teams collaboratively analyzed and prioritized standards. The others did so on their own. Because teachers generally did not work in schools where using standards strategically was encouraged, the two teachers with the least experience were reluctant to skip anything out of concern that they might skip something that would show up on a test.

To the extent that they could, all 10 teachers organized content around meaningful ideas that were relevant to their students. They taught thematic and interdisciplinary curriculum units as much as possible, embedding skills in meaningful content while making explicit links to the standards. They used the state-adopted textbooks in conjunction with other materials, giving priority to thinking and meaning-making over textbook coverage. Examples included linking science with reading/language arts, substituting children's literature for some of the textbook coverage, and creating spaces for students to bring their life experience into the classroom. They used their familiarity with students' cultural backgrounds to guide them in making the curriculum culturally relevant.

For example, a reading/language arts standard Isabel was expected to teach was to distinguish between cause and effect in expository text. Her textbook taught this concept through a story about the iditarod race in Alaska. But since the great majority of her students were Mexican American, she decided to teach the concept through a lesson about immigration and the Mexican Revolution. Field notes described the following:

> "As we study immigrants, we always have to ask ourselves why someone would immigrate to another country and leave his or her home." Gesturing to a poster that appears to have a list of reasons for immigrating, the teacher continues, "We already know something about this topic, don't we?"
>
> With this, Isabel launches into an animated account of the Mexican Revolution, told in her own words. As she talks, the students move in more closely around her; they watch her attentively and intensely. They appear to be mesmerized by the story.
>
> When she finishes she says, "The purpose of this lesson is to learn about cause and effect since it will be on the big tests you'll take in the spring. But cause and effect can also help us to understand our history, culture, and our present lives." (November 16, 2004)

Following demonstrations of her own thinking and writing on chart paper, Isabel made connections to students' prior knowledge about immigration and migration. She included the song "La juala de oro" as a means of tapping into and building on students' prior knowledge and experiences. Through an account of Mexican history, she addressed the history of her students—a history characterized by class oppression, resistance and immigration—and supported them in applying cause and effect to their lives.

Kathy designed and taught an interdisciplinary unit about Monterey County agriculture, which she linked to reading/language arts, math, and science standards, and the "Farm Fresh" unit of her English Language Development text. Using various books, guest speakers, and pictures, Kathy explored with students the differences between large-scale corporate farms and small family farms. They studied where food comes from, including the history and struggles of the United Farm Workers, particularly the work of local organizers. Students planted seeds to observe how plants grow, and examined which foods are grown locally. They learned plant vocabulary, and developed a fruit and vegetable alphabet book. For the math portion of the unit, rather than using textbook examples, Kathy drew on students' family experiences with agriculture. To teach graphing, she had the class construct a bar graph using 3 x 3 cards on which each student indicated the crop in which their parents worked, then placed their cards above the vegetable that corresponded to their parents' work so that cards placed vertically became bars. Kathy made notes on a xeroxed copy of first-grade content standards regarding how all of this addressed the standards.

Teachers actualized their commitment to college preparation by creating explicit college-going cultures in their classrooms. One way they did this was by bringing reference to college into their classrooms regularly. For example, one teacher had students work from a syllabus, learn to take notes on minilectures, and learn to give oral presentations. Another teacher named students' cooperative seating groups after six of the Ivy League universities, and another had explicit discussions about college on a daily basis.

More importantly, the teachers emphasized higher-order thinking, student production of knowledge, and college-preparatory academic expectations. They designed challenging projects that engaged students, interested them, and were well-scaffolded to support student success. Both Xitlali and Juanita created books of students' research. Juanita's second-grade class produced five books per year, each of which included a paper written by every student. Juanita taught students to use Microsoft Word, augment text with pictures (such as scanned photos or clip art) and other decorative touches, and do Internet research. For a book featuring biographies, each child chose a person to research on the Internet, wrote a page about the person's life, and inserted a downloaded photo of the person. Each book had a table of contents, was bound with a decorated cover, and had a pocket with a library card so children could check them out. Juanita started teaching her students to produce books when she realized that too much of the standard instructional program was boring. High school teachers had pointed out to her that a good way to prepare children for college was to teach them to do research and produce documents, so she figured out how to use standards strategically to teach college preparatory work.

Middle school teacher Gina designed her Spanish course to prepare her students for Advanced Placement Spanish in high school. Spanish was the first language of most of her students, but Gina explained that a system designed to transition students away from Spanish leaves them without very good academic language in either Spanish or English. By the middle school level, most students came to her Spanish class with below-grade-level Spanish vocabulary and comprehension. To prepare them for Advanced Placement work, she used grade-level literature in Spanish and taught them literary analysis, embedding specific skills in more complicated work, and using explicit instruction, scaffolding, or modeling as needed. She explained that usually students struggle at first, but "eventually they do get it, it comes together" (January, 2004).

All 10 teachers valued a sociocultural approach to learning, so all of them used small group work regularly. This practice stands in contrast to the whole-class content-delivery approach that is currently widely used in low-performing schools. Most of the teachers seated students in small groups, which they used for cooperative learning projects on a regular basis. Some of the teachers also used centers. For example, Juanita structured her entire approach to teaching reading, language arts, and computers around learning centers. For them, however, small group work was not just a technique or way of organizing student seating. It was a way of making academic learning more authentic, allowing for students to bring their own knowledge and questions into the classroom, and providing a venue through which students could learn from each other.

Supports and Struggles

We selected teachers who brought to their work a clear vision for teaching culturally and linguistically diverse students. In our experience, to borrow from Bartolomé and Trueba (2000), "ideological clarity" is essential to the work of teachers. If unclear about how teaching connects to one's own students as well as broader political social structures, teachers are likely to replicate prevailing practices. But teachers' visions and ideologies interact with the administrative context in which they work, as well as with their skill and experience in implementing their visions. The administration, and the experience and skill teachers bring, can serve as a support or a source of struggle for them.

The teachers experienced varying degrees of pressure to meet No Child Left Behind's Annual Yearly Progress (AYP) and California's Academic Performance Index (API) targets. The nature of that pressure depended on the degree to which school site and district administrators, particularly the school principal, supported teachers in making decisions about curriculum and instruction. Almost all of the teachers talked (often at length) about the impact of principal support. Some principals buffered teachers from accountability pressures and supported their pedagogical expertise; others personified those pressures. For instance, Kathy credited her principal for giving her freedom to construct an interdisciplinary, culturally relevant curriculum, as long as it met key state standards; Jorge's principal went to great lengths to shelter teachers from demands of the district that would hamper their teaching. Gina, on the other hand, had experienced administrative site visits in which the main concern appeared to be whether teachers had standards posted on the wall and could recite which standard they were addressing at any given time. Two teachers experienced a change in principals during the study. Both had one principal with deep pedagogical expertise who supported the teachers' student-centered, culturally relevant inquiry-based approach to teaching enthusiastically, followed by another who insisted that teachers follow the standards and texts, undermining teachers' active and culturally relevant teaching strategies.

What teachers were able to do also appeared to depend on having enough teaching experience to be confident in their judgments and expertise. The two teachers with the least amount of experience—a second-year teacher and a fourth-year teacher who was new to the district in which she was teaching—expressed the most uncertainty about their work. Cheryl, for example, was expected to follow a scripted reading/language arts program all morning everyday. An early career teacher, she found it more systematic and clearly planned than one she would be able to construct on her own:

> If you would have asked me a few years ago, I'd have been totally against it, but actually using this program, I can say it works quite well. It is heavily phonics based, you know, and it gives them every thing that they need, and it's designed to adhere to the standards, so you get standards-based material, that works quite well. Because when you're designing your own thing, I used to just pull out a book and say, OK, I'm gonna hit this one, and this, and this. This program is very systematic. (Sleeter, 2005, p. 155)

At the same time, she was concerned that the program left too little time for other things she valued, such as guided reading, extensive writing, hands-on science, social studies, and authentic literature. Similarly, Angela felt overwhelmed by the number of standards she was expected to cover in all the subject areas fifth graders would be tested on. She said, "The standards make it really hard to be a creative teacher, and really hard to put those values and those really key beliefs that you want to instill in the children. Because you almost have to make it a timed test, make everything like a timed test and drill and drill and drill, and rote memorization, to be able to get through everything" (January, 2004). The more experienced teachers had figured out where they could trim back use of mandated curriculum, but the newer teachers were not sure how to do so without hurting their students' tested achievement.

Teachers' expertise also influenced what they could envision and carry out in the classroom. Most demonstrated a passionate intellectual interest in something, and sought ways to engage students in this interest. For example, two teachers with extensive expertise in multicultural children's literature, despite pressure to follow standards and reading/language arts packages, found creative ways to weave multicultural children's literature into their curriculum. Gina had an exceptionally rich background in Mexican dance, history, and culture, which she had developed by spending summers studying in various Mexican universities. Her passion and content background greatly enriched her teaching. Juanita's ongoing interest and expertise in computers gave her the background and impetus to teach her second graders how to do research and write using computers. Jorge regularly taught content through arts-based activities, such as having students paint maps, sketch how they see a concept, and create miniplays. The arts background he brought enabled him to visualize connecting the arts with literacy and social studies.

Even though all of the teachers had found ways to successfully apply their knowledge and expertise to their work, several veteran teachers simultaneously experienced profound demoralization as they attempted to actualize their visions of effective teaching and learning in the face of high-stakes accountability demands. Teachers who worked in contexts with the least principal support tended to carry the heaviest burden.

On several occasions, for example, Isabel broke down crying after school, explaining that the pressure was simply too much to bear. In her opinion, attempts to align the school's instructional programs with district demands did very little, if anything, to placate district or local administrators. According to her, regardless of how hard she worked, she would never be able to meet the expectations put forth by policymakers and district administrators. Isabel's reservations were validated during one memorable visit to her school site. On that day, teachers had learned that the school's Academic Performance Index—California's school evaluation system— had increased by 63 points because of students' improved performance on state standardized tests. The staff room was abuzz with the news and, understandably, filled with an air of relief and celebration. Needless to say, teachers' palpable excitement was abruptly crushed when, instead of receiving a congratulatory call from the district, teachers were immediately told to prepare for the next visit from the district's red team, who would scrutinize classrooms for more standards-based student work.

Given such events, it makes sense that some teachers interpreted tight monitoring of the standards as a backlash against students of color and English learners, rather than as an innocent effort to improve educational outcomes for these students (Gutiérrez, Asato, Santos, & Gotanda, 2001). Not surprisingly, such occurrences also compelled the most committed and talented teachers to question how long they would be able to endure working under such disheartening, not to mention, stressful conditions.

CONCLUSION

The teachers portrayed in this chapter are highly qualified by anyone's definition, and elected to teach historically marginalized students in underperforming schools. Although it takes considerable effort to enact an ambitious and rich view of excellent teaching in the context of high-stakes accountability-driven reforms, rather than leave these schools, as research on teacher retention suggests they might do, they persisted. Their creative and deeply intellectual labor appears to facilitate both their survival and professional satisfaction in the face of accountability-driven reforms. Below, we offer three recommendations aimed at supporting the work of teachers like them.

First, administrators and policy makers need to gain familiarity with "best practices" for teaching culturally and linguistically diverse students. A considerable body of research and theory depicts the kinds of strategies and approaches that most effectively engage such students in academic learning (see, for example, Baker, 2001; Banks & Banks, 2004; Gay, 2000; Tharp, Estrada, Dalton, &Yamauchi, 2000). Although its direct links with increased student achievement scores have not been well-documented,[1] links with increased student engagement in academic work have been documented. All 10 teachers we studied were well versed in this research and theory, but most struggled with pedagogical directives from their school or district administrators that not only did not reflect it, but got in the way. In particular, several experienced a conflict between the model of teaching as responding to one's students (learner-centered teaching, as discussed in Chapter 3 of this volume), which they were trying to implement, and an imposed model in which all students are taught the exact same content, at the same time, in the same way. Teachers' strategic use of standards was their way of attempting to reconcile conflicting models of teaching, similar to Achinstein and Ogawa's (2006) description of principled resistance. In Chapter 2 of this volume, Skrla, McKenzie, and Scheurich point out that schools that are closing achievement gaps center on the improvement of teaching, rather than on direct control over teachers' work. If more professionals (including policy makers, administrators, and teacher educators) were well versed in research and theory that focuses specifically on teaching culturally and linguistically diverse students well, it is likely that teachers would experience more support for such teaching. It is also likely that more underperforming schools would experience authentic increases in student learning and sustain a better record of retaining highly qualified teachers.

Second, attempts to increase student learning need to engage teachers as professionals, rather than discarding teachers' knowledge. All 10 teachers talked about the extent to which their school and district administrators did or did not value their professional knowledge. Two veteran teachers spoke of having experienced highly controlled (and, in their experience, ineffective) approaches to teaching when they were novices. They described the pendulum as having swung from prescriptive, skill-based approaches to teaching, to open-ended meaning-based approaches. With experience, they had learned to embed skills in meaningful content, and resented attempts to force teachers back into the earlier prescriptive skills-based approach. The newer teachers brought training in embedding skills in meaningful content, as well as in accessing and working with students' interests and community-based knowledge. What the newer teachers did not bring was a fully developed, systematic curriculum for teaching reading or math at their specific grade levels. As noted previously, one commented that she appreciated having access to a structured curriculum. At the same time, she and others resented being treated as if they had no professional knowledge. Clearly, teachers vary in their familiarity with strategies and approaches to teaching culturally and linguistically diverse students well. But it was this treatment of teachers as problems needing to be controlled rather than as committed professionals whose knowledge should be engaged, that the highly qualified teachers discussed in this chapter found deeply painful. Indeed, we wonder how children make sense of intellectual growth when they see teachers treated as lacking intellect.

Third, we concur with Achinstein and Ogawa (2006) in their recommendation that teachers like those we studied form professional networks to help them sustain and deepen their practice. Creating professional networks that support teachers to actively grapple in the ways described in this chapter would help them navigate accountability demands without abandoning the theories and practices they believe in and that research has shown to be best for culturally and linguistically diverse students. One of the veteran teachers commented on an early draft of this chapter that dedicated colleagues made a huge difference in her ability to remain true to her beliefs about teaching in the No Child Left Behind context. She speculated that it would be quite difficult to be a lone voice in one's school. Another veteran teacher draws ongoing sustenance from active community-based professional groups of which she is a member. Cochran-Smith (2004) argued that today's generation of teachers needs tangible support systems that will sustain their "work over the long haul." Teachers who find themselves trying to buck the tide alone should seek out or establish such networks. School leaders and teacher educators who work with teachers like those in our study should find ways to link teachers with such professional networks.

In their quest to understand why two excellent novice teachers whose students were outperforming those of their colleagues left their schools, Achinstein and Ogawa (2006) found that, "It was their critical thinking, questioning, and commitment to reaching all students that was seen as 'resistance' and 'infidelity'" to mandated curriculum programs (p. 59). Like Achinstein and Ogawa, we believe that if schools that serve historically underserved students are to attract and retain well-qualified teachers who are committed to the students and who will want to stay, administrators and policy makers need to value what such teachers bring, support their ability to make decisions in their own classrooms, and become much more familiar with the research and theory that undergirds the student-centered pedagogical approaches such teachers instantiate. Their instructional practices demonstrate how real teachers can mediate broad-based policies, such as No Child Left Behind, to benefit poor students and students from culturally and linguistically diverse backgrounds; and in the process, continue to find possibility in their work. But their struggles to remain true to their vision of what good teaching is, and the discouragement we too often witnessed, threaten to further compromise historically underserved students' access to a qualified teacher.

CHAPTER 2

Supporting Excellent Teaching, Equity, and Accountability

Linda Skrla
Kathryn Bell McKenzie
James Joseph Scheurich

Texas A&M University

"You don't make the pig fatter by weighing it." This piece of folk wisdom in recent years has become a mantra for individuals and groups opposed to standardized testing and accountability policies, appearing regularly in scholarly articles, newspaper editorials, and political speeches (see National School Board Association, 2006; Thomas, 2004). It often seems to be delivered as a punch line, one apparently intended to end all further debate. However, the issues associated with testing and accountability in U.S. public schools—like the issues associated with weighing pigs—just are not that simple; the value of any type of information depends upon the use to which it is put. Extending the porcine analogy a bit, we completely agree that the act of weighing one's pig, by itself, does not contribute to fattening the pig. Nonetheless, swine researchers, pork producers, and 4-H kids all weigh their animals with great regularity; otherwise, it would be impossible to know if their pigs were becoming fatter, staying the same, or losing weight. People raising pigs would also not know if the feed they had chosen was nourishing their pigs, if some other food or combination of foods might produce better results, if individual animals thrived on differentiated diets, if some animals required extra food in order to keep pace with the rest of the group, and so on. Furthermore, if there were not some standard unit of weight and uniform calibration of scales, the pork industry would have no way of determining quality among pigs raised by different producers; nor would it be possible to determine fair prices for the pigs when sold.

Of course, children are not livestock, but the point we are making here is that, just as the superficially appealing aphorism about weighing pigs and fattening pigs fails to hold up upon more careful consideration, policy debates that cast testing and accountability as all bad (or all good) often minimize the enormous complexity of the situation and ignore evidence that does not support a particular predetermined conclusion. We have emphasized this point repeatedly in our work throughout the past 10 years, and extended discussions of it have appeared in other venues (see McKenzie, 2003; Scheurich, Skrla, & Johnson, 2000; Skrla, 2001, 2003; Skrla & Scheurich, 2003). In this earlier body of work, although we acknowledged the dangers and negative outcomes of accountability policies, we concentrated on the possibilities for leveraging equity that such policies also provide. This work was based on research conducted in school districts that had made substantial and sustained progress in raising student achievement and in narrowing gaps among socioeconomic and racial groups. Our discussion in this chapter extends that earlier body of research and is drawn from our more recent work on teaching and equity in a context of high accountability.

Our focus on teaching in our recent work and in this chapter is driven by the need for a deeper and more complex understanding of how policies enacted in Congress and state legislatures ultimately change (or fail to change) instruction at the classroom level. The alignment of policy intent with policy outcome in public schools ultimately depends on how the policy impacts the nearly 3 million teachers in individual classrooms throughout the United States. This impact is, of course, mediated by a chain of intermediary groups and individuals that lies between the policy enactors and teachers. Intermediaries such as local school boards, central office staff, and campus principals act as street level bureaucrats and can have substantial influence (negative, neutral and/or positive) on policy enactment (Lipsky, 1980; Rorrer & Skrla, 2005), but, ultimately, if any educational policy (including accountability) is going to change student achievement levels or reduce achievement gaps, it must first change what is happening between teachers and students in classrooms. Furthermore, a growing body of research points to the quality of teaching as a key determinant of student success, independent of other factors that impact student learning (Hill, Rowan, & Loewenberg Ball, 2005; Rice, 2003; Rowan, Correnti, & Miller, 2002).

For these reasons and others, as we have continued our research on schools and school districts that are making progress on educational equity in high accountability environments, we have focused more closely on the links between policy and teaching. Additionally, all three of us have strong commitments to the practical applications for our research. We all work regularly with highly diverse schools and school districts that are engaged in efforts to raise student achievement and to close their achievement gaps.

Thus, our discussion in this chapter is drawn from two sources. The first is an ongoing, multiyear, grant-funded research project of instructionally successful school districts in three states.[1] The second is our work as advisors and collaborators in school improvement efforts in five school districts that serve mainly Latino and African American students, four of which are located in large urban areas and one of which is in a smaller city.

This research and collaborative work in schools, then, grounds our discussion of *excellent teaching*, *equity*, and *accountability*. Many people reading the title of this chapter might, however, find it oxymoronic to see the words excellent teaching, equity, and accountability in the same title. The research literature and the popular press are replete with discussions of accountability and testing's negative influences on teaching (see Abrams, 2004, for a useful summary). Furthermore, there is little doubt that the influence of accountability and testing can have negative or unintended consequences (McKenzie, 2003). The possibility of detrimental impacts of accountability policy remains a source of significant concern for policy makers, researchers, and practitioners. Nonetheless, based on our research and on our work with practitioners engaged in the struggle to improve equity and quality in their schools, we argue that the negative view of accountability policy's impact on teaching tells only part of the story. There are also other positive relationships among accountability, equity, and teaching. Moreover, it is possible for high-quality, equity-oriented teaching and high accountability to coexist (O'Day, 2002). In fact, we would go so far as to say that to have schools that serve all children well, both accountability and excellent teaching must exist, because neither one alone is sufficient to address the extensive and complex set of challenges today's schools face. In the following paragraphs we discuss three ways in which high accountability and improved teaching can interact to produce better and more equitable student achievement, centering improved teaching, diffusing effective teaching practices, and increasing teachers' equity consciousness.

CENTERING IMPROVED TEACHING

Excellent teaching for every child is a goal that U.S. schools are far from reaching. Even in the schools and districts in which our research has been conducted, which were identified for study based on empirical evidence of substantial progress toward equity and high student performance, the average level of teaching quality is not at a level we would call excellent. Moreover, in the schools and districts in which we work that are engaged in improvement efforts, the quality of teaching is typically even lower, on average, with wide variation among schools and among classrooms within individual schools. Additionally, research by other scholars has shown low teaching quality to be pervasive in schools that serve populations that are majority low income and/or majority children of color (Haycock, 2001; Ingersoll, 1999; Lankford, Loeb, & Wyckoff, 2002). Furthermore, raising the average quality of teaching in these schools to a level of excellence cannot be accomplished overnight or in one step; stages of incremental progress are required. It might be more accurate, therefore, to say clearly that our discussion here focuses on *improved* teaching, with excellent teaching for all students being the ultimate goal. The first area, then, in which accountability can play a supportive role in the advancement of equity is *centering the improvement of teaching* in schools and school districts. This positive aim of accountability policy is also known as increased *academic press* (Diamond & Spillane, 2004).

This clear and sustained focus on the improvement of teaching—placing teaching and good instruction at the center of school life regardless of what else might be going on in the school, is part of a productive leadership response to accountability (Skrla, 2003). The idea that the improvement of teaching *might not be* the central focus of most schools or of their leaders might seem odd or counterintuitive. However, schools are complex organizations situated within multilayer political arenas subject to the demands of a variety of constituencies and pressure groups (Rowan & Miskel, 1999). In short, in many cases, schools and their leaders in the past have focused primarily on maintaining the appearance of providing "good schooling" (however local communities defined it, order and discipline, successful athletic programs, attractive buildings, low taxes, and so forth) whether this resulted in high quality or equitable education for their students or not (Rowan & Miskel, 1999). The advent of accountability, however, has created a context in which the improvement of teaching (or instructional leadership) must be central to what schools do, as illustrated by a quote from a central office administrator in one of the districts participating in our research.

> Previous principals were not instructional leaders. . . .We've had other individuals who are good at managing their buildings, and had a lot of other strengths, but instruction was not one of those. And *in this day and age we can't afford not to have a building principal who has that instructional leadership ability and vision and focus and feels comfortable on the instructional side* [emphasis added].

Centering the improvement of teaching in their schools has clearly become a requirement for leaders in today's climate of high accountability, at least in the successful districts we have studied.

One might argue that good teaching should always have been central to what schools do, but the typical reality in most schools, especially those serving high populations of racially and economically diverse students, is that the instructional mission has been pushed to the back burner. Teachers in the schools in our research districts, in contrast, report that their schools have a strong focus on the core instructional mission, one that is constantly reinforced by the principal and other instructional leaders. In the words of one participant, "The district is very focused, and very focused on the instruction of children." Other researchers have linked this type of strong instructional focus at the campus level to improved math and reading performance (Newmann, Smith, Allensworth, & Bryk, 2001). Our interviewees link the emergence of this focus in their districts and schools to the accountability system and to the pressure to improve student performance. Although this type of pressure can impact teachers negatively in some circumstances, it also can be harnessed as a positive force. A strong and consistent focus on improving teaching (one supported by accountability pressure) helps schools and individuals in schools avoid the numerous microdiversions that exist in the daily life of schools and that typically pull focus and energy away from teaching.

We are not claiming, however, that this type of central focus on the improvement of teaching is the only possibility created by accountability, nor does it automatically arise. As accountability pressure has intensified over the past 20 years, there has been wide variation in the quality of responses superintendents, principals, and other school leaders have made in their efforts to meet state and federal goals for student performance and to avoid negative sanctions. The negative and inept responses by administrators, including institution of regimented or scripted instruction, have received considerable attention (McNeil, 2000; Valencia, Valenzuela, Sloan, & Foley, 2001). Other responses by school and school district leaders to the demands of accountability, such as the central focus on the improvement of teaching discussed here, have been more positive but perhaps less widely reported or less sensationalized.

DIFFUSING EFFECTIVE TEACHING PRACTICES

The second area in which we have observed high accountability advancing the goal of excellent teaching for all children is in providing support for the diffusion of effective teaching practices through focused and sustained professional development. Accountability policies, with their heavy reliance on standardized testing, in the past have been sharply criticized for having detrimental effects on the professional development that schools and districts provide for teachers, including narrowing professional development to sessions focused on test-taking tricks, and so forth. In contrast to this widely reported negative view of accountability's effects on teacher professional development, in the research districts and schools in which we work, accountability pressure has lead to *increased* support for high quality and sustained professional development focused on the dissemination of effective teaching practices.

This could, perhaps, be a result of Texas' evolution into a second generation of accountability that features more coherent curriculum standards and tests with higher degrees of difficulty. Superficial instructional responses, such as wholesale reliance on practice tests and attempts to game the system by focusing on a narrow band of students on the "bubble" of passing, might have been effective (at least in the short term), in raising performance on the earlier generation of state assessments (Texas Assessment of Academic Skills or TAAS); but these sorts of approaches are less likely to work with the newer assessments (Texas Assessment of Knowledge and Skills or TAKS). For example, the following quote from a high school math teacher illustrates the difference between the kind of knowledge tested by TAAS (Texas' first generation exams) and that required by TAKS (Texas' second generation exams):

> We were at basic skills on TAAS. . . . Here [with TAKS] there is a lot of critical thinking. And they have to know concepts. Let's say *slope.* They can't just know slope is rise over run. That means nothing. The question of slope will be presented to them five or six different ways on that test, so they really have to understand the concept and the critical thinking behind it.

As this teacher explained, the new assessments require higher level thinking from students. This has meant that teachers have to be able to teach in different ways, which has driven the districts to ramp up the level of professional development provided for teachers.

Furthermore, the increased support for teacher professional development that has arisen in these districts has not been generic support. It has been, instead, focused on a specific kind of professional development—the type that increases teachers' content knowledge and teaching skills for the grade levels, subjects, and students they are assigned to teach. Desimone, Smith, and Ueno (2006) emphasized in a recent research report that this type of professional development is definitely *not* the norm for most teachers nationwide:

> Current reform efforts rely on teachers' in-service professional development to help teachers improve their practice in response to the demands of high-stakes accountability. We know the characteristics of professional development that make it effective in increasing teachers' knowledge and skills and improving teaching practice in a way that increases student achievement. We know how to deliver such professional development; we know that most teachers do not get

such professional development, and from this study, we know that those teachers that do participate in sustained, content focused professional development are more likely the ones who need it least. (p. 209)

These researchers went on to suggest that school leaders should play a more proactive role in ensuring that all teachers participate in the type of professional development most likely to lead to increases in student performance:

> We suggest that policymakers and administrators use this information as a solid foundation for emphasizing policies such as scaffolding and linking activities to the school's vision. . . . Administrators [should] develop their role as brokers, to play a more definitive role in guiding teachers into high-quality professional development. (p. 209)

This recommendation aligns closely with what has happened in the districts that served as our research sites.

Additionally, our interviewees linked their districts' support for (and insistence on) professional development designed to advance effective teaching practices to accountability. For example, consider this exchange between two teachers who participated in one of our focus group interviews in response to our question about what had changed in the district that had lead to its success in raising student achievement and in closing achievement gaps:

Teacher 1: Our teachers are now being given [through professional development] more *strategies* as opposed to "look, this is what you've got to cover." Now we are looking at and being trained in "this is how you get there."

Teacher 2: I think so too. Because there is no training that we have asked for that we have not gotten. And we're given a multitude of different ways to get the kids there. It's very beneficial because you have so many kids that learn in different ways that all that multitude of training is really coming in helpful a lot.

Teacher 1: They don't just tell you, "You need to learn this." It's, "Let me show you how you're going to get the information to the child."

Teacher 2: Absolutely.

As these teachers' comments illustrate, they find the professional development provided by their district and campus to be very relevant and focused on specific ways in which to teach their content successfully to the children in their classrooms.

RAISING TEACHERS' EQUITY CONSCIOUSNESS

The third area in which accountability policy can work in support of equity and excellent teaching is in increasing the level of awareness, concern, and responsibility for high and equitable student performance among teachers. We call this *equity consciousness*. By equity consciousness we mean that teachers are aware of, accept, and act on four central beliefs:

1. That all children (except only a very small percentage, i.e., those with profound disabilities) are capable of high levels of academic success
2. That this academic success equitably includes all student groups, regardless of race, social class, gender, sexual orientation, learning differences, culture, language, religion, and other similar factors
3. That the adults in schools are primarily responsible for seeing that all children reach this success
4. That traditional school practices result in inequity for individual students and groups of students and that these must be changed to ensure success for every child (See McKenzie, Skrla, & Scheurich, 2006)

This list may not seem particularly startling or innovative to scholars, especially critical scholars, who operate daily in fields in which the profound inequities in U.S. public schooling are well understood and are widely discussed. However, the world in which most public school practitioners work day-to-day is very different. Overall, the degree to which inequity is systemically structured into schooling is *not* well understood, and overt discussions of race as a factor in inequitable school outcomes are avoided (Pollock, 2001). Thus, we have found it highly useful in our work with practitioners to have a clearly stated, easily understood definition of what we mean by equity consciousness.

Obviously, teachers' willingness to embrace and act on these equity consciousness beliefs varies widely among individual teachers in schools, among groups of teachers in different schools, and even within the same individual teacher depending on circumstances. In other words, equity consciousness among teachers is highly complex. Furthermore, efforts by school leaders to systematically increase levels of equity consciousness in order to advance school improvement goals are often unsuccessful. In our study districts, however, as well as in the schools with which we work as collaborators on improvement efforts, we see that elements of accountability policy can be used as tools to start and sustain individual teachers and groups of teachers on a path of growth with respect to equity consciousness.

We offer two examples of the ways in which accountability and improved equity consciousness can be linked.

The first is that the accountability system provides data that teachers can use to track individual progress for children. And as children make progress, teachers see their success and hold increasingly higher expectations for each child's performance based on past successes. Put another way, having systematic, tracked data on each child concretely refutes assumptions about the educability of children when the progress is visible and readily accessible. In fact, the districts that participated in our research study had all developed systems of tracking student learning that provide up-to-date, readily available data for each child on state and local learning objectives. One teacher explained a district's database system: "We have software available that we have loaded on the server where any teacher, any staff member, can pull up a student's previous [state assessment and local benchmark assessment] scores and what they need to improve on." This accessibility of data provides teachers with the information they need to make curricular and instructional decisions tailored for the individual student. This, then, can prevent achievement gaps from emerging and can provide timely information for teachers to use in closing gaps before they widen.

The second way in which accountability can operate to improve teachers' equity consciousness is by making visible teachers' *zone of self-efficacy* (McKenzie & Lozano, 2006), thereby leading to the possibility of an expansion of this zone. The concept of *zone of self-efficacy is* drawn from Bandura's social cognitive theory, specifically his concept of self-efficacy. According to Bandura (1982), "People tend to avoid situations they believe exceed their capabilities, but they undertake and perform with assurance activities they judge themselves capable of handling" (p. 201).

Certainly, Bandura's concept of self-efficacy applies to teachers who, consciously or unconsciously, have a zone in which they place students they believe they can successfully teach, that is "teachable" students. Conversely, teachers may believe there are certain students or types of students that they cannot successfully teach. If a teacher feels she is unable to teach a particular student, this student is, consciously or unconsciously, placed outside a teacher's zone of self-efficacy. This student, then, is either not taught, or not taught at the level that the students who are included in the zone are taught. Furthermore, this outside-the-zone student is oftentimes, literally, taken out of the teacher's classroom. In other words, the student may be placed in special education, or tutorials, or an alternative placement center, or timeout, or given a pass to walk the halls during class time (McKenzie & Lozano, 2006).

Our point, then, is that the data used for accountability can make visible this otherwise invisible zone of self-efficacy. If well used, these data can clearly show which students are learning or not learning and which students are being taught or not taught. This understanding of a teacher's zone of efficacy shifts the focus away from an effort to blame the victim—the student—and toward a critical engagement with our foundational beliefs about our abilities to teach all students, including those students who are unlike us. This critical introspection, which can be started and driven by accountability data, is needed at both the individual and the organizational levels and is the first step in expanding the zone of self-efficacy, so that it includes *all* students.

CONCLUSION

As we have said in numerous other venues, we clearly understand the possibilities for detrimental effects on teaching that can and do result from today's context of high accountability in U.S. public schools. However, we have been consistent in our call for researchers, policy makers, and practitioners to attend to the complexity of various state accountability systems and their equally complex effects in thousands of individual classrooms, schools, and districts. We have also been consistent in our call for everyone not to ignore or dismiss, in a summary or totalistic fashion, positive outcomes from accountability policy systems. Therefore, to communicate our more recent work and to further a more balanced conversation on accountability and its effects, we have identified three areas that our research and consulting work on school improvement efforts has shown are arenas in which accountability can support improved teaching and advance equity in public school classrooms. These areas included centering improved teaching, diffusing effective teaching practices, and increasing teachers' equity consciousness.

What then, might be the implications of this work for those interested in maximizing the improvement of teaching and the advancement of equity in a context of high accountability? The experiences of teachers and administrators in the successful districts we have studied and in the schools and districts where we have worked as partners in improvement processes suggest two additional, overarching factors that are important to creation and maintenance of school environments in which good teaching and strong accountability can coexist and interact successfully.

First, a sense of agency in the face of high accountability that is shared by school leaders and teachers is characteristic of these successful and improving schools and districts. Rather than seeing accountability policy as a monolithic monster demanding some particular (and most often negative) response, educators in the schools and districts with whom we have worked tend to view accountability as a force to be shaped, integrated, and *actually used to advance* the goals they have for their schools. In other words, they feel empowered to determine how "this [accountability] will go here." Centering the improvement of teaching is how they choose to meet the demands of accountability, rather than defaulting to some other, less productive, choice such as test tricks or drill-and-kill workbooks.

Second, recognition of and appreciation for complexity is another important characteristic present in these successful and improving schools and districts. Leaders and teachers on these campuses tend not to characterize their work or their students in either/or terms, and they neither seek nor support simplistic, silver bullet solutions for the complex problems their schools face. For example, working as a campus using accountability data to systematically increase teachers' equity consciousness requires attendance to the complexity of interactions among people's backgrounds, training, experiences, beliefs, and practices. It requires a coexistence of what O'Day (2002) calls *professional accountability*—the ability and willingness among professionals to hold one another accountable for standards of practice that lead to improvement of instruction and enhanced student learning— along with the bureaucratic accountability provided by state and federal legislation.

In sum, what we advocate in this chapter is that all of us—teachers, school leaders, researchers, and policy makers—should carefully consider the full range of possibilities in our discussions of, debates about, and efforts to implement accountability policy in ways that support the improvement of teaching and the advancement of equity. To put it another way, "you don't make the pig fatter *only* by weighing it."

CHAPTER 3

Balancing Accountability Demands with Research-Validated, Learner-Centered Teaching and Learning Practices

Barbara L. McCombs

University of Denver

There is growing recognition that current reform policies, including the accountability agenda as specified under No Child Left Behind (NCLB), are creating a conflict in perspectives about which approaches best enhance student learning and achievement. What underlies conflicting perspectives between learner-centered and accountability-centered advocates? Many in the first category are urging holistic and learner-centered practices as the *means* to best raise student achievement scores. On the other hand, those in the second category advocate standardized testing and measures of accountability as the policy framework for ensuring achievement gains. Which resolutions are most likely to resolve these conflicting perspectives?

In this chapter I will argue that what appears to be a conflict between holistic and democratic practices for enhancing student achievement versus testing and accountability practices can be resolved by turning to a research-validated model of learning and motivation. This conflict is largely the result of differing assumptions and philosophies about the purposes of schooling and what best supports learning of desired knowledge and skills. The resolution can be found in better understanding the nature of the conflict and what a research-validated model can contribute to balancing both views within the larger framework of education for democracy.

THE PROBLEM: CONFLICTING PERSPECTIVES

Effective approaches, beyond testing academic achievement, are needed for preparing all students for productive and creative lives in a democratic society. But there is a significant dispute about which approaches might be most effective. Rich (2005) argues that school reform efforts often failed because they were based on mistaken and misleading assumptions: that schools are the primary source of education, test scores are the best measures of student achievement, punishment works to help students learn, raising standards means students will meet them, and better teaching alone can close the achievement gap.

Many educators are now presenting compelling results showing that one of the biggest factors responsible for the achievement gap is poverty, which is a function of social and economic policies, rather than of schools. According to Berliner (2006), reform efforts external to schools, that help to reduce the social and economic gap, will be more effective than reform within the schools. Since achievement is consistently correlated with poverty, increasing the income of the poor and allowing for good nutrition, high quality child care, good medical care and insurance, and quality summer programs promise to have the biggest payoff in terms of increased achievement. Test results only reflect these broader socioeconomic gaps. Many organizations within states are taking a stand against standardized tests because of their socioeconomic bias. An example is the Colorado Coalition for Better Education, whose members have consistently opposed the Colorado Student Assessment Program (CSAP) because of its strong correlation between family income and test performance (Babbidge, 2006). This group has studied CSAP scores and reports that as the percentage of students receiving free and reduced lunches in a school goes up, test scores go down.

Other educators and researchers point to the current testing and accountability policies themselves as part of the crisis, arguing that high-stakes testing will not improve schools (see Amrein & Berliner, 2003; Neill, 2003). Research is consistently showing that high-stakes testing narrows curriculum and dumbs down instruction. From over a decade of research, Amrein and Berliner (2003) report that those states without high-stakes tests had (1) more improvement in average scores on the National Assessment of Educational Progress (NAEP) than states with such tests, (2) improvement at a faster rate on a variety of standardized tests, (3) higher student motivation and levels of critical thinking, and (4) lower dropout rates. In schools focusing on student performance on high-stakes tests, teachers are less inclined to encourage students to explore concepts and subjects of interest to them, obstructing students' path to becoming lifelong, self-directed learners. As a result, students disengage, and many drop out mentally and emotionally, if not physically. For example, Barton (2006) found that high school dropout rates have substantially increased in the last decade. Depending on which sources are studied, these rates vary from a low of 12.9 % in some states to a high of 45% in other states. Minorities have higher dropout rates, with Black males faring the worst (61% in some urban schools). Further, many schools are induced to push students out, increase grade retention, force many teachers to leave, and impede needed improvements.

Part of the nature of the conflict in perspectives over approaches to school reform derives from opposing viewpoints of those arguing for humanistic, organic, and ecological educational models versus those arguing for business models that emphasize competition, choice, and efficiency. Saltzman (2005) suggests that current business models that seek to privatize education (e.g., the Edison Schools) threaten the ideal of equal educational opportunity because they maintain the way of life enjoyed by those with money and power. The real threat in privatizing public education is that it removes public accountability and assistance in solving inequities between rich and poor; it also maintains corporate interests. Saltzman believes learning is not just about assimilating current knowledge and existing social order, but also about remaking society in more free, just, and democratic ways.

Ayers (2004) points out dialectical tensions within the politics of education, which at their core involve how the purpose of education and schooling are conceived. If education is to be a humanizing endeavor that fosters, develops, and expands human capacities, it has the potential to empower and enable educators and their students to gain a deeper awareness or *critical consciousness* to better serve the interests of the human community. Beyond that, Ayers sees the role of education as empowering those in the system to create possibilities for transforming the world. This role includes helping students and schools work toward ending social injustices and inequities with self-education models that allow students to produce new forms of being and knowing that are productive, empowering, and liberating. Similarly, Mulcahy (2006) examines the racial pain in both Black and White communities that involves a felt absence of power and presence of guilt and shame. When we fail to recognize the racialized experience of students, however, we make little progress toward social and racial healing. Ayers' and Mulcahy's visions capture education's aim as teaching for freedom and democracy through epistemological and ontological investigations of what could and ought to be, and contrast that with education models aimed at reproducing and maintaining asymmetrical relations of power and privilege.

A way forward involves engaging students to transform themselves and the larger social systems of which they are a part. Rich (2005) contends that the impact of school reform initiatives depends on the positive attitudes, behaviors, and habits that students bring into and learn in the classroom. Recognizing the importance of these social and emotional factors, in addition to the more academic factors, is the most critical lever in effective school reform. Failing to implement student-focused practices—such as encouraging students' innate curiosity to interpret and make meaning of the world—has been a major stumbling block. When we do not build on research-validated principles of learning, motivation, development, and individual differences, we place students in the role of passive learners, a role that conflicts with both the goal of education for democracy as well as natural laws of learning.

ADDRESSING GOALS OF EDUCATION FOR DEMOCRACY

Educating students for democracy is a good starting place in articulating how current tensions in public education reform can best be resolved. The *Brown v. Board of Education* decision defined educating enlightened citizens as a top function of public education (Wraga, 2006). As Fuhrman and Lazerson (2005) point out, most Americans agree that education should be about citizenship. Democratic deliberation is cited as a key process, in addition to academic content, with teachers having the greatest potential influence on what students as future citizens think. Without these deliberations in school settings, students fall victim to media influences that are part of the continuing deterioration in public discourse. The authors advocate a more pervasive role for civic education, where students learn to debate and appreciate, understand and criticize, persuade and collectively decide on moral terms of how to deal with ongoing disagreements that are part of the American democracy.

Grappling with real issues, diverse perspectives, and challenges to one's assumptions and beliefs promotes both democratic engagement and intellectual growth. McQuillan's (2005) case studies of two high schools' efforts to promote student empowerment demonstrate that empowerment strategies promote greater student participation, engagement, and responsibility in their education. McQuillan defines student empowerment as involving the academic, political, and social dimensions, wherein students have a say in how to understand the realities that affect their lives, and are provided opportunities for participation in changing curriculum, institutional leadership, and institutional structures and policies. Students then take part in creating a safe social environment that supports and nurtures the expressing of diverse views. McQuillan found these dimensions to be synergistic and mutually reinforcing, because as students and teachers became more empowered, they were more likely to empower others. As Moses and Chang (2006) argue, educational benefits that flow from a racially diverse student body depend on engaging students with diverse perspectives, which both promote intellectual development and also make democracy stronger. Gurin and Nagda (2006) describe an intergroup dialogue model for engaging students in exploring commonalities and differences in group identities and experiences. This model moves beyond most diversity initiatives by not masking conflicts but rather giving students opportunities to understand commonalities as well as differences between groups and foster active thinking about causes of inequalities.

Grappling with conflict, then, promotes both intellectual growth and democratic habits of mind. Although U.S. schools may express a commitment to preparing students for the responsibilities of democratic citizenship, most define students as passive and subordinate and treat them in undemocratic ways. But, as Wraga (2006) argues, recent reform efforts, and notably the NCLB Act, have replaced the democratic ideal with emphasis on training *productive workers*. The question then becomes, how do we strengthen student learning and also educate students for democratic life?

A recent report of the National Study Group for the Affirmative Development of Academic Ability (2004) crafted a vision for affirming academic ability, nurturing intellective competence, and moving all students to high levels of academic achievement. What emerged was a vision for a transformed education system, particularly for minority and low-income students, and the development of intellective competencies that could eliminate academic achievement gaps. Intellective competence is a holistic set of affective, cognitive, and situative mental processes. Specific competencies included literacy and numeracy, mathematical and verbal reasoning, problem solving, sensitivity to multiple contexts and perspectives, relationship skills, self-regulation, resource recognition, and information management skills. The study group contended that "Affirmative development of academic ability is nurtured and developed through (1) high-quality teaching and instruction in the classroom, (2) trusting relationships in school, and (3) supports for pro-academic behavior in the school and community" (p. 1).

The National Study Group also recommended a systemic approach that addresses classroom, school, and community. At the classroom level, inquiry-based approaches help all students acquire knowledge, followed by deep learning techniques and practice of basic skills and concepts until they become automatic. Collaborative learning and social interaction involving authentic, naturalistic situations are recommended, along with teaching students strategies for transferring what is learned from one task to another through problem-based approaches that emphasize metacognitive strategies. In this way, students gain insights into strategic knowledge and monitoring of their learning processes. At the school level, there should be emphasis on relationships that build relational diversity and trust among the students. At the family and community levels, supports must be in place to promote the economic, health, and personal welfare of all. Community service projects as well as strategies to provide education supports to families are recommended. Overall, the study group recommended that academic environments be learner-centered.

It is *urgent* that we transform education systems in this direction. Darling-Hammond and Ifill-Lynch (2006) report that by ninth grade, 40% of urban students fail multiple classes and that 50% or more in many schools leave without graduating. Of those who enter high school, many lack the learning and study skills they need to be good students (e.g., knowing how to take notes, study on their own, engage in classwork, and finish their homework). Consistent with research by motivation researchers (e.g., Covington & Teel, 1996; Dweck, 1999; Meece, Herman, & McCombs, 2003), to protect their self-esteem, many adolescents maintain they don't care about school and the boring or "stupid" work they have to do. Echoing recommendations of the National Study Group, Darling-Hammond and Ifill-Lynch (2006) urge educators to engage students by creating a strong academic culture in which students pursue relevant, meaningful, and authentic work, such as inquiry- and project-based learning. Involving students, collaborating with them, and making them part of the solution are also very effective strategies. In short, Darling-Hammond and Ifill-Lynch propose learner-centered approaches that recognize the learning and life needs of struggling students.

The remainder of this chapter discusses the types of solutions needed to make our public educational system conform more closely to research-validated principles of human functioning while addressing current inequities that exist within and outside of school walls. My own work with a number of colleagues on a transformed learner-centered educational model is then presented, along with research evidence supporting its potential for addressing the preceding critical issues while educating for democracy.

The Mismatch Between Human Learning Principles and Existing Educational Systems

It has long been recognized that humans have a need and tendency to form social connections. Humans also have common qualities such as empathy, kindness, compassion, love, friendship, and hope that represent their spirituality. Sociality is foundational to these spiritual qualities in the sense that in social relationships these qualities emerge and are developed. Making sense out of life via the creation of relationship-supporting organizational structures is also central to both sociality and spiritually. Many researchers emphasize these more complex metaphors in describing the human mind and behavior. They move us away from the mechanical or solitary computer metaphors that do not do justice to the interconnectivity of humans (see Cacioppo, Hawkley, Rickett, & Masi, 2005).

Eisner (2005) contends the current policies that advocate having clear outcomes defined by measurable performance standards and holding schools and teachers accountable for attaining them are highly rational with impeccable logic. However, such policies narrow the vision of education to intellectual capacities only, neglecting the social and emotional qualities of students and situations. They promote a technical rather than organic, humanistic, or personal orientation to teaching that does not work well with living beings. Eisner argues that we need to return to the vision of progressive education (Dewey, 1938) that recognized distinctive talents of individual children and created environments to actualize those potentialities. This vision also means that teachers should design experiences that allow students to respond not just in cognitive ways, but also emotionally, imaginatively, and socially. The basic argument is that in human organisms, there are no independent parts—all are interconnected.

Decades of research have confirmed the importance of student-teacher relationships in student motivation, social outcomes, and classroom learning (see Davis, in press, 2005). Low levels of conflict and high levels of closeness and support define good relationships. Through a good relationship with teachers, students experience their academic work as meaningful, personal, complementing their goals, and promoting their understanding, as contrasted with poor relationships where students see their academic work as coercive, repetitive, isolated, irrelevant, and contrary to their social and academic goals. These positive teacher-student relationships teach students how to regulate their behavior, and affect and develop social competence.

The foregoing findings and the principles behind them apply to all learners across economic, social, and cultural lines. A recent national study of low socioeconomic status and minority elementary students indicated that the most powerful school characteristics for promoting resiliency (academic success) included a supportive school environment model that was safe and orderly and promoted positive student-teacher relationships (Borman & Overman, 2004). Students in these environments displayed greater engagement in academic activities, a stronger sense of math efficacy, higher self-esteem, and a more positive outlook toward school (Phillips, 1997). This is particularly needed in today's culture with fewer stable family and social institutions that promote resilience.

Situating learning principles within the larger framework of human and systems functioning helps to clarify the fundamental cause of current imbalances in our educational models and philosophies. The industrial paradigm that characterizes most 21st century organizations, including schools and school systems, reflects the mismatch between principles of nature and human functioning, and institutions. Wielkiewicz and Stelzner (2005) argue that the industrial paradigm be replaced with an ecological paradigm. Principles that define ecological systems include: interdependence (components with bi-directional influences, such as subgroups within the organization, families, communities); open systems and feedback loops (dependence on inflow of materials, resources, and information from internal and external systems such as the economic, political, social, and environmental systems that surround the organization); cycling of resources (making multiple uses of resources such as human talents without relying on a single individual); and adaptation (providing structures and processes for adaptive learning to meet challenges and changes in technology, economics, student populations, etc.). In the ecological perspective, leadership is an emergent process in keeping with learner-centered principles and practices that share leadership among all learners.

Addressing the mismatch between learning principles and education systems will address a range of pressing issues schools face. As noted in Chapter 1 of this book, one of the big issues facing our nation's schools is that as many as 33% of new teachers leave within 3 years and another 46% leave in the first 5 years (Rubalcava, 2005). Many teachers go into teaching because they want to connect with students as individuals, create a sense of community, and help students develop their personal creativity and talents— goals that are very different from teaching realities that focus on economic efficiency, testing, accountability, and predetermined content objectives. In learner-centered environments, however, Rubalcava found teachers are able to balance current policies with nurturing students' emotional health and creativity. They engage students in critical thinking and creative expression, using strategies such as cultural exchanges, environmental projects, story writing, integrated physical education, and inquiry-based collaborative learning. Helping new teachers connect meaningfully with their students is the key to the success of any of these strategies.

WHAT SOLUTIONS ARE NEEDED?

It is clear that we need an educational system that embraces academic competence *and* the development of human potential and life competencies that prepare students for democracy and lifelong learning. The solutions must represent a balanced and transformed view of education. At the heart of such a view is simplifying and realigning our educational priorities and values based on research-validated principles.

Few would disagree that we want to prepare all students for productive lives and to be lifelong learners. In spite of differing politics, most would favor solutions that are empowering and in keeping with natural learning principles and laws of human functioning. These principles and laws include the natural range and diversity in human talents, abilities, and interests. In trusting natural principles that sort learners into the range of skills and interests needed to support a productive democratic society, we move away from standardized one-size fits all educational paradigms. We move into a transformed view of systems that rewards and support diversity and the development of individual potential in the context of democratic social ideals. Naturally, we want these transformational solutions to be evidence-based and lead to high levels of learning and achievement. The conflict is in the how. Even if we accept the value of high stakes tests, most people acknowledge, and research supports, that to be motivated to work hard on high stakes tests, low achieving students need incentives such as feedback on their progress and personalized teacher support. Such practices are essential if students are to find meaningfulness in the experience and take responsibility for their own learning. Outcome-based policies will not work without these extra learner-centered supports.

The increased pressure on high-poverty schools to spend the majority of time on test preparation does not engage students in the types of strategies that will pay off in the long run (Moon, Callahan, & Tomlinson, 2003). Through more curriculum redesign, more time will be found to teach students to deal with a changing world. Students need to know who they are as learners and how to go about learning, in addition to knowing how the world works. Such redesign efforts reflect an international movement to bring a new set of values to education (Russell, 2004). It is a movement that parents favor, because it would allow their students to see their learning improve, develop necessary skills, and be prepared for higher education as well as the workplace and larger society (Diamond, 2005).

Implementing less is more suggests centering education on basic life competencies. In fact, this is something more and more American parents are undertaking. According to the Coalition for Self-Learning (2003), the number of students being homeschooled has grown from about 20,000 in 1980 to over 2 million in 2003, and their test results are currently averaging higher than public schooled children. Homeschool students are also reported to have more self-confidence, creativity, optimism, and courage to explore, key qualities of lifelong learners as verified in United Kingdom (UK) studies (Deakin Crick & McCombs, in press). Transformative educational systems that develop basic life competencies, offered by others working in the UK (see Hargreaves, 2004), lead to lifelong and self-directed learning. Such systems focus on curriculum that is *competency-led* rather than information-led, enhancing motivation and students' natural interest in learning (which begins at birth) through strategies that are learner-centered. Strategies include listening and respecting student voices, providing relevance in topics to be learned, using collaboration in learning activities, and engaging students in vital projects that allow them to be involved in meaningful problem solving, thinking, communication, teamwork, social and interpersonal skills, and leadership development. In short, transformative educational systems provide meaningful academic content around fewer, central competencies.

But there is another feature of this transformational view: It acknowledges and respects human potential, the creative capacity at individual and collective levels. Friedman (2005) describes innovative organizations and systems as those made up of collaborative (and competitive) parts. They empower people with responsibility and tools and connect them in collaborative structures. The result can be imagination and initiative that results in innovation. Organic principles replace mechanistic approaches in transformative ways that capitalize on natural principles of learning and change, bridging the tension between a traditionalist focus on academic achievement (measured by mechanistic tests) and progressive education principles focused on student engagement. By looking at students and teachers as innovative human beings, both systems balance and a vibrant learning experience can be realized.

We can see the power of creative capacity in students' responses to technology. Technology is clearly a tool of innovation that is underutilized and inequitably distributed in public schools. In spite of these inequities, most educators and many parents are aware of the gap between students' use and understanding of the latest digital technologies and how these technologies are used or not used in the schools. Prensky (2006) contends that schools are stuck in the 20th century while students have rushed into the 21st century. Today's school-age students were born into the digital age and are fluent in the digital language of computers, video games, and the Internet. Many even report learning to read from games rather than teachers and school. Because students are empowered by technology in so many ways outside their schools, more than ever they need a meaningful voice in their own digital-age education. March (2006) argues that in this era of instant gratification, schools must provide education that is real, rich, and relevant. With this challenge comes the opportunity to shift students from consumption to action and creativity. It is more imperative than ever that teachers stay on top of innovative ways to use technology in learning. Most promising are collaborative partnership models shown to be highly effective, such as Dennis Harper's Gen Y program (Harper, 2002). What makes this program so innovative is that teachers and students are partners in using technology in learning. Students are taught to work with teachers to use technology in ways that are interesting and relevant while teachers are taught to work with students to design the lessons in ways that promote learning. Together, both teachers and students learn the best ways to learn with technology.

A LEARNER-CENTERED EDUCATIONAL MODEL

In our work with research-validated learner-centered principles, we have learned that learner-centered practices do not look the same from school to school, classroom to classroom, day-to-day, or even moment to moment within the same classroom. When teachers are attentive to learners and their learning needs, and understand basic principles of human learning, motivation, development, and individual differences, they go with the flow and create innovative environments that are flexible and dynamic. The most learner-centered teachers we have studied are not afraid to share power and control with students in a collaborative learning partnership (McCombs & Miller, 2006).

The benefits of faculty and students sharing academic goals and working together have been recognized at all educational levels (Summers, Beretvas, Svinicki, & Gorin, 2005). They lead to the development of a sense of community, which has been shown to have a number of positive benefits, including reduced high school dropout rates and increased student retention at the college level, as well as meeting basic human needs for connectedness.

As a grounding for such transformed practices, the American Psychological Association (APA) adopted the *Learner-Centered Psychological Principles* (LCPs) in 1997. This was mostly a response to what the APA considered ill-informed decisions being made based on *A Nation at Risk* (National Commission on Excellence and Education, 1983), which concluded that student achievement in the United States showed an alarming decline, especially in comparison with other countries such as Japan. The APA was concerned that the push toward testing and accountability was not informed by evidence regarding what best supports and fosters learning. Members of the APA Task Force working on the LCPs believed that psychology, as a scientific field that has studied learning for over 100 years, had a responsibility to clearly present to educators and policy makers its accumulated and research-validated knowledge base about learning and learners.[1] When work on the LCPs began, no one knew what the final product would look like or what it would be called. The Task Force saw it as a "living document" that would be revised and reissued as more was learned about learning, motivation, development, and individual differences that must be addressed to achieve optimal learning for all. The LCP document is now in its second iteration and continues to be widely disseminated to educators and researchers in this country and abroad (American Psychological Association [APA], 1997).

The LCPs, shown in Figure 3.1, serve as the foundation for the Learner-Centered Model (LCM) that colleagues and I developed over the past decade (McCombs, 2003, 2004; McCombs & Lauer, 1997; McCombs & Miller, 2006; McCombs & Whisler, 1997). Based on years of research, the LCPs were adopted by the APA (1997) as a definition of the psychological principles with the greatest positive effect on learners and learning. The 14 Learner Centered Principles, organized into four categories or domains, define what is known about learning and learners as a result of research into both. Many of these principles are consistent with recent discoveries from psychology relating to positive youth development and prevention interventions (see Seligman & Csikszentmihalyi, 2000).

The LCPs apply to all learners, in and outside of school, young and old. Research underlying the LCPs confirms that learning is nonlinear, recursive, continuous, complex, relational, and natural in humans. The evidence also shows that learning is enhanced in contexts where learners have supportive relationships, have a sense of ownership and control over the learning process, and can learn with and from each other in safe and trusting learning environments (McCombs, 2003, 2004). The key processes involved in developing learner-centered principles and practices are:

- Building ways to meet learner needs for interpersonal relationships and connections
- Finding strategies that acknowledge individual differences and the diversity of learner needs, abilities, and interests
- Tailoring strategies to differing learner needs for personal control and choice
- Assessing the efficacy of instructional practices to meet diverse and emerging individual learner and learning community needs

As an overriding principle, not only is it necessary to look for the match or mismatch of instructional practices with learning principles, but also their match or mismatch with learners and their diverse needs. A balance of supports can then be provided with a variety of learning opportunities, content requirements, and communities of learning.

Defining the Learner-Centered Model (LCM)

When the 14 LCPs are applied to schools and classrooms, they address each of the four learning domains. The resulting learner-centered framework provides a systemic approach to content, context, assessment, and individual learner needs. In addition, basing educational practices on the LCM and its associated LCPs provides a means for transforming education. The role of teachers changes to that of co-learners and contributors to the social and interpersonal development of students. In partnership with their teachers, students become responsible for their own learning and participate equally in determining what, how, and when they learn. The learner-centered framework adds a constant reminder that the human element cannot be left out of even the most advanced educational systems, including technology-supported networked learning communities (see McCombs & Vakili, 2005).

Taken together, the four domains of the LCPs offer a holistic way of looking at how individual principles combine and interact to influence

Figure 3.1. The Learner-Centered Psychological Principles

COGNITIVE AND METACOGNITIVE FACTORS

Principle 1: Nature of the learning process. The learning of complex subject matter is most effective when it is an intentional process of constructing meaning from information and experience.

Principle 2: Goals of the learning process. The successful learner, over time and with support and instructional guidance, can create meaningful, coherent representations of knowledge.

Principle 3: Construction of knowledge. The successful learner can link new information with existing knowledge in meaningful ways.

Principle 4: Strategic thinking. The successful learner can create and use a repertoire of thinking and reasoning strategies to achieve complex learning goals.

Principle 5: Thinking about thinking. Higher order strategies for selecting and monitoring mental operations facilitate creative and critical thinking.

Principle 6: Context of learning. Learning is influenced by environmental factors, including culture, technology, and instructional practices.

MOTIVATIONAL AND AFFECTIVE FACTORS

Principle 7: Motivational and emotional influences on learning. What and how much is learned is influenced by the learner's motivation. Motivation to learn, in turn, is influenced by the individual's emotional states, beliefs, interests and goals, and habits of thinking.

Principle 8: Intrinsic motivation to learn. The learner's creativity, higher order thinking, and natural curiosity all contribute to motivation to learn. Intrinsic motivation is stimulated by tasks of optimal novelty and difficulty, relevant to personal interests, and providing for personal choice and control.

Principle 9: Effects of motivation on effort. Acquisition of complex knowledge and skills requires extended learner effort and guided practice. Without learners' motivation to learn, the willingness to exert this effort is unlikely without coercion.

DEVELOPMENTAL AND SOCIAL FACTORS

Principle 10: Developmental influence on learning. As individuals develop, they encounter different opportunities and experience different constraints for learning. Learning is most effective when differential development within and across physical, intellectual, emotional, and social domains is taken into account.

Principle 11: Social influences on learning. Learning is influenced by social interactions, interpersonal relations, and communication with others.

INDIVIDUAL DIFFERENCES FACTORS

Principle 12: Individual differences in learning. Learners have different strategies, approaches, and capabilities for learning that are a function of prior experience and heredity.

Principle 13: Learning and diversity. Learning is most effective when differences in learners' linguistic, cultural, and social backgrounds are taken into account.

Principle 14: Standards and assessment. Setting appropriately high and challenging standards and assessing the learner and learning progress—including diagnostic, process, and outcome assessment—are integral parts of the learning process.

Note. Summarized from the APA Work Group of the Board of Educational Affairs (1997, November). *Learner-centered psychological principles: Guidelines for school reform and redesign.* Washington, DC: American Psychological Association.

learners and learning. Research on which the LCPs are based confirms the
four domains as follows:

- *Cognitive and metacognitive*—what the intellectual capacities of
  learners are and how they facilitate the learning process
- *Motivational and affective*—the roles played by motivation and
  emotions in learning
- *Developmental and social*—the influence of various diverse aspects of
  learner development and the importance of interpersonal interactions
  in learning and change
- *Individual differences*—how individual differences influence learning,
  how teachers, students, and administrators adapt to learning
  diversity, and how standards and assessment can best support
  individual differences in learners

Each of the four domains affects each learner in a unique way, as does the
synergy resulting from the interaction of the domains.

Putting learners first is at the heart of learner-centered teaching. It requires
knowing individual learners and providing a safe and nurturing learning
environment before the job of teaching can begin. Teachers who engage in
learner-centered teaching also understand that learning is a natural lifelong
process and that motivation to learn is also natural when the learning context
is supportive. If these teachers see evidence that students are not learning or
do not seem motivated to learn, they do not blame the student (or his/her
parents). They look at what is not happening in the teaching and learning
process or in the learning context that result in these natural processes being
blocked. Learner-centered teachers know that listening to students provides
a blueprint for finding the most effective practices and for engaging students'
voices in the process of learning. They encourage students to talk about how
they would meet their own learning needs, satisfy their natural curiosity,
and make sense of things. Since we know that teachers are learners, too, our
research and that of others confirms fundamental qualities of teachers that
are essential to their ability to provide learner-centered practices in ways that
authentically respond to student learning, motivation, and social needs.

What the General Research Evidence Shows

The Hay McBer Report (2000) includes these descriptions of how 8th
grade students define their ideal teacher: Is kind, is generous, listens to you,
encourages you, has faith in you, keeps confidences, likes teaching children,
likes teaching their subject, takes time to explain things, helps you when
you're stuck, tells you how you are doing, allows you to have your say,
doesn't give up on you, cares for your opinion, makes you feel clever, treats

people equally, stands up for you, makes allowances, tells the truth, is forgiving. These students' descriptions illustrate that the qualities that make teachers effective and learner-centered are more than their practices. Who teachers are—their qualities and characteristics—are as critical to being learner-centered as the practices, programs, and strategies they use.

A recent review of alternative educational models examined learner-centered, progressive, and holistic education (Martin, 2002). Growing numbers of alternative schools include: democratic schools, Quaker schools, Montessori education, Waldorf schools, and homeschooling. The alternative models tend *not* to be rooted in an overly rational or objective way of knowing and they acknowledge interdependencies and values. They include the emotional, ecological, spiritual, social, physical, and intellectual aspects of learning and living. These models address needs of the whole learner in balance with the needs of the community and society at large (Forbes, 1999). They hold in common a respect for diversity and are all person-centered approaches expressed in a diversity of ways. What makes learner-centered transformative (holistic) is its recognition that meaning is co-constructed, self-regulation occurs through interdependence, with a focus on being and becoming fully functioning.

In a comprehensive metaanalysis, White (2005) found that person- and learner-centered education are associated with large increases in student participation/initiation, satisfaction, and motivation to learn, which indicated high levels of engagement in learner-centered classrooms. Student perspectives were stronger predictors of student success than teacher perspectives. The major teacher variables associated with positive student outcomes included positive relationships, nondirectivity, empathy, warmth, and encouraging thinking and learning skills. White also found that universal learner-centered practices are particularly important for poor and minority students who traditionally do not receive this level of support.

Students As Meaningful Partners: International Evidence

Including students as meaningful partners in school reform is occurring internationally, particularly in the UK and Australia. In a study of student voice in British school reform, Fielding (2001, 2002) describes a 4-year Student as Researcher project in which high school students identified important issues in their daily experience of schooling. Together with students, staff gathered data, constructed meaning, shared recommendations for change with fellow students and staff, and presented their recommendations to the governing body of the school.

Fielding (2001) found that students began challenging the curriculum to move it away from a delivery model to a jointly derived, negotiated curriculum and pedagogy with meaning and relevance to their own lives. As the project continued, several student-led changes emerged from the dialogue engendered by the partnership model. As they gained new understandings and insights into their learning and the nature of the learning experience, students demonstrated the quality of their research and ability to identify and articulate insights into curriculum practices. The ongoing dialogue between teachers and students showed that both groups came to view their joint efforts as reflective of a genuine community. Teachers and students developed a commitment to teaching and learning as a shared responsibility, and each redefined what it means to be a student and a teacher.

Learner-Centered Model Components: Our Research Evidence

This simple idea—listening to kids in meaningful partnerships with adults as a foundation for addressing youth and public policy issues—is central to learner-centered teaching, to empowering youth, and to changing many systemic inequities and failures. When translated into practice, the LCM consists of a variety of materials, guided reflection, and assessment tools that support teacher effectiveness and change at the individual and school levels. Staff development workshops and videos exemplify learner-centered practices in diverse school settings. As an additional support for teachers changing their practices, my colleagues and I (McCombs, 2001, 2003; McCombs & Lauer, 1997; McCombs & Whisler, 1997) developed a set of self-assessment and reflection tools for K–20 teachers, called the Assessment of Learner-Centered Practices (ALCP). The ALCP includes surveys for teachers, students, and administrators that facilitate reflection and a willingness to change instructional practices. The teacher surveys offer an opportunity for reflection on how personal beliefs about learners, learning, and teaching coincides with the knowledge base underlying the LCPs. More importantly, they allow teachers to become aware of their students' perceptions about the frequency of their teacher's learner-centered practices.

In over a decade of research with the LCM and its associated tools, we have verified the benefits of learner-centered practices at the school and classroom levels. Research with the ALCP self-assessment surveys for teachers and students confirms that learner-centeredness is not solely a function of particular instructional practices or programs. Rather, it is a complex interaction of the programs, practices, policies, and people as perceived by the individual learners, that is, how teachers are perceived (their qualities and characteristics) as well as how instructional practices are implemented in terms of meeting student learning needs defines learner-centeredness. Ongoing data of over 35,000 students and their teachers in kindergarten through graduate school have now been collected with the ALCP surveys (McCombs, 2001; McCombs & Lauer, 1997; McCombs &

Pierce, 1999; McCombs & Quiat, 2002) to evaluate programs and practices that enhance the teaching and learning process.

In our research (McCombs, 2004), qualities related to being perceived by students as engaging in high levels of learner-centered practice in domains most related to high achievement and motivation include: high learner-centered beliefs (consistent with the APA principles) and low nonlearner-centered beliefs (more traditional), high levels of self-efficacy about their ability to reach and teach diverse learners, high reflective self-awareness, and high degrees of autonomy support. In schools and districts where the LCPs have been widely shared, teaching practices are achieving a more balanced approach that encourages high student learning and achievement while also promoting learner-centered approaches. These approaches, recognized in many of the nation's most excellent schools, lead to effective schooling and to positive mental health and productivity of our nation's children, their teachers, and the systems that serve them. A summary of these follows.

Grades K–3 results. The most important finding with K–3 teachers and students is that even young children can reliably and validly assess the degree to which their teachers engage in learner-centered practices. For young children, three validated domains most relate to positive learning and motivation outcomes: (1) creates positive interpersonal relationships/climate, (2) provides motivational support for learning, and (3) facilitates thinking and learning. Results indicated that when students perceived more learner-centered teacher practices, they had higher academic achievement and also reported greater interest in and liking of school and academic subjects (McCombs, Perry, & Daniels, in press).

Grades 4–8 results. With upper elementary and middle school students, learner-centered practices begin to have even stronger impacts on learning and motivation. Four domains of practice have been validated to most impact learning, motivational, and behavior outcomes: (1) creating positive relationships, (2) honoring student voice, (3) supporting higher order thinking and learning skills, and (4) adapting to individual differences (McCombs & Quiat, 2002; McCombs, 2004; Meece, Herman, & McCombs, 2003). At this developmental stage, students' perceptions of classroom practices are more strongly related to valued outcomes than teachers' perceptions.

Grades 9–12 results. For high school students, the importance of learner-centered practices increases. At this level, although there are different items from the Grades 4–8 level, the same four domains of practice exist (McCombs, 2004). Students' perceptions that their teachers frequently perform the four learner-centered domains of classroom practice are significantly correlated with all motivation variables, and are particularly highly related to student self-efficacy, epistemic (knowledge-seeking) curiosity, active learning strategies, and task mastery goals. In addition, students' perceptions that their teachers significantly perform these four domains of practice are positively correlated with classroom achievement and negatively correlated with classroom absences.

Connecting People, Principles, and Practices at all System Levels

One of the strongest implications of the LCPs and LCM is that education must address the whole learner. This is certainly not a new idea (see Combs, 1986, 1991; Noddings, 2005). The evidence base for this approach was less clear in earlier years than now, making a stronger case in terms of positive outcomes that extend beyond academic achievement. William Glasser (1990) has maintained that students will be more motivated to work harder and learn more, or have lower dropout rates, when we create more need-satisfying schools. These new schools will provide environments where students can really get to know their peers and teachers and develop a sense of trust, potentially also avoiding school violence issues. It is essential that students have an opportunity to study real world problems and learn for understanding in self-directed ways. In the new school paradigm, Patterson (2003) argues that decisions will be made based on what makes educational and personal sense for students. Combining this model with general education that contributes to the development of citizenship in a democratic society increases the usefulness and long-term impact of this model.

Vanhuysse (2006) contends that a general education contributes to the development of creativity and the role of the future in education. He relates that Albert Einstein defended generalism in schools on the basis that it promotes better adaptability to change. Further, those who study creativity in artistic and scientific endeavors such as Csikszentmihalyi (1996) have also argued that breakthroughs depend on linking information that is usually not thought of as related, by having a breadth of general knowledge beyond the limits of a specific knowledge domain. Vanhuysse (2006) points to general education as a way that the scientific and intuitive orientations of the human mind can avoid being kept separate, as their cross-fertilizing relates to the creation and production of knowledge. As shown by Simon (1983), liberal arts curricula help students learn better and remember longer than in narrowly defined or rigid curricula. Students can attend to issues longer and think harder about them, leading to deeper impressions that last longer, particularly when this curriculum is taught in the context of critical dialogue.

National studies conducted by the Just for the Kids (2003) organization suggest that the first key is to focus on the student, followed by high quality teaching and research-based instructional practices. Teachers are given the materials, training, and support they need and the time to plan together, discuss student progress, and reflect on best practices. In one such high performance school in Los Angeles, teachers work together to help students take risks so that they develop character and the skills to succeed in life (Mathews, 2004, January 20). As with the Central Park East program, students were taught to develop their minds by weighing evidence, seeing other ways of looking at the same data or situation, comparing and contrasting, seeking patterns, conjecturing and arguing (Meier, 2002). This type of transformational learner-centered paradigm can help students develop into the creative and critical thinkers, self-directed learners, problem solvers, time managers, and lifelong learners needed in our complex society.

Now let's revisit the question posed at the beginning of this chapter: How can we resolve the tensions between learner-centered and accountability focused perspectives in educating for democracy? I offer the following new model.

A NEW MODEL: THE LEARNER-CENTERED EDUCATIONAL SYSTEM AS AN INTELLECTUAL SUPPLY CHAIN

A number of colleagues and I have been working over the past 2 years to develop the Center for Innovation Science (CIS).[2] Our work is driven by the vision of creating and implementing a transformed educational systems model. To this end, we have developed a framework called the *intellectual supply chain* (ISC). The ISC supports the LCPs and is a system for integrating all key stakeholders in education and the workplace so that each has input at every level. It also discourages silos of isolated interest, allowing equitable access to the entire system by all learners. The major goal of the ISC is the alignment of all functions, content, and processes across the educational system and the workplace in order to nurture and further develop the natural human capacities of Collaboration, Learning, and Creativity (CLC). Together, these capacities form a meta-competency needed for a positive and productive life in all aspects of the personal, interpersonal, life work, and broader social-economic system levels. The end result of the ISC is an educational system that will be more responsive to technological changes and the need for innovation in the global economy.

Our vision for the CIS grew out of our shared understanding and concern over the fundamentally flawed current public education system and the policies surrounding its operation. We observed that the public education system is presently incapable of developing the intellectual capital and innovation that will drive the economy in the 21st century. We reviewed empirical evidence showing that schools willing to step outside the narrow testing and accountability agenda and implement practices consistent with research-validated principles of human learning, motivation, development, and individual differences are achieving higher levels of student learning across academic and social-emotional domains. Thus, we verified that the balance of high achievement and positive personal development is possible.

The challenge is to capture these best practice principles into a new educational systems design that prepares all learners (students and adults alike) to be lifelong learners and innovators in the workplace and in life. The positive outcomes at an individual level can to transfer to the ultimate establishment of new human social, economic, and political systems on a global scale. These new systems further promise to result in a more competent, more productive, more collaborative, and more creative world. The long-range goal of the CIS is to create a transformed view of educational systems that transfers to enlightened corporate settings. These systems must be grounded in an understanding of nature's natural sorting system and principles of human learning, motivation, development and individual differences.

WHAT'S NEXT—A CALL TO ACTION: CREATING THE EVOLVING MODEL TOGETHER

My colleagues and I believe the new metacompetency and ISC—implemented in keeping with the LCPs and the LCM—are needed to develop and enhance creativity, learning, and collaboration competencies in all learners. Beyond these goals, we believe it is what is needed to resolve the conflicting perspectives identified at the beginning of this chapter and to move us to a balanced resolution to current accountability demands.

How do we realize these transformational and systemic solutions? I believe it is by coming together and acknowledging our shared visions and values. The means for coming together are becoming easier than ever with existing and emerging technologies (e.g., chat rooms, virtual meetings). We can find each other, communicate across physical, economic, social, and cultural boundaries while building a network of diverse people, all of whom are ready to create the kind of educational system we need. The time for these activities is now. The seeds we plant now will affect the growth of our citizens for the future. And who knows what may get started. I hope it is the movement we have been aiming for that finally allows us to apply research-validated principles that result in learner-centered education for democracy equitably provided for all students.

CHAPTER 4

The More Things Change, the More They Stay the Same: Lessons from the Past on Diversity and Teaching

Cherry A. McGee Banks

University of Washington, Bothell

In 1944, when editors of *Educational Leadership* decided to devote the March 1945 issue to intercultural understanding, Ruth Cunningham contacted Leonard Covello, principal of Benjamin Franklin High School (BFHS) to ask for his support. The editors wanted to craft an issue that would be provocative and represent the perspectives of young people. Cunningham asked Covello to identify students who could write about intercultural education at Benjamin Franklin and share their understanding of the nature of intercultural problems and possible solutions to those problems. Ten years earlier no one would have believed that students from East Harlem would be asked to write for a national publication. In a relatively short period of time, a dedicated group of educators had helped improve the lives of young people in East Harlem, their education, and the community in which they lived.

Can we learn from what these educators in the past did? George Santayana (1905), the renown philosopher, said that to ignore history is to doom oneself to repeat its mistakes. As our nation grapples on an unprecedented scale with how to make schools work for diverse students, we have much to learn from educators who faced similar issues stemming from the arrival of immigrants from southern and eastern Europe in the late nineteenth and early twentieth centuries (Banks, 2005). An understanding of the past, when coupled with technical expertise and professional competence, can help educators and policy makers solve current problems (Presseisen, 1985; Tanner, 1997).

Identifying and applying lessons from the past to the present, however, is a challenging task. Even though problems related to language, social class, racial, ethnic and cultural diversity are perennial, we cannot simply assume that the problems educators confronted in the past are essentially the same as those we confront today. The unique character of the problems, the contexts in which they surface, and the specific groups they are associated with are never exactly the same. However, by examining the programs, strategies, and curricula that educators in the past used to address diversity, and the beliefs and values that informed their decision-making, readers can deepen their understanding of the complexities of school reform in a pluralistic society.

Benjamin Franklin High School, a school that was located in East Harlem, New York, can serve as a case study on school reform in a diverse community. As such it can help readers better understand how educators can respond to the challenges of a student population whose ethnic, religious, and cultural backgrounds place them on the margins of mainstream society. During the 1930s and 1940s, East Harlem was a diverse immigrant community. One could hear Yiddish, Russian, German, Italian, and various dialects of those and other languages while walking from block to block. People who lived outside the community viewed East Harlem and the people who lived there as something to be feared and avoided. Teachers at BFHS, however, saw the diversity of the community and the people who lived there as an asset.

This chapter describes how teachers at BFHS actualized their belief that diversity was an asset. The school's programs, teacher training, curricula, and the values and vision underpinning them are discussed. The chapter also highlights the role that Leonard Covello, who served as the school's first principal, played in implementing and sustaining school change. Throughout the chapter lessons from BFHS are identified and discussed. The lessons can be used as a departure point for readers to reflect on diversity and the role it should play in contemporary discussions about testing, standards, accountability, and other components of school reform. Readers will also learn that addressing diversity while maintaining a sense of accountability in schools is not new.

While the core idea of addressing diversity in schools is not new, many things have changed from the 1930s to present. The student population in urban schools changed from predominantly low-income European immigrants to predominantly students of color. The extent to which education is a requirement for employment has dramatically changed from the 1930s to the present. Public support for education has also changed. Immigrants in the early 20th century benefited from an unquestioned link between public schools and democracy. Today there is a growing acceptance of privatization of schools and little discussion about the role of public education in maintaining a democracy. Willingness to invest in schools like

BFHS, which was not only a beautiful building with the best equipment, labs, and teachers, seems to have disappeared. Today in its place, we have urban schools that Kozol (2005) describes in *The Shame of the Nation* as being similar to prisons.

As readers reflect on the challenges they are addressing with respect to diversity, they will know that while the specific issues that they are grappling with are unique to their time, they share a commitment to addressing diversity with BFHS teachers and administrators. This is the first lesson that readers can take from this chapter. Teachers who are committed to responding constructively to diversity are part of a long tradition of educators who envisioned high quality schools for all students and worked to create them. The educators at BFHS were a part of that tradition. They worked to close the gap between ideal American creed values of justice, freedom, and equality and the reality of those values as they were reflected in the daily lives of their students. In reading this chapter, contemporary educators who are committed to addressing diversity in their schools will know that they are not alone. They are standing shoulder to shoulder with teachers, social activists, and scholars who, early in the 20th century, centered diversity in their work.

THE MORE THINGS CHANGE, THE MORE THEY STAY THE SAME

By the beginning of the 21st century White ethnics, whose ancestors were on the margins of U.S. society in the early 20th century, were comfortably settled in mainstream America (Ignatiev, 1995; Jacobson, 1998). The margins, however, didn't disappear. They continued to be vibrant and were populated by indigenous people of color and by new waves of immigrants from Asia, Mexico, Latin America, and the Caribbean Islands (Pollard & O'Hare, 1999).

Even though the ethnicity of immigrant groups changes over time, the ways in which they are characterized within mainstream society remains essentially the same. This point is cogently made in *Shadow of Hate* (Teaching Tolerance, 1992), a video, text, and set of activities produced by the Southern Poverty Law Center for used with middle and high school students. *Shadow of Hate* illustrates how arguments made about the limitations of people from Russia, Italy, and other southern and eastern European countries who came to the United States at the turn of the 20th century were resurrected and used to describe immigrants who came after them. It is ironic that people who are members of ethnic groups that were once commonly described as delinquents and truants and as lacking ambition and intellectual ability would use similar language to characterize others. It is also ironic that teachers whose European ancestors may have been described in a similar way, wonder aloud how they can be expected to teach in schools where many of their students and their parents do not speak English, where conflict between groups require that they police the hallways, and where the economic and family patterns of their students are so different from theirs.

Understanding how and why immigrants who came to the United States at different times, spoke different languages, and had different phenotypes and other distinguishing characteristics, are viewed in such similar ways provides a concrete reference for drawing the following lesson from the past about the meaning of diversity. Diversity does not encompass a static set of characteristics that are exclusively associated with a particular group. It is a concept that encapsulates a broad and dynamic constellation of characteristics that, over time, have been associated with people who are now apart of the mainstream as well as people who are on the margins of society. As readers delve into a study of BFHS and the European immigrants it served they may find that learning about diversity and equity isn't simply an intellectual exercise, it is an encounter with the other that is within all of us.

BENJAMIN FRANKLIN HIGH SCHOOL: A SCHOOL THAT EMBRACED DIVERSITY

From the day its doors opened, Benjamin Franklin High School was a beacon of hope for a struggling and underprivileged community. To the immigrant and minority community it served, BFHS was *their* school, a place where they were welcome, understood, and appreciated. Its location on 116th Street near the East River in East Harlem, New York represented a real chance for a new beginning for people who had little more than the dreams that they had brought with them when they came to the United States. Benjamin Franklin High School gave them a sense that things were changing for the better. "A New School in a New Community" was a phrase heard throughout the community when BFHS opened in 1934.

Leonard Covello, an Italian immigrant, served as the first principal of the school. Covello grew up in an Italian American community and understood the people of East Harlem. He believed that America could be "enriched by the cultural heritage of all the world without sacrificing any degree of that which is essentially American" (Covello, 1939b, p. 11). That belief was reflected in BFHS's outreach programs, curriculum, and teacher-student interactions. He also believed that teachers needed opportunities to develop the intercultural skills and knowledge necessary to work effectively with second generation immigrants and their parents. To that end he, along with a cadre of dedicated teachers and administrators, created school structures that linked the school to the community.

Soon after BFHS opened it was clear that the school would not only have to focus on education, it would also have to address the social and economic needs of its students. The school provided free lunches, carfare, clothes, shoes and other necessities of life to its students. In talking about the challenge he faced at BFHS, Covello (1939b) stated that, "the work of the school became so intimately associated with the life of the community that it became inconceivable to think of the school in terms other than a neighborhood agency dispensing not only education but many other necessary aids to a happier community life" (p. 14). Covello understood students had a life outside of school. Problems they faced in their homes and communities didn't disappear as soon as students stepped inside BFHS (Perrone, 1998).

Benjamin Franklin was a child-centered, not a subject-centered, school. As such, the school was concerned with students' home life and social background. Teachers recognized that there were powerful disruptive as well as constructive forces in their students' communities and homes that both contributed to as well as detracted from their education. To get a better understanding of their students' home life, needs, handicaps, and emotions, teachers designed questionnaires that students and their parents completed. Information from the questionnaires was used to improve school services for students.

When problems of truancy and delinquency occurred or whenever there was a need for special assistance with students, teachers had the support of a special staff of home visitors who were hired to go into the homes of the students and talk with their parents. The home visitors were particularly helpful in working with parents because they spoke the language of the student's parents and were familiar with the students' home communities. Covello (1939a) argued that "the failure to approach the foreign-born through a familiar language leaves them stranded" (p. 324). Communicating with parents in their language helped make them feel comfortable coming to the school for conferences when problems occurred. Consequently, problems could be responded to quickly and positively before they developed into something more serious.

Long before educators recognized the importance of engaging students' preconceptions about how the world works (Donovan, Bransford, & Pellegrino, 1999), teachers at BFHS sought to identify and build on their students' home and community knowledge. By linking BFHS to the community, teachers were able to see their students as they were seen in the community and thus challenge their own preconceptions about their students and their students' parents. Teachers were also able to better understand their students' ideas and beliefs about gender roles as well as the social limits they placed on interacting with people who were ethnically, racially, and even regionally different from them. Through their connections with the community BFHS teachers were able to uncover, challenge, and ultimately provide adults and young people in East Harlem with new ways of viewing the world and their position in it.

The BFHS faculty's demonstrated commitment to working closely with parents and community members suggests the following lesson for contemporary educators to consider: Students' homes and communities are an important part of the educational equation. The connection between home and school, however, is complex because it involves elements of both assimilation and pluralism. Educators at BFHS wanted their students to assimilate into the mainstream of U.S. society, but they did not believe it was necessary for them to abandon all aspects of their ethnic culture in order to do so. They tried to balance diversity and unity by embracing aspects of both pluralism and assimilation, two competing ideologies. Pluralism was reflected in the BFHS faculty's outreach to the community and their efforts to learn more about their students' homes and community. Assimilation was reflected in how the faculty used that information to help them better understand how to help their students gain the skills and knowledge necessary for them to move into the mainstream. The combination of assimilation mediated by pluralistic perspectives that included sensitivity, appreciation, and recognition of their students' home and community culture, helped them balance unity with diversity.

The assimilation ideology, which was embedded in BFHS's commitment to linking the school to the community, continues to have primacy in schools today. The tension between assimilation and pluralism, however, has not been resolved. Educators and policy makers tend to avoid engaging in discussions that could help resolve the tension. This is because such discussions are often too emotional and personally situated for a dispassionate analysis to occur. Taking an historical perspective and using the work done by educators at BFHS, to open and frame discussions about how unity and diversity can be balanced in your school, may provide enough emotional distance for insights on contemporary educational problems to surface. It may also provide an opportunity for people to step back from the assumptions that they have about others who hold positions that are different from theirs and gain a better understand of the real values and beliefs that undergird various positions.

ADULT EDUCATION AT BENJAMIN FRANKLIN HIGH SCHOOL

There were two educational programs at Benjamin Franklin High School, a regular high school for boys and the adult school. While conceptually separate, the two schools were linked together through school–community committees, a shared facility, and families that had siblings in the regular school and the adult school. The school building was open continuously from 8:30 a.m. to 10:00 p.m. Monday through Friday. The regular program ran during the morning and early afternoon and the adult school operated during the late afternoon and evening. The curriculum at the adult school included academic subjects, crafts, and courses designed to build vocational skills. It was also a place were members of the community could go for help in addressing their day-to-day problems. For example, multilingual naturalization aides were available to assist members of the community who were having difficulties with their naturalization papers.

In addition to providing educational services and assistance to people in East Harlem, a major aim of the adult school was to increase intercultural understanding among the more than 36 different ethnic groups who lived in the immediate community. Covello's experience growing up in an ethnic community helped him understand that adults did not always realize the extent to which their attitudes and opinions were reflected in the attitudes and behaviors of their children and how their intolerance of outside groups could ultimately harm their children (Covello & D'Agostino, 1958). He and his colleagues understood that if they were to reduce prejudice among students in the high school, they had to move beyond the walls of the regular classroom. They had to go out into the community and find ways to increase understanding and appreciation of differences among the various groups who lived there. The adult school provided just the outreach vehicle that the BFHS staff needed to examine and transform intolerance in East Harlem.

The faculty and the administrators at BFHS were committed to using education to reduce prejudice and discrimination and to helping students recognize that the United States was a diverse society. They worked with ethnic organizations such as The Anti-Defamation League, community-based groups like the Young Men's Christian Association (YMCA), educational groups like the Service Bureau for Intercultural Education and religious groups such as the Churches of Christ in America to bring that message to their students. Those were particularly effective groups to work with because many of their staff members had parents who were immigrants. As members of a second generation they understood the challenges that BFHS students, who were also members of a second generation, had as they tried to bridge their parents' world and mainstream society. They could also appreciate and support BFHS's core value that ethnic, racial, and religious diversity added to the richness of American life.

When the adult school opened there was some concern that people in East Harlem would not be interested in an afternoon or evening educational program. However, as a result of an intense outreach program mounted by Covello, who served as principal of both the regular and adult school, and the BFHS faculty, enrollment in the adult school grew. By 1939, Covello reported that more than 1700 hundred adults had enrolled in English language, sewing, cooking, and other classes at the school. At its height the adult school had 46 classes and 26 teachers, some of whom also worked in the regular school.

A lesson that we can draw from the BFHS adult school is that schools do not operate in a vacuum. This lesson builds on the previous lesson where I argued that the link between schools and communities is complex. Even though parents and other members of the community are critical members of the school community, their ability to reinforce school values and goals is tied to their understanding of them and their sense that their concerns are reflected in them. Covello and the educators at BFHS designed the adult school as a place where adults could improve their skills, increase their job opportunities, get accurate information on immigration issues, and meet other concrete needs. While helping adults meet their needs, educators at BFHS were learning more about East Harlem and the people who lived there, and the adult students were learning about the school's goals and values. Most importantly, the adult school was a place were people from different ethnic, religious, and cultural groups could come together and through their interactions challenge their perceptions about people from other groups and identify characteristics that they shared with people they thought were different from them. The assumption that undergirded the faculty's efforts to reduce student prejudice was that once people got to know each other they would see their similarities and pay less attention to their differences. While this assumption may be viewed as somewhat naïve today, it was a radical idea in the 1930s. It also highlights the importance of intergroup contacts and interactions.[1]

WHAT TEACHERS AT BFHS WERE TAUGHT ABOUT DIVERSITY

One of the problems that Covello faced in implementing intercultural education at BFHS was the preparation of his teachers. Many of them were concerned about discrimination and prejudice and were aware of intercultural tensions particularly those in New York City. However, for the most part, the teachers were subject matter specialists who did not know how to deal with issues related to race and culture in the classroom.

Covello worked with the Service Bureau for Education in Human Relations and his long-time friend Rachael Davis DuBois to provide intercultural training for teachers at BFHS (DuBois, 1937). BFHS teachers and administrators met in Covello's office with representatives from the Service Bureau to design an in-service training plan. The plan they designed had teacher and student components. The teacher component involved small group meetings between representatives from the Bureau and teachers. In the meetings, which were essentially in-service training sessions, Bureau staff and BFHS teachers discussed intercultural education, read material on the contributions of immigrant groups, and teachers were trained in the intercultural program that was implemented with students. The student program employed a three-level approach (DuBois, 1939; DuBois with Okorodudu, 1984). The three levels were:

- *An Emotional Approach:* Teachers worked with members of the community to organize assembly programs where different ethnic groups performed and people from their group were featured as guest speakers. The goal was to give students a chance to see the rich cultural traditions of their classmates.
- *A Situational Approach:* Small groups of students engaged in informal conversations with community members who talked about ethnic or cultural issues. These talks were arranged to give students a chance to get to know people on a personal basis who were from a different ethnic group.
- *An Intellectual Approach:* During homeroom, students read and discussed information about ethnic groups that wasn't available in their school texts. The information was provided in the form of pamphlets and booklets produced by the Service Bureau.

BFHS teachers were also encouraged to expand their intercultural knowledge and skills by attending summer workshops in human relations. Scholarships covering registration fees, tuition, and room and board were offered to teachers who wanted to attend workshops at New York University, Stanford University, University of Michigan, and other U.S. universities. The summer workshops primarily focused on learning how to work more effectively with racial, religious, class, national and ethnic groups.

A lesson that readers can take from the BFHS in-service program is that teachers can't teach what they don't know. Becoming an effective teacher in a diverse society requires in-depth subject matter knowledge as well as multicultural knowledge. The combination of subject matter knowledge and multicultural knowledge is difficult to obtain without support. BFHS teachers were given the support they needed to become effective teachers for a diverse student body. It is important to note, however, that while deep subject matter and cultural knowledge is necessary, it isn't sufficient. Once teachers obtain that knowledge, it has to be translated into curriculum with appropriate instructional strategies. That also requires support. As you will read below, Covello asked his teachers to incorporate their newfound knowledge into their curricula.

DIVERSITY: FROM A CONCEPT TO A CURRICULUM

BFHS's in-service program in intercultural education drew heavily on social science knowledge. Teachers learned about concepts such as stereotypes, prejudice, and scapegoating. After they learned about these and other key concepts, they decided to make reducing student prejudice a key component of their curriculum. However, before designing curricula that addressed prejudice reduction, BFHS teachers wanted to better understand what their students knew and felt about people who were different from them. Using a questionnaire designed by The Service Bureau, BFHS teachers surveyed their students and identified knowledge gaps and misunderstandings that students had about outgroups. Next teachers assessed what students learned in their classes about diversity. Last, using the data they collected they designed curricula and formulated policies for future intercultural education programs.

Living Together with Others, Mankind Grows Up, Understanding America, and The Literature of Moral Attitudes and Social Problems are examples of themes that teachers wove through the English curriculum. Joseph Gallant, the head of the English Department at Benjamin Franklin High School, reported that those themes provided a basis for exploring issues related to race relations, nationality, prejudice, stereotypes, and the interrelationships of world religions. Readings such as *The ABC's of Scapegoating* (Allport, 1966) by Central YMCA College, *The Footprints of the Trojan Horse* (1940) by the Citizenship Educational Service, and *Divide and Conquer* (1942) by the Office of War Information were used to teach students how to analyze propaganda.

The Races of Mankind by Ruth Benedict and G. Wetfish (1943), along with its companion 35-minute silent film titled "We Are All Brothers," was used in biology classes to challenge the myth of the supremacy of the Aryan race. *The Races of Mankind* was an accessible text that simply yet scientifically explained why intelligence, character, and other positive human traits could not be singly attributed to one race. Science teachers also developed a number of lessons on racial attitudes (Bleifeld, 1939; Bleifeld, Goldstein, Nestler, Robinson, Rock, Sygoda, Weinberg, and Nagler, 1939). Teachers believed it was important to confront these kinds of issues because BFHS students were continually exposed through the societal curriculum to ideas that suggested that there was a hierarchy of races. Teachers also used excerpts from films such as *Black Legion, Fury, The Life of Louis Pasteur,* and *Men in White* to engage students in discussions about prejudice and other social issues. See Figure 4.1 for a brief description of the films.

A lesson from the past that remains relevant today is that when teachers are treated like professionals, they can add an important dimension to schools. BFHS teachers were given support in the form of in-service education where they were exposed to programs, materials, approaches, and strategies. Interestingly they were not expected to replicate those new ideas in their classrooms. They were expected to learn from them, rethink them, adapt them and then pilot their transformed ideas, strategies, and curricula in their classrooms. Teachers at BFHS were seen as skilled professionals who added important insights and perspectives to the curriculum.

It was, for example BFHS teachers, not school administrators, who were the force behind using contemporary films as classroom texts. Louis Relin, who taught in the BFHS English Department, spent three and a half weeks at Sarah Lawrence College learning how to incorporate films into school curricula. He brought the information he learned at Sarah Lawrence back to BFHS and beginning in October 1937, along with other BFHS teachers, began what was termed the Films Works Project. Mr. Relin captured the sense of professionalism that BFHS teachers felt after the implementation of the Films Works Project when he said, "We are duly proud, here at Franklin, to take our place in the ranks of forward-looking educators. It is impossible to even summarize adequately what we are doing for our students through the medium of the film. . . . We are learning the attitudes and prejudices which pervade the thinking of our youngsters, attitudes of which we have taken too little cognizance in the past" (Relin, 1937, p. 3). This is the statement of a person who sees himself and is seen by others as a professional and a leader among his peers.

Teachers today are often encouraged to look for the magic bullet, in the form of a perfect curriculum, strategy, or set of materials that when implemented according to the developer's directions will magically raise their students' test scores. The goals BFHS teachers had for their students went well beyond doing well on tests. They wanted their students to be well-rounded citizens. By treating BFHS teachers as professionals, Covello was able to draw on their energy, expertise, and enthusiasm to work toward meeting the school's goals.

ENRICHING LEARNING THROUGH COMMUNITY INVOLVEMENT

Earlier in the chapter we discussed why BFHS educators believed that community involvement was important, and we discussed the adult school as one venue for forging that link. Here we will discuss another approach that the educators used to link the school to the community. This approach involved setting up school-community committees where community members and teachers worked together (Covello, 1942).

The Committee for Racial Co-operation is an example of the kind of community-school committees Covello established. A core belief at BFHS was that the tensions and overt conflicts that occurred in the community between various racial and ethnic groups had to be addressed at school. The Committee for Racial Co-operation provided an effective vehicle for BFHS to operationalize that goal. The Committee began with BFHS staff, teachers, and administrators and then expanded to include community members. Covello encouraged community members to join the committee by inviting local leaders to a meeting to discuss racial discord in East Harlem. The group was told that the committee wanted to plan ways to counteract racial tension and prevent any further negative activity. That meeting resulted in a coalition of parents, teachers, students, and community leaders who were willing to join together to publicly voice their concerns about racial discord in the community. Committee activities included:

- Meeting periodically to maintain open lines of communication between the school and the community
- Organizing a speaker's bureau, visiting community organizations, and making presentations on BFHS's intercultural goals in the language of the group
- Presenting radio addresses on intercultural education. These addresses were designed to reach larger audiences than those that attended community meetings
- Writing articles on intercultural education for local foreign-language publications

The Committee was a visible statement to the community about the values of BFHS teachers, students, and parents. It did not, however, eliminate intergroup conflict in the school and community. Conflict between ethnic and racial groups surfaced again and again through the years. However, the coalition of teachers, students, and parents was always there to assert the values of the school and to temper intergroup tensions.

For example, in 1945, a series of incidents between African American and White students at BFHS and James Otis Junior High School threatened to erupt into a student strike. The trouble began on Thursday, September 27, with a dispute between Black and White students in the school gymnasium. It continued after school when several White boys, some of whom were not connected with BFHS, attacked a group of African American students who were waiting for their bus to take them home. Tensions continued to run high on Friday, September 28th, when a group of African American boys, some of whom had knives for their protection, walked en mass from their bus toward BFHS. When White residents in East Harlem saw the large group of African American students, some went into the street to confront the students. Eventually the police were called. On learning what was going on in the streets surrounding BFHS, school officials went outside, defused the

Figure 4.1. Films Used by BFHS Teachers

In an attempt to better understand and mediate students' attitudes and perceptions about a wide range of issues, BFHS teachers used films to engage students in open-ended discussions. Because the discussions centered on popular culture, students did not feel compelled to express "correct" answers, but instead could express their real thoughts and feelings. Using films as classroom texts is still viable today.

1. *Black Legion.* In this film Humphrey Bogart plays Frank Taylor, a man who, after losing a job to an immigrant, joins the Black Legion, a nativist group that engaged in crime and taught hatred of Catholics, Jews, Blacks, and others. The Black Legion wasn't simply a name given to a fictitious group in the film. The Black Legion was a group that actually existed and was involved in numerous ruthless acts of violence. This gave the film a type of authenticity when issues of scapegoating, projection, and violence were discussed.

2. *Fury.* This award-winning 1936 film, which starred Spencer Tracy, told the story of a man's dogged attempt to seek retribution after he narrowly escapes from a lynch mob. The film provided an opportunity for teachers to talk with students about the ways that rumors, prejudice, and groupthink can lead to tragedy.

3. *The Life of Louis Pasteur.* This Warner Brothers film chronicles the challenges that Louis Pasteur, a French chemist, faced in getting his ideas on germs and disease accepted by the medical establishment. The film highlights the importance of resilience and perseverance, especially when a person is an outsider whose ideas not viewed as being worthy of recognition. This story resonated with BFHS students, many of whom were immigrants or members of the second generation.

4. *Men in White.* Clark Gable and Myrna Loy starred in this 1934 MGM controversial film about crossing social boundaries and social taboos. Abortion, which was illegal at that time, is hinted at in the film. The film opened a door for discussions about decision-making and the catastrophic ways that poor decisions can affect one's life.

situation, and then escorted the African American students into the school. School was dismissed 20 minutes early that day and the African American students were allowed to board their bus near the school under the watchful eye of school officials. Rumors were rampant in the tense atmosphere following the incidents and parents commonly expressed fears about their children's safety. The rumors and fears were exacerbated by reports on the incidents in the *New York Times* with headlines such as "Student Strikes Flare into Riots in Harlem Schools" and "Knives Flash in Street Fights as Elders Join Pupils in Battling the Police."

Covello immediately convened a committee of teachers to investigate the incidents and draft a statement of facts. The statement, written in English and Italian, was shared with students and parents. In a letter inviting parents to attend a meeting at the school where they would be able to hear reports on the incidents in English and Italian from community leaders as well as himself, Covello implored the school community to pull together saying, "For 11 years I have worked all year 'round, day and night, 7 days a week, motivated only by my deep interest in the welfare of your children and families. I have always been willing to assume the responsibility of the school's program. The responsibility, however, is not mine alone. It is a joint responsibility, yours as parents, and ours as teachers. I know that I can count on your help" (Covello, 1945).

The parent meeting was followed by an all-day student assembly, where it was decided that students would work with their English teachers to draft slogans that would be used in the Columbus Day Parade.[2] Teachers were encouraged to ask their students to write brief slogans that expressed the democratic spirit of the unity of races, respect for all individuals, and BFHS school unity.

The Columbus Day Parade became a focal point for the school to reassert its values and commitments to the community. There would be a large turnout of parents and community members, and Covello wanted to make sure that BFHS would make a strong showing. So in addition to encouraging a large turnout of students, Covello sent a memo to the faculty in which he said in part, "A week ago Friday our school went through a difficult and trying experience. Every member of the faculty stood by fully allaying the fears of our boys and of their parents and thus making it possible by the middle of last week for us to have normal attendance and normal programs. Let us again stand as a group by marching with our boys on Friday. Let us affirm by positive action how deeply we feel on the question of segregation, discrimination and the fermenting of race hatred." (Covello, 1945). The Columbus Day Parade was a tremendous success for Covello and BFHS. The school reclaimed its position of leadership in the community and distanced itself from another incident of racial discord.

The Columbus Day incident illustrates how educators can use conflict to strengthen rather than fragment the school community. It also illustrates the extent to which racial discord and issues related to intergroup tensions cannot be fixed in a final sense. When they are addressed in one area, they may surface in another. The goal at BFHS wasn't to create a conflict-free school, but rather to create a school where students could be enriched through authentic intercultural contacts and experiences. Instead of allowing conflict to become dysfunctional, the actions of Covello and the teachers at BFHS demonstrate a way to learn and grow when confronted with conflict. The lessons of open and clear communication with parents and students, taking advantage of teachable moments, not being afraid to state your values and commitments, and working together as a school community are as sound today as they were in the mid-20th century.

ACCOUNTABILITY AT BFHS

During the 1930s when BFHS was established, it was not uncommon for educators to voice concerns about the intellectual ability of the second generation. Immigrants from southern and eastern Europe were widely believed to be incapable of reaching high levels of academic achievement. That idea was turned on its head at BFHS where teachers were expected to teach and students were expected to learn.

While the concept of accountability was not used in the way that it is used today, there was a clear sense that both teachers and students were accountable to the community. That sense of accountability was manifested in several ways. Students evaluated teachers and felt comfortable in complaining to the Covello if they believed a teacher was unprepared or not performing at an expected level. Students who dropped out of school were interviewed by Works Progress Administration (WPA) workers to find out why they left school and whether the school had failed them in some way. The information that was gathered from school dropouts was the impetus for a recommendation that BFHS establish a way to maintain a communication with these students. It was hoped that the students would, at a later date, enroll in the adult school or make themselves available to help in school programs designed to encourage students to stay in school. With this in mind, Covello worked with teachers to organize the Old Friendship Club. A major goal of the club was to maintain contact with boys after they left BFHS. The club included students who had dropped out as well as those who graduated. The club held periodic meetings in which the boys and their families and friends were invited to the school or a school clubhouse for entertainment, advice, and friendship.

Educators at BFHS teach us that accountability does not have to be framed in a punitive structure. Success and failure were not viewed as diametrically opposed at BFHS. Instead, accountability was framed by the school's values and goals that were embodied in school pride, inquiry, and a deep concern for students who were currently enrolled in the school as well as those who had dropped out. Moreover, accountability at BFHS did not exist in a vacuum. It was broadly defined, inclusive of the community, and the individuals who were held accountable were supported with the resources necessary for them to achieve success.

THEY MADE A DIFFERENCE

Human values guided the work done by Covello and his dedicated cadre of educators at Benjamin Franklin. Among the many values espoused by

BFHS educators, community was one of the most important. Covello and the educators at BFHS blurred the lines between community and school by bringing the community into the school and the school into the community. By doing so they were better able to understand and work effectively with their students. Covello captured this perspective when he noted that students should not be viewed as clay to be molded in the hands of skilled craftsmen. He believed that they were alive, vibrant, ever changing young people who were being shaped by forces both within and outside the school (Covello, 1936).

Many educators viewed Benjamin Franklin High School as a success in educating students who were on the margins of society. Covello and his teachers were sought after as experts who could provide insights to educators, politicians, the business community and others about how to teach underprivileged students. Commenting on intercultural education at Benjamin Franklin, Ione S. Eckerson, Field Secretary for the New York State Board of Higher Education, said:

> There is no doubt that the minority groups in this school have already become more interested in and proud of their own backgrounds.
> They seem to have gained a new conception of American culture and what their people have contributed to it. The inferiority complexes sublimated in bravado and mischief will gradually fail away. . . . The so-called majority group is having an eye-opening experience, finding out how very unique and rich American culture and life is because of its gifts from many lands and races. (Covello Archives, 1943)

The innovations at Benjamin Franklin High School were achieved as a result of an actively involved community, a dedicated and committed group of socially minded teachers, and the visionary leadership of Leonard Covello. Human values were paramount at Benjamin Franklin and Covello led through values. Leadership through values, however is a difficult kind of leadership because values are often in conflict. While teachers, students and community members at BFHS shared many values and beliefs, they also had conflicting ones. For example, some individuals saw community involvement as detracting from the school's central mission while others saw it as an integral part of the school's mission. Covello had to acknowledge those and other perspectives as he built coalitions and environments where differences could be discussed and negotiated. His success is an example of transformative leadership.

School change frequently involves tensions among values and beliefs as well as tensions between different political and ideological perspectives. Covello's experience at BFHS teaches us that a school leader has to draw upon the strength of his/her personality, leadership skills, and respect in the school system while maintaining a focus on values and goals. It also highlights the central role that vision plays in creating a sense of direction and in executing change.

By the late 1940s, African Americans and Puerto Ricans had become a more sizable component of the student population at BFHS. As East Harlem changed, it became harder for Covello and the teachers to identify and utilize common values to motivate people to come together and to garner the resources necessary for the school's extensive community outreach program. By the late 1950s, community schooling was only a shadow of what it had been in the 1930s and early 40s (Johanek, 1995). In addition, BFHS lost the skillful and visionary leadership Covello provided. Covello retired from the NYC schools in 1956 and in 1972 he returned to Italy. By the end of the 1982-83 school year, Benjamin Franklin High, the school on the hill, was no more. It closed amid accusations about its failed programs, high dropout rate, and declining teaching quality.

We've come full circle in our discussion of Benjamin Franklin High School, a school that fully embraced its mission to give its students, for whom society expected little, the finest education that it could provide. With lessons from the past as a backdrop, readers can begin to sort out the values that will guide their leadership, the vision that will serve as a foundation for school change in their communities, and the sources of motivation that will challenge teachers, students, and community members to work together for common goals. An understanding of the pioneering work done by educators at BFHS can serve as a departure point for educators to hone their skills and judgment as they work to address the challenges that they face as teachers in a pluralistic democratic society.

CHAPTER 5

Standards, Accountability, and School Reform

Linda Darling-Hammond

Stanford University School of Education

The education reform movement in the United States has focused increasingly on the development of new standards for students: Virtually all states have created standards for student learning, new curriculum frameworks to guide instruction, and new assessments to test students' knowledge. School districts across the country have weighed in with their own versions of standards-based reform, including new curricula, testing systems, accountability schemes, and promotion or graduation requirements.

The rhetoric of these reforms is appealing. Students cannot succeed in meeting the demands of the new economy if they do not encounter much more challenging work in school, many argue, and schools cannot be stimulated to improve unless the real accomplishments, or deficits, of their students are raised to public attention. There is certainly merit to these arguments. But will standards and tests improve schools or create educational opportunities where they do not now exist? What evidence do we have about the success of standards-based reform strategies, especially for the students in America's urban school systems where educational needs are greatest? In this chapter I review evidence about the outcomes of different approaches to standards-based reform in states and districts across the country with an eye toward evaluating whether and how they improve educational opportunities and student learning.

ALTERNATIVE VIEWS OF STANDARDS-BASED REFORM

Some proponents of standards-based reforms have envisioned that standards that express what students should know and be able to do would spur other reforms that mobilize more resources for student learning, including high quality curriculum frameworks, materials, and assessments tied to the standards; more widely available course offerings that reflect this high quality curriculum; more intensive teacher preparation and professional development guided by related standards for teaching; more equalized resources for schools; and more readily available safety nets for educationally needy students (O'Day & Smith, 1993). For others, the notions of standards and accountability have become synonymous with mandates for student testing, which may have little connection to policy initiatives that directly address the quality of teaching, the allocation of resources, or the nature of schooling (see Educate America, 1991).

In addition to these differences, distinct change theories have emerged around the idea of standards-based reform. Some argue that standards for learning and teaching should be used primarily to inform investments and curricular changes that will strengthen schools. They see the major problem as a need for teacher, school, and system learning about more effective practice combined with more equal and better-targeted resource allocation. Others argue that standards can motivate change only if they are used to apply sanctions to those who fail to meet them. They see the major problem as a lack of effort and focus on the part of educators and students.

Policy makers who endorse the latter view have emphasized high-stakes testing—that is, the use of scores on achievement tests to make decisions that have important consequences for examinees and others—as a primary strategy to promote accountability. Some high-stakes decisions affect students, such as the use of test scores for promotion, tracking and graduation. Others affect teachers and principals when scores are used to determine merit pay or potential dismissal. Still others affect schools, as when schools are awarded recognition or extra funds when scores increase or are put into intervention status or threatened with loss of registration when scores are low. Some policies take into account differences in the initial performance of students and in the many nonschool factors that can affect achievement. Some do not, holding schools to similar standards despite dissimilar student populations and resources.

Many questions arise from this policy strategy. Will investments in better teaching, curriculum, and schooling follow the press for new standards? Or will standards and tests built upon a foundation of continued inequality simply certify student failure more visibly and reduce access to future education and employment? In states where standards accompanied by high-stakes tests have been imposed without addressing inequalities in access to qualified teachers, a new generation of equity lawsuits has emerged. Litigation in California, Florida, New York, and elsewhere has followed on the heels of recently successful "adequacy" lawsuits in Alabama and New Jersey.

A growing body of research has found unintended consequences of high-stakes tests. Some studies have found that high-stakes tests can narrow the curriculum, pushing instruction toward lower order cognitive skills, and can distort scores (Klein, Hamilton, McCaffrey, & Stretcher, 2000; Koretz & Barron, 1998; Koretz, Linn, Dunbar, & Shepard, 1991; Linn, 2000; Linn, Graue, & Sanders, 1990; Stecher, Barron, Kaganoff, & Goodwin, 1998). In addition, grade retention as a response to low test scores appears not to improve educational achievement for those who are held back and increases their likelihood of dropping out (Hauser, 1999). Finally, there is evidence that high-stakes tests that reward or sanction schools based on average student scores can create incentives for pushing low scorers into special education, holding them back in the grades, and encouraging them to drop out so that schools' average scores will look better (Allington & McGill-Franzen, 1992; Darling-Hammond, 1991, 1992; Figlio & Getzler, 2002; Haney, 2000; Koretz, 1988; Shepard & Smith, 1988; Smith, 1986). School rankings tied to test scores have sometimes punished schools for accepting and keeping students with high levels of special needs and rewarded them for keeping such students out of their programs through selective admissions, transfer, and even push out policies (Smith, 1986).

In a recent paper citing concerns about the negative outcomes of test-based promotion and graduation policies, Robert Hauser (1999) voiced skepticism about whether many states' or districts' high-stakes testing policies are likely to result in positive consequences for students:

> It is possible to imagine an educational system in which test-based promotion standards are combined with effective diagnosis and remediation of learning problems, yet past experience suggests that American school systems may not have either the will or the means to enact such fair and effective practices. Such a system would include well-designed and carefully aligned curricular standards, performance standards, and assessments. Teachers would be well trained to meet high standards in their classrooms, and students would have ample notice of what they are expected to know and be able to do. Students with learning difficulties would be identified years in advance of high-stakes deadlines, and they and their parents and teachers would have ample opportunities to catch up before deadlines occur. Accountability for student performance would not rest solely or even primarily on individual students, but also, collectively, on educators and parents. There is no positive example of such a system in the United States, past or present, whose success is documented by credible research. (p. 3)

Hauser's concerns appear apt, given the research on such policies that has been available to date. In this chapter, I review additional data on the outcomes of test-based accountability systems. I also examine research on urban districts that have substantially improved their students' performance by focusing on the improvement of teaching through attending to professional accountability—rather than on sanctions for students—by emphasizing test-based accountability. In this chapter, I argue for a broader conception of accountability that examines whether the actions undertaken by policy makers in fact produce better quality education and higher levels of learning for a greater share of students and whether they work to address shortcomings in children's opportunities to learn.

Types of Educational Accountability

To expand our frame for examining accountability, it may be useful to recognize that there are many different conceptions of accountability that have influenced U.S. education policy and interact with one another in today's systems. They include at least the following:

- Political accountability: Legislators and school board members, for example, must regularly stand for election and answer for their decisions.
- Legal accountability: Schools are to operate in accord with legislation, and citizens can ask the courts to hear complaints about the public schools' violation of laws.
- Bureaucratic accountability: Federal, state, and district offices promulgate rules and regulations intended to ensure that schooling takes place according to set procedures.
- Professional accountability: Teachers and other staff are expected to acquire specialized knowledge, meet standards for entry, and uphold professional standards of practice in their work.
- Market accountability: Parents and students may in some cases choose the courses or schools they believe are most appropriate (Darling-Hammond, 1989).

All of these accountability mechanisms have their strengths and limitations, and each is more or less appropriate for certain goals. Political mechanisms can help establish general policy directions, but they do not allow citizens to judge each decision by elected officials, and they do not necessarily secure the rights of minorities. Legal mechanisms are useful in establishing and defending rights, but not everything is subject to court action and not all citizens have access to the courts. Bureaucratic mechanisms are appropriate when standard procedures will produce desired outcomes, but they can be counterproductive when clients have unique needs that require differential responses by those who must make nonroutine decisions. Professional mechanisms are important when services require complex knowledge and decision making to meet clients' individual needs, but they do not always take competing public goals (for example, cost containment) into account.

Market mechanisms are helpful when consumer preferences vary widely and the state has no direct interest in controlling choice, but they do not ensure that all citizens will have access to services of a given quality.

Because of these limits, no single form of accountability operates alone in any major area of public life. The choices of accountability tools—and the balance among different forms of accountability—are constantly shifting as problems emerge, as social goals change, and as new circumstances arise. In most urban public school systems, legal and bureaucratic accountability strategies have predominated over the last 20 or more years. These have especially focused on attempts to manage schooling through standardized educational procedures, prescribed curriculum and texts, and test-based accountability strategies, often tied to tracking and grouping decisions that are meant to determine the programs students will receive.

Few have experimented with market accountability until very recently. Most notable among them are New York City, which launched more than 150 small schools of choice in the 1990s to add to the many dozens that existed before that time, and Cambridge, Massachusetts, which has had a system of choice-based schools for more than 20 years. Finally, a very few urban districts have launched well-developed professional accountability strategies tied to standards for teaching as well as student learning. New York City's District #2, New Haven, California, and several cities in Connecticut, a state that launched a highly successful statewide reform focused on teaching quality are among these, and are described later.

Standards as Assessment: Attempts to Create Accountability Through High-Stakes Testing

Since the mid-1800s, urban school systems have periodically used student test scores to allocate rewards or sanctions to schools or teachers. (For an historical account, see Tyack, 1974.) Many states and districts have approached standards-based reform through this familiar strategy, claiming to implement new standards even when the tests are not aligned to the standards and when students are not assured of receiving qualified teachers, curriculum aligned with the standards, or schools organized to support them. Standards-based reform strategies that have used test scores as the basis for promoting students from grade to grade, determining program placements (e.g., to compensatory or gifted and talented classes), and making graduation decisions have received a great deal of publicity in the mid- to late-1990s as "new" reforms; however, they replicate policies that have come and gone many times before.

In contrast to schools in most European and Asian countries, U.S. schools have a long tradition of retaining students in a grade if they seem not to be succeeding at school. It has been estimated that the United States has an overall retention rate of 15 to 20% of its students annually (most of them at-risk students in central cities), placing U.S. public schools on a par with countries like Haiti or Sierra Leone and in stark contrast with countries like Japan, which has less than a 1% rate of grade retention, and European nations that bar grade retention (Smith & Shepard, 1987; Hauser, 1999). During the early 1980s, grade retentions increased as school districts instituted policies that linked standardized test scores to student promotion and placement decisions. Many of these policies failed and were repealed by the late 1980s, only to be reinstated less than a decade later.

For example, New York City experienced many of the problems associated with grade retention when the Promotional Gates Program was put in place in elementary and junior high schools during the early 1980s. At that time, gateways in Grades 4 and 7 were created through which students could pass only if they demonstrated a specified level of performance on the standardized citywide reading and mathematics tests. Students who did not meet the minimum standards were retained, sometimes repeatedly, until they were able to achieve the necessary score on the tests. Instead of strengthening most students' academic performance, however, the program created cohorts of students who had been retained repeatedly without learning gains; sometimes they had been held back for so long that their advanced age and physical size led to increased misbehavior and decreased achievement for both the retained students and others in their classrooms. The students retained had lower achievement, greater incidences of disciplinary difficulties, and higher dropout rates than students at similar achievement levels who had previously been promoted. A district study found that 40% of the students retained in seventh grade had dropped out within 4 years, as compared to 25% of a comparison group, and that, while those who received intensive services in the Gates year improved their achievement temporarily, neither the services nor the students' progress were sustained (New York City Division of Assessment and Accountability, 2001). Eventually, in the face of national and local evidence about the failures of this approach, the program was ended by Chancellor Fernandez in the late 1980s (Gampert & Opperman, 1988).

A decade later, with no sense of irony or institutional memory, the New York Times reported in September, 1999, that 21,000 students would be held back under the City's "new" policy to end social promotion (Wasserman, 1999). Two weeks later the newspaper reported that the social promotion policy was in disarray as two-thirds of the 35,000 students forced to take summer school still did not pass the tests and, further, that 4,500 students' test scores had been misreported and as many as 3,000 had been forced to take summer school by mistake (Hartocollis, 1999). Similar news headlines appeared in Los Angeles, where a policy to "end social promotion" resulted in more than 10,000 students being threatened with grade retention, only to find that the schools could not accurately identify who had passed or failed and could not find qualified teachers to teach the summer school programs that were supposed, miraculously, to catch these students up. The New York City Division of Assessment and Accountability (2001) noted that a sharp increase in dropout rates between the classes of 1998 and 2000 (from 15.6% to 19.3% of each class) was likely a function of both the "new" city promotional standards and the state's new test-based graduation requirements.

These outcomes have been replicated in other recent test-based promotion and graduation reforms. For example, the much publicized Chicago effort, which sought to end social promotion by requiring test passage at Grades 3, 6, and 8, appears to have failed to improve the learning of the thousands of students it retained. In the first 2 years under the policy, more than one-third of third, sixth, and eighth graders failed to meet the promotional test cutoffs by the end of the school year. Despite the fact that there were large-scale waivers for students with limited English proficiency and special education students, more than 20,000 students were retained in grade in 1997 and 1998, during the first 2 years of the program. Although average test scores improved, an evaluation by Consortium on Chicago School Research concluded that:

> Retained students did not do better than previously socially promoted students. The progress among retained third graders was most troubling. Over the 2 years between the end of second grade and the end of the second time through third grade, the average ITBS reading scores of these students increased only 1.2 GEs (grade equivalents) compared to 1.5 GEs for students with similar test scores who had been promoted prior to the policy. Also troubling is that one-year dropout rates among eighth graders with low skills are higher under this policy. . . . In short, Chicago has not solved the problem of poor performance among those who do not meet the minimum test cutoffs and are retained. Both the history of prior attempts to redress poor performance with retention and previous research would clearly have predicted this finding. Few studies of retention have found positive impacts, and most suggest that retained students do not do better than socially promoted students. The CPS policy now highlights a group of students who are facing significant barriers to learning and are falling farther and farther behind. (Roderick, Bryk, Jacob, Easton, & Allensworth, 1999, pp. 55–56)

These findings confirm those of a substantial body of research that has demonstrated that retaining students does not appear to help them catch up with peers and succeed in school; however, it does contribute to high rates of academic failure and behavioral difficulties. Studies comparing the learning gains of students who were retained with those of academically comparable students who were promoted have typically found that retained students actually achieve less than their comparable peers who move on through the grades. Students do not appear to benefit academically from grade retention regardless of the grade level or the student's initial achievement level (for reviews, see Baenen, 1988; Holmes & Matthews, 1984; Illinois Fair Schools Coalition, 1985; Labaree, 1984; Meisels, 1992; Oakes & Lipton, 1990; Ostrowski, 1987). Shepard and Smith (1986) conclude in their review of research: "Contrary to popular beliefs, repeating a grade does not help students gain ground academically and has a negative impact on social adjustment and self-esteem" (p. 86).

When students who were retained in a grade are compared with students of equal achievement levels who were promoted, the retained students consistently suffer poorer self–concepts, have more problems of social adjustment, and express more negative attitudes toward school at the end of the period of retention than do similar students who are promoted (Eads, 1990; Holmes & Matthews, 1984; Illinois Fair Schools Coalition, 1985; Shepard & Smith, 1988; Walker & Madhere, 1987).

In addition, many studies have found that grade retention increases dropout rates (Hess, 1986; Hess, Ells, Prindle, Liffman, and Kaplan, 1987; Safer, 1986; Smith & Shepard, 1987). Researchers have found that the odds of dropping out increase significantly for retained students, increasing the probabilities from 40% (Jimerson, Anderson, & Whipple, 2002) to as much as 250% (Rumberger & Larson, 1998) above those of similar students who were not retained.

The notion of holding students back is a crude remedy for educational problems derived from the factory assembly line model of schooling developed during the early years of the twentieth century: The assumption was that a sequenced set of procedures would be implemented as a child moved along the conveyor belt from 1st to 12th grade. If a particular set of procedures didn't take, the procedures should be repeated until the child was properly processed. There are a number of reasons why grade retention is not generally a productive answer to low achievement, however. First, students develop at very different rates, and in the early grades the wide range of development that produces many of the differences in achievement measures evens out by about third or fourth grade. However, students who are held back often develop a conception of themselves as incapable, which then often becomes a self-fulfilling prophecy as it affects their motivation and willingness to attempt difficult tasks. Second, if there is a real problem with a student's learning, wholesale grade retention does not typically lead to diagnosis of special learning needs or the use of more appropriate teaching strategies targeted to those needs. Finally, grade retention does not address system problems of poor teaching; nor does it promise better teaching in the subsequent year. In fact, low-achieving students are generally assigned to the least experienced and qualified teachers, exacerbating their learning difficulties.

Generally, the premise of grade retention as a solution for poor performance is that the problem, if there is one, resides in the child, rather than in the school setting. Rather than looking carefully at classroom practices and student needs when students are not achieving, schools send students back to repeat the same experience over again. Very little is done to ensure that the experience will be either higher in quality or more appropriate for the individual needs of the child. In short, grade retention provides little accountability for the quality of the educational experience students receive.

While it is certainly true that both students and their parents bear a measure of accountability for attending school, putting forth effort, and striving to meet expectations (and policies that set standards appropriately seek to mobilize those efforts), it is important for accountability policies to fairly assess what children and parents can do and what the system must do to enable successful efforts. This is especially important given the clear evidence that children in the United States receive dramatically unequal access to high-quality curriculum and teaching, and that these differentials are strongly related to their achievement (see Darling-Hammond, 1997, for a review).

Despite the rhetoric of American equality, the school experiences of students of color in the United States continue to be substantially separate and unequal. More than two thirds of minority students attend predominantly minority schools, and one third of Black and Latino students attend intensely segregated schools (i.e., 90% or more minority enrollment), most of which are in central cities (Orfield & Gordon, 2001). Currently, about two thirds of all students in central city schools are Black or Hispanic (National Center for Education Statistics, 1997a). This concentration facilitates inequality. Not only do funding systems and tax policies leave most urban districts with fewer resources than their suburban neighbors, but schools with high concentrations of low-income and minority students receive fewer resources than other schools within these districts. And tracking systems exacerbate these inequalities by segregating many minority students within schools, allocating still fewer educational opportunities to them at the classroom level.

In their review of resource allocation studies, MacPhail-Wilcox and King (1986) summarized the resulting situation as follows:

> School expenditure levels correlate positively with student socio-economic status and negatively with educational need when school size and grade level are controlled statistically. . . . Teachers with higher salaries are concentrated in high income and low minority schools. Furthermore, pupil-teacher ratios are higher in schools with larger minority and low-income student populations. . . . Educational units with higher proportions of low-income and minority students

are allocated fewer fiscal and educational resources than are more affluent educational units, despite the probability that these students have substantially greater need for both. (p. 425)

The situation has not improved in most states over the last decade and has grown substantially worse in some, as recent lawsuits challenging inequalities in Alabama, California, Louisiana, New Jersey, New York, and elsewhere have demonstrated. In combination, policies associated with school funding, resource allocations, and tracking leave poor and minority students with fewer and lower quality books, curriculum materials, laboratories, and computers; significantly larger class sizes; less qualified and experienced teachers; and less access to high quality curriculum. The fact that the least qualified teachers typically end up teaching the least advantaged students is particularly problematic, given recent studies that have found that teacher quality is one of the most important determinants of student achievement (for a review, see Darling-Hammond, 2000). Low-income and minority students are least likely to receive well-qualified, highly effective teachers (National Center for Education Statistics, 1997a; Sanders & Rivers, 1996). Some evidence suggests that differences in the quality of teachers available to poor and minority children may explain nearly as much of the variance in student achievement as socioeconomic status (Ferguson, 1991; Strauss & Sawyer, 1986).

Unequal access to qualified teachers exacerbates the disparate effects of test-based promotion and graduation policies. Nationally, retention rates for low-income children are at least twice those for high-income students. Students who are retained in grade are disproportionately representative of racial and ethnic and populations whose dominant language is other than English (Illinois Fair Schools Coalition, 1985; Shepard & Smith, 1986; Walker & Madhere, 1987). Thus, the students who receive the scantiest resources, the least qualified teachers, the poorest physical facilities, and the most restricted access to quality learning opportunities are supposed to be fixed by being held back.

The Chicago study noted that the failure to invest in improved teaching was an unrecognized problem in the city's reform strategy, which had tried to rely on a highly scripted centrally developed curriculum (which by design assumes, inaccurately, that students learn in the same ways and at the same pace) and grade retention as its major tools. The authors noted: "Thus the administration has worked to raise test scores among low-performing students without having to address questions regarding the adequacy of instruction during the school day or spend resources to increase teachers' capacity to teach and to meet students' needs more successfully" (Roderick et al., 1999, p. 57).

Where the failure to learn is a result of inadequate teaching and where the system's primary response is to require children to experience that inadequate teaching again, it is doubtful that such a policy increases the system's accountability to parents and students. The educational system's accountability to the greater society is also reduced when a side effect of the policy is that large numbers of students drop out of school, thus creating a societal burden of undereducated youth who are unable to function in the labor market and who increasingly join the welfare or criminal justice systems rather than the productive economy. Society as a whole does not benefit from school policies that claim to heighten accountability by pushing low achievers out of school to make test scores look better—a result that has been documented in several studies—or by failing to offer education that enables these students to learn.

INSTITUTIONAL RESPONSES TO TEST-BASED INCENTIVES

Unfortunately, most cities and states have used test-based reform strategies that rely on cross-sectional measures of student scores for different populations of students (e.g., average scores for eighth graders in a given year are compared to average scores for a different group of eighth graders in the prior year), rather than longitudinal assessments of student gains for students who remained in a given school over a period of time. Because schools' average scores on any measure are sensitive to changes in the population of students taking the test, and such changes can be induced by manipulating admissions, dropouts, and pupil classifications, policies that use schools' average scores for allocating sanctions have been found to result in several unintended negative consequences. As noted earlier, these include labeling low-scoring students for special education placements so that their scores won't count in school reports, retaining students in grade so that their relative standing will look better on grade-equivalent scores, excluding low-scoring students from admission to open enrollment schools, and encouraging such students to leave schools or drop out. This occurs because the policies create incentives for schools to keep out of the testing pool, or the school itself, students who will lower the average scores. Smith and colleagues explained the widespread engineering of student populations that he found in his study of New York City's implementation of performance standards as a basis for school level sanctions:

> Student selection provides the greatest leverage in the short-term accountability game. . . . The easiest way to improve one's chances of winning is (1) to add some highly likely students and (2) to drop some unlikely students, while simply

hanging on to those in the middle. School admissions is a central thread in the accountability fabric. (Smith, 1986, pp. 30–31)

In some cases, policies that reward or punish schools for average test scores have created a distorted view of accountability, one in which beating the numbers by manipulating student placements overwhelms efforts to serve students' educational needs well. These policies may also further exacerbate existing incentives for talented staff to opt for school placements where students are easy to teach, and school stability is high. Capable staff are less likely to risk losing rewards or incurring sanctions by volunteering to teach where many students have special needs and performance standards will be more difficult to attain. This outcome was recently reported as a result of Florida's recent use of aggregate test scores, reported as cross-sectional averages and unadjusted for student characteristics, for school rewards and sanctions. Qualified teachers were leaving the schools rated D or F "in droves" according to news reports at the start of the 1999 school year (DeVise, 1999), to be replaced by teachers without experience and often without training. As one principal queried, "Is anybody going to want to dedicate their lives to a school that has already been labeled a failure?"

Ironically, this approach to accountability compromises even further the educational chances of disadvantaged students, who are already served by a disproportionate share of those teachers who are inexperienced, unprepared, and underqualified. This outcome will be further exacerbated by policies that plan to reduce federal funds to schools that have lower test scores. Critics have argued that applying sanctions to schools with lower test score performance penalizes already disadvantaged students twice over: Having given them inadequate schools to begin with, society now punishes them again for failing to perform as well as other students who attend schools with greater resources. Such sanctions can discourage good schools from opening their doors to educationally needy students and place more emphasis on manipulating scores by eliminating or keeping out low-scoring students than on improving schools.

These outcomes have been noted of reforms in several states. For example, after the Regents Test reforms of the early 1980s in New York State, studies found evidence of schools retaining students and placing them in special education to increase average school performance in critical grade levels used as benchmarks for accountability policies (Allington & McGill-Franzen, 1992) and encouraging low-scoring secondary students to leave school entirely (Smith, 1986). By 1992, New York's four-year graduation rate had dropped to only 62%, leaving the state ranked 45th in the country on this measure (Feistritzer, 1993).

Similarly, Atlanta, Georgia, instituted a pupil progression policy in 1980 based on test score thresholds for each elementary grade. High failure rates and repeated retentions led to increased dropout rates. The high school completion rate in Atlanta dropped to 65% by 1982 and to 61% by 1988. A 1988 state policy set up additional test thresholds for promotion and graduation. This policy exacerbated the declines in graduation in Atlanta and elsewhere across the state. As Gary Orfield and Carole Ashkinaze (1991) noted:

> Although most of the reforms were popular, the policymakers and educators simply ignored a large body of research showing that they would not produce academic gains and would increase dropout rates. In other words, this was a policy with no probable educational benefits and large costs. The benefits were political and the costs were borne by at-risk students. The damage was psychological as well as educational, increasing the likelihood that at-risk students would drop out before receiving their diplomas; school districts were also hurt by the diversion of resources to repetitive years of education for many students. (p. 139)

An analysis of the test-based reform strategies enacted in 1983 and 1984 in Georgia and South Carolina, both of which tied rewards and sanctions to annual tests at each grade level found that neither state realized gains in achievement on the National Assessment of Educational Progress during the 1990s, although both experienced declines in high school graduation rates (Darling-Hammond, 2000).

Recent analyses of test-based reforms instituted in Texas in the 1980s have pointed to these and other problems. Although there were ostensible gains in scores on the TAAS tests have caused the state's reforms to be hailed as the Texas Miracle, a number of studies have suggested that the outcomes may be less positive than they appear. First, studies by the Center for Research and Evaluation on Testing (Haney, 2000) and by the Intercultural Development Research Association (1996) have found that both retention rates in ninth grade and dropout or attrition rates for high school students increased substantially since the 1980s. Both studies found that fewer than 50% of African American and Latino ninth graders progress to graduation 4 years later, and only about 70% of White ninth graders reach graduation. Haney (2000) found evidence that a growing number of low-scoring students leave school as early as eighth or ninth grade, before their scores are factored into school accountability rankings. The effects are most pronounced for students of color:

> In 1990–91, Black and Hispanic high school graduates relative to the number of Black and Hispanic students enrolled in grade 9 three years earlier fell to less than 0.50 and this ratio remained just about at or below this level from 1992 to

1999. (The corresponding ratio had been about 0.60 in the late 1970s and early 1980s). . . . From 1977 until about 1981 rates of grade 9 retention were similar for Black, Hispanic, and White students, but since about 1982, the rates at which Black and Hispanic students are denied promotion and required to repeat grade 9 have climbed steadily, such that by the late 1990s, nearly 30% of Black and Hispanic students were "failing" grade 9 and required to repeat that grade.

Haney's report and Texas Education Agency (TEA) analyses agree that dropout rates in Texas are substantially higher for students retained in ninth grade than for any other group.

TEA data find that rates of dropping out are at least 3 times higher for this group, even though they provide a rosier picture of overall graduation rates, since they do not count as dropouts the large number of students who are transferred to GED programs and fail to finish them.

Several recent studies have produced empirical data that cast doubt on the gains noted on the state TAAS tests, observing that Texas students have not made comparable gains on national standardized tests or on the state's own college entrance test (Haney, 2000; Gordon & Reese, 1997; Hoffman, Assaf, & Paris, 2001; Klein et al., 2000; Stotsky, 1998). These studies have variously suggested that teaching to the test may be raising scores on the state high-stakes test in ways that do not generalize to other tests that examine a broader set of higher order skills; that many students are excluded from the state tests to prop up average scores; and that passing scores have been lowered and the tests have been made easier over time to give the appearance of gains.

The American Psychological Association, American Educational Research Association, and the National Council on Measurement in Education have issued standards for the use of tests that indicate that test scores are too limited and unstable a measure to be used as the sole source of information for any major decision about student placement or promotion. A recent report of the National Research Council on high stakes (Heubert and Hauser, 1999) testing concluded:

> Scores from large-scale assessments should never be the only sources of information used to make a promotion or retention decision. . . . Test scores should always be used in combination with other sources of information about student achievement. (p. 286)

The test-based accountability systems in dozens of states and urban school systems stand in contravention to these professional standards. However, the negative effects of grade retention and graduation sanctions should not become an argument for social promotion, that is, the practice of moving students through the system without ensuring that they acquire the skills that they need. What are the alternatives? There are at least four complementary strategies that evidence suggests can improve student learning without grade retention:

1. Enhancing preparation and professional development for teachers to ensure that they have the knowledge and skills they need to teach a wider range of students to meet the standards
2. Redesigning school structures to support more intensive learning— including creating smaller school units (within an optimal size of 300– 500) and schools that team teachers to work with smaller total numbers of students for longer periods of time
3. Employing schoolwide and classroom performance assessments that support more coherent curriculum and better inform teaching
4. Ensuring that targeted supports and services are available for students when they are needed

Some urban districts have used these strategies to upgrade student learning and to create a more genuine accountability to parents and students. Though all of these districts continue to face difficulties and challenges, their substantial successes offer a very different model for standards-based reform, one that rests on the use of standards and assessments as a stimulus for professional development and curricular reform rather than as punishments for schools and students. Three examples are offered here: the statewide reforms in Connecticut that have supported substantial improvements in a number of cities (featured here are New Britain, Norwalk, and Middletown, among the state's lowest-income and once lowest-achieving districts); New York City's School District #2, and New Haven, California.

Connecticut

Connecticut provides an especially instructive example of how state level policy makers have used a standards-based starting point to upgrade teachers' knowledge and skills as a means of improving student learning. Since the early 1980s, the state has pursued a purposeful and comprehensive teaching quality agenda. The Connecticut case is a story of how bipartisan state policy makers implemented a coherent policy package over more than 15 years. They used teaching standards, followed later by student standards, to guide investments in school finance equalization, teacher salary increases tied to higher standards for teacher education and licensing, curriculum and assessment reforms, and a teacher support and assessment system that strengthened professional development.

Connecticut's teacher assessments and preparation requirements ensure that every entering teacher has strong content and pedagogical knowledge to enable him or her to teach a wide range of diverse learners well, including those who have special education needs and English language learning needs. Standards-based professional development opportunities have dramatically upgraded the knowledge and skills of the veteran teaching population. Student assessments are aimed at higher order thinking and performance skills and are used to evaluate and continually improve practice. While the public reporting system places strong pressure on districts and schools to improve their practice, the student assessments are not used for rewards or punishments for students, teachers, or schools. Rather than pursue a single silver bullet or a punitive approach that creates dysfunctional responses, Connecticut has made ongoing investments in improving teaching and schooling through high standards and high supports.

Dramatic gains in student achievement (accompanied by increases rather than declines in student graduation rates) and a plentiful supply of well-qualified teachers are two major outcomes of this agenda. By 1998, Connecticut's fourth grade students ranked first in the nation in reading and mathematics on the National Assessment of Educational Progress (NAEP), despite increased student poverty and language diversity in the state's public schools during that decade (National Center for Education Statistics, 1997b; National Education Goals Panel, 1999). (See Figure 6.1). The proportion of Connecticut eighth graders scoring at or above proficient in reading was also first in the nation, and Connecticut was not only the top performing state in writing, but the only one to perform significantly better than the U.S. average. A 1998 study linking the NAEP with the Third International Math and Science Study (TIMSS) found that, in the world, only top-ranked Singapore outscored Connecticut students in science (Baron, 1999). The achievement gap between white students and the growing minority student population was decreasing, and the more than 25% of Connecticut's students who are Black or Hispanic substantially outperformed their counterparts nationally (Baron, 1999).

In explaining Connecticut's reading achievement gains, a National Educational Goals Panel report (Baron, 1999) cited the state's teacher policies as a critical element, pointing to the 1986 Education Enhancement Act, as the linchpin of the teacher reforms. In this omnibus bill, Connecticut coupled major increases in teacher salaries with greater equalization in funding across districts, higher standards for teacher education and licensing, and substantial investments in beginning teacher mentoring and professional development. An initial investment of $300 million was used to boost minimum beginning teacher salaries in an equalizing fashion that made it possible for low-wealth districts to compete in the market for qualified teachers. The average teacher's salary increased from a 1986 average of

$29,437 to a 1991 average of $47,823 (Fisk, 1999). These grants were provided on an equalizing basis to enable poor districts to better compete in the market for qualified teachers. Districts were given incentives to hire qualified teachers because salary grants were calculated on the basis of fully certified teachers only, and emergency credentials were phased out.

To further ensure an adequate supply of qualified teachers, the state offered incentives including scholarships and forgivable loans to attract high-ability teacher candidates, especially in high-demand fields, and encouraged well-qualified teachers from other states to come to Connecticut through license transportability reforms. An analysis of the outcomes of this set of initiatives found that they eliminated teacher shortages, even in the cities, and created surpluses of teachers within three years of its passage (Connecticut State Department of Education, 1990). These surpluses were maintained throughout the decade, allowing districts, including urban school districts, to be highly selective in their hiring and demanding in their expectations for teacher expertise.

At the same time, the state raised teacher education and licensing standards by requiring a major in the discipline to be taught plus extensive knowledge of teaching and learning as part of preparation (including knowledge for all teachers about literacy development and the teaching of special needs students); instituted performance-based examinations in subject matter and knowledge of teaching as a basis for receiving a license; created a state-funded beginning teacher mentoring program that supported trained mentors for beginning teachers in their first year on the job; and created a sophisticated assessment program using state-trained assessors for determining who could continue in teaching after the initial year.

Connecticut also required teachers to earn a master's degree in education for a continuing license and supported new professional development strategies in universities and school districts. In the late 1990s, the state further extended its performance-based licensing system to incorporate the new Interstate New Teacher Assessment and Support Consortium (INTASC) standards[1] and to develop portfolio assessments modeled on those of the National Board for Professional Teaching Standards. As part of ongoing teacher education reforms, the state agency has supported the creation of professional development schools linked to local universities and more than 100 school-university partnerships. In addition, Connecticut has developed courses on teacher and student standards that can be applied toward the required master's degree. The state also funds and operates a set of institutes for teaching and learning.

Connecticut's portfolio assessments for beginning teacher licensing are modeled on those of the National Board for Professional Teaching Standards; they examine directly whether a teacher is able to teach to Connecticut's student learning standards in specific content areas. The performance assessments examine teacher plans, videotapes of lessons, student work, and teacher analyses of their practice. They are developed with the assistance of teachers, teacher educators, and administrators. Hundreds of educators are convened to provide feedback on drafts of the standards, and many more are involved in the assessments themselves, as cooperating teachers and school-based mentors who work with beginning teachers on developing their practice, as assessors who are trained to score the portfolios, and as expert teachers and teacher educators who convene regional support seminars to help candidates learn about the standards and the portfolio development process. Preparation is organized around the examination of cases and the development of evidence connected to the standards.

Together, these activities have had far-reaching effects. By one estimate, more than 40% of Connecticut's teachers have gone through the process as new teachers or have served as assessors, mentors, or cooperating teachers. By the year 2010, 80% of elementary teachers, and nearly as many secondary teachers, will have participated in the new assessment system as candidates, support providers, or assessors. Because the assessments focus on the development of teacher competence, are tightly tied to student standards, and lead to sophisticated analysis of practice, the assessment system serves as a focal point for improving teaching and learning.

In addition to the state's major investments in teaching quality, the Goals Panel report also pointed to the thoughtful use of student standards and assessments in Connecticut. In 1987, following the teaching reforms, student learning standards were adopted in an early effort to link teacher education standards with expectations for teaching. In 1993–1994, the student standards were updated to emphasize higher order thinking skills and performance abilities, and new assessments were developed; these include constructed response and performance assessments that measure reading and writing authentically and reflect more challenging learning goals than the previous tests.

Also critical is the fact that, in line with professional standards for testing, the law precludes the use of these assessments for promotion or graduation of students. Instead, they are used for ongoing improvements in curriculum and teaching. The Goals Panel report noted the benefits of the state's low-stakes testing approach, which emphasize reporting and analysis strategies that support the wide dissemination of the standards and test objectives along with widespread professional development around literacy and the teaching of reading. The State Department of Education also supports the use of test results for educational improvement by giving districts computerized data that allow analyses at the district, school, teacher, and individual pupil level. The department assists districts in analyzing the data in ways that permit diagnosis of needs and areas for concentrated work (Baron, 1999). The state then provides targeted resources to the neediest districts to help them improve, including funding for professional development for teachers and administrators, preschool and all-day kindergarten for students, and smaller pupil–teacher ratios, among other supports.

The Goals Panel study notes that this approach to assessment has enabled districts to clarify their teaching priorities and has helped galvanize district efforts to make major revisions and improvements in their reading instruction. At the same time, the targeted provision of resources to the state's neediest districts through categorical grants has enabled these districts to enhance their reading initiatives and to begin to close the gap between their scores and those statewide (Baron, 1999).

Among the 10 Connecticut districts that made the greatest progress in reading between 1990 and 1998, three—New Britain, Norwalk, and Middletown—are urban school systems in the group identified as the state's neediest districts based on the percentage of students eligible for free lunch programs and their state test scores (see Table 5.1).

Follow-up studies in these districts identified a number of state-level policies and related local strategies as contributing to this success (Baron, 1999). Among them were teacher policies that enabled the districts to hire and retain highly qualified teachers who had been prepared to teach a wide range of learners, and the required beginning teacher program that provided state training for all mentors, thus increasing the knowledge and skills of veteran teachers along with beginners involved with the program. In addition, district respondents described state and locally supported intensive professional development around the teaching of reading. Consistent with the student standards and the state assessments, professional development funds were orchestrated to improve teachers' knowledge of how to teach reading through a balanced approach to whole language and skill-based instruction, how to address reading difficulties through specific intervention strategies, and how to diagnose and treat specific learning disabilities. Most of the districts had developed cadres of teacher trainers or coaches who were experts in literacy development and who were available to work with colleagues in the schools, offering demonstration teaching as well as classroom coaching. A number used state grants to sponsor intensive summer literacy workshops focused on the teaching of at-risk readers.

The approaches to reading instruction used in sharply improving districts rely on the enhanced teacher knowledge spurred in Connecticut's teacher education reforms and represented in the state's teaching assessments: systematic teaching of reading and spelling skills (including linguistics training that goes beyond basic phonemic awareness); use of authentic reading materials—children's literature, periodicals, and trade books—along with daily writing and discussion of ideas; ongoing assessment of students' reading proficiency through strategies like running records, miscue analyses, and analysis of reading, writing, and speaking samples; and intervention strategies for students with reading delays, such Reading Recovery, which was used in 9 of the 10 sharply improving districts and is widely used across the state (Baron, 1999).

District administrators noted the importance of the system's coherence in allowing them to pursue these sophisticated strategies for teaching and learning. In addition to their work on teacher development, they described how they had realigned district curriculum and instruction to the student learning standards and assessments, and how they had used the rich information about student performance made available by the CSDE as the basis for school problem solving and teachers' individual growth plans. (The latter are part of the teacher evaluation system.) They also credited the fact that the state assessments measured reading and writing in authentic ways, the preparation and professional development programs were supportive of the same approaches, and beginning teachers were coming to them better prepared to teach to these standards using successful pedagogical strategies, while veterans also had many opportunities to develop.

The quality of teaching in Connecticut can be traced directly to the implementation of an increasingly well-developed statewide infrastructure that has been designed to encourage high quality teaching by (1) linking salaries to high standards for preparing, entering, and remaining in teaching, (2) providing intensive support and assessment of beginning teachers, and (3) requiring and supporting continued high-quality professional development for teachers and administrators. These factors have helped establish a foundation of professional expertise that can ensure the success of other organizational policies and practices, such as analysis of student achievement results, linking school improvement plans and teacher evaluations to student achievement, and aligning expectations and assessments for students with high standards for teachers.

New York City District #2

A remarkably similar set of strategies produced similar results in New York City's Community School District #2 during the decade-long tenure of superintendent Tony Alvarado, from 1987 to 1997. Among the extremely diverse, multilingual district of 22,000 students, of whom more than 70% were students of color and more than half were from families officially classified as having incomes below the poverty level,[2] the district families spoke more than 100 different languages. Over the course of a decade, the district rose from 11th to 2nd in the city in student achievement in reading and mathematics, scoring above New York State norms as well as New York City averages, even while the population of the district grew more more language diverse.

Studies of District #2 attributed these gains to the district's decision

Table 5.1. Progress in Reading Achievement in Three Connecticut Districts, 1990–1998

District	Grade Level	1993 CMT Index Score	1998 CMT Index Score	Gain in Average CMT Score
State	Grade 4	56.9	65.5	18.6
Average	Grade 6	68.0	74.2	16.2
	Grade 8	69.9	75.5	15.6
Middletown	Grade 4	51.8	65.7	13.9
	Grade 6	67.0	74.2	17.2
	Grade 8	64.7	75.6	10.9
Norwalk	Grade 4	46.6	58.6	12.0
	Grade 6	55.3	62.7	17.4
	Grade 8	53.8	66.4	12.6
New Britain	Grade 4	36.3	47.4	11.1
	Grade 6	35.0	45.6	10.6
	Grade 8	38.5	52.3	13.8

to make professional development the central focus of management and the core strategy for school improvement. The strong belief governing the district's efforts is that student learning will increase as the knowledge of educators grows (Elmore & Burney, 1999). Rather than treating professional development as a discrete function implemented with a set of disparate nonsystemic activities, District 2 makes professional development around common standards of teaching the most important focus of all district efforts, its most prominent discretionary budgetary commitment, and a key part of every leader's and every teacher's job.

After consolidating categorical funds and focusing them on a coherent program of professional learning, District 2 moved most of its central office personnel positions back to school sites to focus on the improvement of practice. In a set of moves intently focused on enhancing professional accountability, Alvarado aggressively recruited instructionally knowledge-able teachers and principals, created pointed expectations and opportunities for professional development around the deepening of instructional practice—first in literacy and then in mathematics—and replaced through retirements, counseling out, and personnel actions those underskilled principals and teachers who were unable or unwilling to develop their practice. Both principals and teachers were expected to learn about best practices in teaching literacy and mathematics, and school leaders were held accountable for their own and their colleagues' increasing skill, for the quality of instructional practice in their buildings, for recruiting well-prepared new teachers, and for moving ineffective teachers out of the district.

While he was transforming the composition and skill set of the district staff, Alvarado created 17 Option Schools, small alternative schools that reorganized instruction to focus on greater personalization and more performance-based assessments to guide teaching, while encouraging the redesign of other schools. These efforts leveraged the creation of more small schools along with grouping practices that keep teachers and students together for more than one year, schedules that allow collaborative planning and professional development for teachers within the school day, and more coherent, intellectually challenging curriculum supported by ongoing diagnostic and performance assessments of student learning.

School redesign was joined with professional development in a conscious strategy to improve both teachers' expertise and schools' ability to support in-depth teaching and learning. Well known for his efforts to create restructured schools and schools of choice when he was superintendent in District #4, Alvarado found that the creation of new alternatives, while useful for the schools where dynamic educators coalesced, did not go far enough in building knowledge for better practice in all schools and classrooms. As he explained, "When I moved to District 2, I was determined to push beyond the District 4 strategy and to focus more broadly on instructional improvement across the board, not just on the creation of alternative programs" (Elmore & Burney, 1999, p. 267).

Staff development in District 2 differs substantially from the one-shot workshop that expects teachers to take generic ideas unconnected to their ongoing work and apply them in the classroom. Rather, the prevailing theory is that changes in instruction occur when teachers receive continuous support embedded in a coherent instructional system that is focused on the practical details of what it means to teach effectively. The district's extensive professional development efforts, which have paid off in rapidly rising student achievement, include several vehicles for learning. Instructional consulting services allow expert teachers and consultants to work within schools with groups of teachers in sustained ways to develop particular strategies, such as literature-based reading instruction. Intervisitation and peer networks are designed to bring teachers and principals into contact with exemplary practices. The district budgets for 300 days each year to provide the time for teachers and principals to visit and observe one another, to develop study groups, and to pair up for work together. Off-site training includes intensive summer institutes that focus on core teaching strategies and on learning about new standards, curriculum frameworks, and assessments. These are always linked to follow-up through consulting services and peer networks to develop practices further. The Professional Development Laboratory allows visiting teachers to spend 3 weeks in the classrooms of expert resident teachers who are engaged in practices they want to learn. Oversight and evaluation of principals focuses on their plans for instructional improvement in each content area, as does evaluation of teachers. There is close, careful scrutiny of teaching from the central office as well as the school and continual pressure and support to improve its quality. As Elmore and Burney (1999) explain:

> Shared expertise takes a number of forms in District 2. District staff regularly visit principals and teachers in schools and classrooms, both as part of a formal evaluation process and as part of an informal process of observation and advice. Within schools, principals and teachers routinely engage in grade-level and cross-grade conferences on curriculum and teaching. Across schools, principals and teachers regularly visit other schools and classrooms. At the district level, staff development consultants regularly work with teachers in their classrooms. Teachers regularly work with teachers in other schools for extended periods of supervised practice. Teams of principals and teachers regularly work on districtwide curriculum and staff development issues. Principals regularly meet in each others' schools and observe practice in those schools. Principals and teachers regularly visit schools and classrooms within and outside the district. And principals regularly work in pairs on common issues of instructional improvement in their schools. The underlying idea behind all these forms of interaction is that shared expertise is more likely to produce change than individuals working in isolation. (p. 268)

A key feature of these strategies is that they have focused intensely for multiple years on a few strands of content-focused training designed to have cumulative impact over the long term, rather than changing workshop topics every in-service day or picking new themes each year. The district has sponsored 8 years of intensive work on teaching strategies for literacy development and 4 years on mathematics teaching. District 2's approach began with reading and writing because this focus provided a readily available way for the district to demonstrate improvement in academic performance in an area that was important on citywide assessment measures and because literacy was important in the context of the district's linguistic and ethnic diversity. New York City's development of more performance-oriented assessments in reading and mathematics in the early 1990s provided more useful targets for these instructional reforms.

As in Connecticut, Reading Recovery training for an ever-widening circle of teachers created the first foundations of the teacher development initiative. This effort was used to improve teachers' knowledge about how to teach reading to their entire classrooms of students, not just to provide one-on-one tutoring to students with special reading needs. Ongoing work focused on whole language approaches to the teaching of reading and writing, with integration of specific work on reading skills and strategies focused by individual student assessment through tools like the Primary Language Record, that helped teachers develop documentation through running records, miscue analyses, and analysis of student work samples. As district staff, consultants, and principals learned how to change teaching practice through the literacy initiative, drawing on local university supports like Teachers College's Writing Institute and the Lehman College Literacy Center as well as district expertise, Alvarado began a parallel effort in mathematics using a similar model that drew in part on mathematics coaches trained at Bank Street's School of Education.

Much of this work occurred within the context of changes in New York State's learning standards and curriculum frameworks that supported district efforts to develop more challenging, performance-oriented standards to be used in assessing student work. District #2, and later New York City, adopted the curriculum frameworks of the New Standards Project and formed an alliance with the University of Pittsburgh's new Institute for Learning, piloting its performance assessments of student learning, which use portfolios and extensive student work samples as well as constructed response tests. Alvarado saw this emerging emphasis on standards as a logical extension of the District's efforts at instructional improvement. At the same time, he argued that introducing the standards and assessments before principals and teachers had had extensive experience with instructional improvement would have been a mistake. "You can kill a lot of the learning that you need in the system by insisting that it all has to line up with some item on a test," he explained. On the other hand, he felt that standards and assessment are logical extensions of an emphasis on professional development as a mechanism of instructional improvement (Elmore & Burney, 1997, p. 283).

While assessments of student learning are a critical element in the overall improvement strategy, the incentive structures are explicitly aimed at improving professional accountability—that is, the capacity and commitment of educators to teach well—rather than hoping for improved learning by increasing the amount of testing or sanctions attached to tests. Elmore and Burney note, "Accountability within the system is expressed in terms of teachers' and principals' objectives for instructional improvement. . . . Management is operationally defined as helping teachers to do their work better, and work is defined in terms of teaching and learning" (p. 283).

Professional accountability has meant high-stakes attached to hiring and retaining high quality teachers and principals, rather than stakes that punish students who do not succeed. While Alvarado replaced 80% of the principals in District 2 in his first 4 years, about 50% of teachers in the district were replaced over the course of 8 years, not through random attrition but through careful recruitment and replacement. Elmore and Burney (1999) report:

> This attitude toward the centrality of personnel decisions has begun to permeate, in turn, principals' attitudes toward the hiring of teachers. Most of the principals we interviewed in the system said spontaneously, without any prompting, that the key determinant of their capacity to meet their school-level objectives was the quality of their teachers and that they had learned how to exercise more influence on the process of recruiting, hiring, nurturing, retaining, and firing, or counseling-out, of teachers in their schools. (p. 282)

The emphasis on professional accountability, while uncomfortable for those not interested in improving, also created a positive professional culture in the district. Elmore and Burney (1999) also note:

> Most principals and teachers with whom we spoke reported that they were gratified, energized, and generally enthusiastic, if sometimes a bit intimidated, by the attention they received through District 2's professional development strategy. They report attending professional development activities outside the district or conducting visits to other schools and districts and being impressed with the amount of attention that teaching and learning receive in District 2. Teachers from outside the district who attend District 2-sponsored summer professional development activities often report that they have heard that the district is the place to be if you are interested in good teaching, and they comment favorably on the range of professional development activities available to District 2 teachers and principals. Outsiders also comment on the unusual practice of principals attending content-centered professional development activities with teachers from their schools. (p. 288)

The District 2 case shows how a district can mobilize resources to support sustained improvement in teaching practice and substantial improvements in student learning. In addition to the highly focused strategies the district uses to improve the quality of teaching practice systemwide, there are targeted efforts for students who do not initially succeed. In addition to the use of Reading Recovery strategies, Alvarado made investments in teacher training to teach English language learners and in highly expert special education services, replacing the common practice of assigning special needs students to untrained paraprofessionals with a strategy of hiring highly trained special educators who work with students but also share their expertise with other teachers, so that regular education teachers, too, can become more expert. Rather than using widespread grade retention, Alvarado focused these services on students with lagging achievement and assigned students with the lowest scores to the most expert teachers, rather than the most inexperienced and least well-trained teachers, as is the custom in most districts.

These practices have been continued in the years since, under the leadership of an interim superintendent who had been Alvarado's deputy and then a superintendent promoted from among the ranks of highly able instructionally knowledgeable principals appointed during the early years of the reform. The combination of these efforts focused first on teaching standards and then on student standards over a period of more than a decade has developed a brand of accountability in which parents in District 2, a growing number of whom are now returning from private schools, are assured that their students will be well taught, not just much tested.

New Haven, California

Another glimpse of the possible can be seen in the New Haven Unified School District, located midway between Oakland and San Jose, California, a district that serves approximately 14,000 students from Union City and south Hayward, three fourths of whom are students of color, most of them low-income and working class.[3] In the 1970s, the district was the lowest-wealth district in a low-wealth county, and it had a reputation to match. Families who could manage to do so sent their children elsewhere to school. Twenty years later, New Haven Unified School District, while still a low-wealth district, has a well-deserved reputation for excellent schools. Every one of its 10 schools had been designated a California Distinguished School, and schools at all three levels had been designated as exemplary by the U.S. Department of Education. All have student achievement levels well above California norms and even further above the norms for similar schools (Snyder, 1999).

One key element of New Haven's success was its commitment, 20 years ago, to high standards for teachers. Like Tony Alvarado in District #2, when superintendent Guy Emanuele first entered his post in the early 1980s, he started by establishing high expectations for teachers. He recalls:

> The presence of . . . teachers who did not perform to high standards lowered academic achievement of students and ultimately led to lower morale among other teachers. . . . One of my first acts as superintendent was to tighten the teacher evaluation process and implement procedures that allowed for due process while still enabling the district to remove teachers who simply were not able or willing to address deficiencies in their performance. A concerted focus upon teacher evaluations resulted in a number of resignations. Now, with performance standards in place and clear expectations as to the need to exceed them, teachers respect the district's effort to maintain high instructional standards, and rarely is a teacher terminated. Furthermore, the district's reputation in this regard draws high-achieving teachers, deters those who are not as committed, and generally elevates the status of the teaching profession. (Snyder, 1999)

   The district held administrators accountable for assessing teachers and providing necessary supports for teachers to meet expectations. New Haven put together thorough evaluation procedures requiring the systematic collection of data—no more drive-by teacher observations. The responsibility for assuring the caliber of all teachers in all schools was a powerful incentive for making good initial hires. Making good hires required the district to revamp its recruitment and retention strategies to guarantee that qualified candidates would know about, wish to come to, and want to stay in the New Haven district.

   Thirty years ago New Haven did what many districts continue to do today: Wait until the last minute and see what is available in the way of teachers. New Haven learned that even in a buyer's market, this is a shortsighted approach. The district began to seek out exceptional teachers, streamline the application process, make decisions, and offer contracts in a timely manner. Over time, the district built support systems and teaching conditions that would retain exceptional teachers, and eventually it became involved in strong partnerships for pre-service teacher education. Today, the district can afford to be selective, recruiting with an eye toward teachers with the skills and dispositions to grow within the teacher learning environments the district supports. Unlike many other urban districts with similar student populations, New Haven does not have recruitment crises annually because of the low attrition rate of its new and experienced teachers (Snyder, 1999).

   While school districts across California have scrambled in recent years to hire qualified teachers and many cities hired 20% or more of their teachers on emergency credentials, New Haven had in place an aggressive recruitment system and a high quality training program with local universities that allowed it to continue its long-term habit of hiring universally well-prepared, committed, and diverse teachers to staff its schools. In 2001, 10 of its 11 schools had no teachers lacking full credentials, and the district average was 0.1% (Futernick, 2001). One factor in this success is that, despite its lower per pupil expenditures than many surrounding districts, New Haven spends the lion's share of its budget on teachers' salaries and then aggressively recruits and works to retain highly qualified teachers. In 1997–1998, salaries in New Haven ranged from $37,604 to $70,373, the highest in the Bay Area and in the state's upper echelon, despite New Haven's historic standing as one of the lowest-wealth districts in the state and the county (Snyder, 1999). New Haven's per-pupil expenditure was at that time $4,103, approximately the fifth percentile in the state and $2,337 per student below the highest per-pupil expenditure in the county. New Haven is not a rich district, but it affords quality because it:

- Has flattened the traditional hierarchy of district and school bureaucracies (with 771 teachers and 50 managers, nearly 94% of certified personnel work with children)
- Allocates resources, including technology, to support and build teaching capacity
- Creates multiple hybrid professional roles that enrich teacher learning while enhancing district policy and practice

Rather than spending money on an array of special programs to address the problems created by inadequate teaching, the district decided to create a cadre of well-paid and highly qualified teachers to avoid such problems in the first place.

A key to this strategy is coupling high salaries with high standards. New Haven's personnel office uses technology and a wide range of teacher supports to recruit from a national pool of exceptional teachers. Its Web site posts all vacancies and draws inquiries from around the country. Each inquiry receives an immediate e-mail response. With the use of electronic information transfer (e.g., the personnel office can send vacancy information directly to candidates and applicant files to the desktop of any administrator electronically), the district can provide information to people urban districts might never think would be available to them. Viable applicants are interviewed immediately in person or via video conference (through a local Kinko's), and if they are well-qualified with strong references, they may be offered a job that same day. Despite the difficulty many out-of-state teachers experience in earning a California teaching credential, New Haven's credential analyst in the personnel office has yet to lose a teacher recruited from out-of-state in the state's credentialing maze.

Among the many factors contributing to the district's success in recruiting teachers and serving students, one significant strategy is the district's long-term investments in teacher education. The district was one of the first in the state to implement a Beginning Teacher Support and Assessment Program that provides support for teachers in their first 2 years in the classroom. All beginning teachers receive classroom support from a trained mentor who has released time for this purpose. Based on the California Standards for the Teaching Profession, the beginning support and assessment program, like Connecticut's, points the attention of beginning teachers—as well as veteran teachers and principals who serve as members of their support teams—to critical aspects of teaching, including effective strategies for diagnosing learning, planning curriculum to meet the needs of diverse learners, organizing and implementing instruction. Beginning teachers are guided by an individual induction plan developed with their support team, and they develop a portfolio that documents their growth toward the plan's goals. This is supplemented by a series of formal observations by support team members that guide additional goal setting and a final assessment conducted in an interview format with the support team.

Many beginning teachers report that they chose to teach in New Haven because of the availability of this strong support for their initial years in the profession. In addition, in collaboration with California State University, Hayward, the district designed an innovative teacher education partnership that combines college coursework and an intensive internship conducted under the close supervision of school-based educators. This program is guided by the same teaching standards as the beginning teacher program, creating coherence in teachers' pathways into teaching. Because interns function as student teachers who work in the classrooms of master teachers, rather than as independent teachers of record, the program simultaneously educates teachers while protecting students and providing quality education.

Throughout their careers teachers have access to a wide range of professional development opportunities throughout the year and in intensive summer work. For example, during the summer of 1997, approximately 65% of the district's teachers participated in district-sponsored staff development activities. The district has organized school schedules so that all teachers have the time to meet for 90 minutes each week to plan collaboratively. In addition, all of the professional work of the district engages teachers, thereby building and sharing their expertise and creating ownership in district reforms. In New Haven, classroom teachers enact the beginning teacher support and assessment program, develop curriculum, design technological supports, and create student standards and assessments.

As in District #2, standards for students have been developed and enacted as a professional development activity, using state and national frameworks as the starting point for engaging teachers in thinking through what students should know and be able to do, how it should be assessed, and which curriculum and instructional strategies could allow them to succeed. For example, using a combination of release time, after-school workshops, and extensive summer institutes, the district involved more than 100 teachers (nearly 40% of its K–4 teachers) in its language arts and mathematics standards committees during the 1996–1997 year.

New Haven began with this teacher-developed district-wide, comprehensive K–4 standards and assessment system that has since served as a prototype for all grade levels. This system consists of:

- Clearly articulated performance standards with clear descriptions of seven different performance levels (from pre-readiness through

    independent) tied to grade-level expectations
- A criterion-based parent reporting system for all K–4 students, including special education and second language learners
- Three strands of assessments
- A database system that pulls together assessment, demographic, and intervention information for analysis and use in program planning and targeting student assistance

    The model is one of the few comprehensive standards systems in the country to incorporate a learner-centered developmental perspective with the more traditional accountability features of standards-setting efforts. The key to the standards and assessment system is not the testing itself but the web of supports activated by the assessments. The most fundamental use of the standards and assessment system is as a tool for classroom-level instructional planning. For example, in August each teacher receives a printout of the levels of each of his or her students' performance in reading, writing, and mathematics. Teachers initially use this information to design guided reading groups, target computer software, and assign home reading levels. Ongoing authentic assessments (e.g., running records of reading) based on the standards help teachers continually modify these groupings. In addition, teachers use this assessment information to identify students needing tutoring during the after-school, extended-day program and/or homework support. On a more personal level, the database also helps maximize the match of primary-age students and intermediate-age reading buddies. And at the school level, educators use the system to guide changes in just about every educational arena, including staffing, instructional programming, resource allocation, and configuring classes (Snyder, 1999).

    Such a program puts a major responsibility on teachers. What children know and are able to do must be clearly documented using students' classroom work, formal and informal assessment data, and teacher observation. This requires more than presenting information; it involves an expectation that the content of the standards be accessible to, and learned by, students at all performance levels. The purpose is not to label a child, but to develop a program that facilitates that child's development. Thus, standards and assessments are used to support the existing professional accountability structure by providing more information to guide collective as well as individual teaching practice. The fruits of these combined efforts to enact high standards for teaching and for learning show in New Haven's steadily increasing student achievement, which is now well above California state norms, as well as its success in finding and keeping good teachers.

IMPROVING THE CHANCES OF STUDENT SUCCESS

Ultimately, accountability is not only about measuring student learning but actually improving it. Consequently, genuine accountability involves supporting changes in teaching and schooling that can heighten the probability that students meet standards. Unless school districts undertake systemic reforms in how they hire, retain, prepare, and support teachers and develop high quality teaching, the chances that all students will have the chance to meet new high standards are slight. There are at least three major areas where attention is needed:

1. Ensuring that teachers have the knowledge and skills they need to teach to the standards
2. Providing school structures that support high quality teaching and learning
3. Creating processes for school assessment that can evaluate students' opportunities to learn and can leverage continuous change and improvement

Building Professional Capacity

The changes in teaching and assessment strategies needed to achieve new content and performance standards require increased knowledge and skills on the part of teachers. Teachers need deep understanding of subject matter, student learning approaches, and diverse teaching strategies to develop practices that will allow students to reach these new standards. To provide this kind of expertise to students, districts must pay much greater attention to the ways in which they recruit, hire, and support new teachers and the ways in which they support veteran teachers. Cumbersome and counterproductive personnel practices in many large district bureaucracies have resulted in the hiring of hundreds of untrained teachers when qualified personnel were available, and in the attrition of far too many beginning teachers who are left to sink or swim without support. These practices create a continuous revolving door of inexperienced and under-prepared teachers in schools where student failure rates are the highest. Neither standards nor assessments will help students learn more effectively if they do not have a stable community of competent teachers to support them in their learning.

Until school systems address the dramatic inequalities in students' access to qualified teachers, other curriculum and assessment policies will prove ineffective in increasing achievement. In addition, schools and districts need to provide systematic supports for ongoing teacher learning in the form of time for shared teacher planning, opportunities for assessing teaching and learning, more exposure to technical expertise and resources, and opportunities for networking with other colleagues. These investments in building the capacities of teachers pay off in improved student outcomes (National Commission on Teaching and America's Future, 1996). In addition, as teachers learn to develop and use performance assessments, they discover more about their students and the effects of their teaching. This allows them to build more responsive and supportive teaching strategies that support the attainment of higher standards for a greater range of students (Darling-Hammond, Ancess, & Falk, 1995).

Providing these opportunities will require a clearer focus on teacher learning as a critical ingredient for enhanced student learning and as the most important preventive for the escalating costs of compensatory education, special education, grade retention, and other manifestations of student and school failure. Allocating resources to support teacher learning includes restructuring school time and staffing patterns to allow teachers time to work and learn together.

Structuring Schools to Support Student and Teacher Learning

As noted earlier, learning arrangements in which students work with the same teachers for more than 1 year facilitate higher levels of learning. In most high-achieving European and Asian countries, students stay with the same teacher for at least 2 years, and sometimes 3 or more. United States research has also found that smaller schools and schools that personalize instruction by keeping the same teachers with the same students for extended periods of time are associated with increased student achievement, more positive feelings toward self and school, and more positive behavior (Gottfredson & Daiger, 1979; National Institute of Education, 1977; Wehlage, Rutter, Smith, Lesko, & Fernandez, 1989). Teachers are more effective when they know students well, when they understand how their students learn, and when they have more time with students to accomplish their goals.

Schools that have restructured to provide more shared planning and professional development time for teachers are also more successful at meeting the needs of diverse learners. When teachers can share knowledge with each other and can access expertise beyond the school, they learn how to succeed with students who require special insights and strategies. This kind of restructuring of time often requires rethinking staffing arrangements as well as schedules. In U.S. schools, where only 43% of total education staff are classroom teachers (as compared to 60 to 80% in many European schools and in Japan, for example), the costs of supporting nonteaching staff absorb the resources needed to provide planning time for teachers.

Thus, whereas teachers in many other countries have as much as 15 to 20 hours per week for joint planning and learning, U.S. teachers have only 3 to 5 hours weekly for class preparation, usually spent alone (National Commission on Teaching and America's Future, 1996). Creating time for teachers to work together often means reducing the number of nonteaching staff, pullout teachers, and specialists and reassigning them to teaching teams to increase person power for classroom teaching.

Ensuring Opportunities to Learn

When students are to be held to the same set of learning standards, there must be means to ensure that all students have access to the conditions and resources needed for them to be able to meet these standards. Differential access to the resources that enable students' learning—qualified teachers, adequate facilities, and high-quality materials—greatly impacts student achievement, disadvantaging those from underresourced schools.

Along with standards for student learning, school systems should develop opportunity-to-learn standards—standards for delivery systems and standards of practice—to identify how well schools are doing in providing students with the conditions they need to achieve and to trigger corrective actions from the state and district. As Jeannie Oakes (1989) argues, information about resources and school practices is essential "if [policy makers] want monitoring and accountability systems to mirror the condition of education accurately or to be useful for making improvements" (p. 182). Those who would attempt to use standards in the quest for accountability and improvement can themselves be held accountable for making sound decisions only if they address questions of why outcomes appear as they do and make necessary changes in the conditions that influence learning.

This framework also suggests a more limited and appropriate role for test data as a component of accountability systems. Assessment data are helpful for creating more accountable systems to the extent that they provide relevant, valid, timely, and useful information about how individual students are doing and how schools are serving them. However, indicators such as test scores are information for the accountability system; they are not the system itself. Accountability occurs only when a useful set of processes exists for interpreting and acting on the information in educationally productive ways. This may seem a straightforward notion, but it is significantly different from the predominant conceptions of accountability in the contemporary policy arena.

This definition of accountability suggests that we should evaluate policy strategies on the basis of whether and for whom they provide greater assurance of high quality teaching and learning. We should ask who is helped and who is harmed by policies that are offered under the name of accountability. Do accountability systems heighten the probability that good practices will occur for students and reduce the likelihood that harmful practices will occur? And do they provide self-correctives in the system to identify, diagnose, and changes courses of action that are harmful or ineffective?

The issue of standards and accountability cannot be separated from issues of teaching, assessment, school organization, professional development, and funding. Efforts aimed at better supporting learning for all students so that they can successfully progress through school must include changes that address the overall fabric of education.

Academic success for a greater range of students will be facilitated by initiatives that:

- Use standards and authentic assessments of student achievement as indicators of progress for improved teaching and needed supports, not as arbiters of rewards and sanctions
- Provide professional learning opportunities for teachers that build their capacity to teach ways that are congruent with contemporary understandings about learning, use sophisticated assessments to inform teaching, and meet differing needs
- Encourage the design of classroom and grouping structures that create extended, intensive teacher-student relationships
- Create strategies for school accountability that examine the appropriateness and adequacy of students' learning opportunities and create levers and supports for school change

Ultimately, raising standards for students so that they learn what they need to know requires raising standards for the system, so that it provides the kinds of teaching and school settings students need in order to learn. Test-based grade retention and denial of diplomas as the major solutions to low achievement are merely a symbol of the failure of the system to teach successfully. Given the effects of these policies, such a strategy for accountability foreshadows the system's greater failure in the years ahead. Genuine accountability requires instead both higher standards and greater supports for student, teacher, and school learning.

CHAPTER 6

Performance Standards:
What Is Proficient Performance?

Robert L. Linn

University of Colorado at Boulder

Educational measurement specialists have devised an abundance of ways of reporting results on tests and assessments. The most common ways of reporting results throughout most of the 20th century sought to give meaning to scores by providing a comparison to the performance of other test takers. For tests such as the ACT and SAT used in college admissions and guidance, the comparison is to the performance of test takers in a reference population for a given year used to establish a score scale with a specified mean and standard deviation. For most standardized achievement tests used in the schools the comparison was to a norm group from which various kinds of norm-referenced scores such as grade-equivalent scores, percentile ranks, and normal-curve-equivalent scores were derived.

The standards movement represented a shift from norm-referenced to criterion-referenced assessments of learning. The shift in orientation placed greater emphasis on interpreting student performance in terms of test content rather than in comparison to the performance of other students. In this regard, the shift might be viewed as supporting equity. This chapter reviews the origins of the performance standards movement, examining reasonable and unreasonable performance goals and uses of criterion-referenced assessments. The origin of the concept of criterion-referenced measurement is considered, followed by a discussion of the standards movement and the desire for ambitious performance standards. The use of performance standards to meet the requirements of the No Child Left Behind Act of 2001 is briefly discussed and comparisons are made between the performance standards on the National Assessment of Educational Progress and on state assessments. The uncertainties associated with performance standards are discussed. Finally, the question of whether performance standards are necessary is considered.

CRITERION-REFERENCED MEASUREMENT

Norm-referenced interpretations of test performance are useful for indicating how a performance on a test compares to that of other students, but they don't provide a direct indication of what a student knows or is able to do. Glaser and Klaus (1962) introduced the concept of criterion-referenced measures as a way of providing interpretations of test performance in terms of the content of the test rather than in reference to the performance of others. Glaser (1963) elaborated the idea of criterion-referenced measures in his classic paper published in the *American Psychologist*:

> Underlying the concept of achievement measurement is the notion of a continuum of knowledge acquisition ranging from no proficiency at all to perfect performance. An individual's achievement level falls at some point on the continuum as indicated by the behaviors he displays during testing.... Along such a continuum of attainment, a student's score on a criterion-referenced measure provides explicit information as to what the individual can or cannot do. (p. 519)

Glaser's notion of a criterion-referenced measure as a continuum of attainment along which individual student performances could be arrayed did not require the establishment of a performance standard or cutscore (Glass, 1978). Although Glaser's conceptualization did not require it, the use of cutscores to determine that a student either did or did not meet a performance standard became associated with criterion-referenced measures (Hambleton & Rogers, 1991; Linn, 1994). According to Popham and Husek (1969), for example:

> Criterion-referenced measures are those which are used to ascertain an individual's status with respect to some criterion, i.e., performance standard. It is because the individual is compared with some established criterion, rather than other individuals, that the measures are described as criterion-referenced. (p. 2)

Criterion-referenced measurement became associated with mastery testing. In mastery testing a performance standard was often set to correspond to 80% of the items correct. Eight years after his classic 1963 article in the *American Psychologist* Glaser recognized that it was common to treat the criterion as a fixed performance standard when he and Nitko stated that a "second prevalent interpretation of the term criterion in achievement measurement concerns the imposition of an acceptable score magnitude as an index of achievement" (Glaser & Nitko, 1971, p. 653). Nonetheless, the setting of a fixed standard or cutscore is not an essential requirement of criterion-referenced measurement as originally conceptualized by Glaser (1963).

THE STANDARDS MOVEMENT

The early efforts to construct and use criterion-referenced tests were usually in low-stakes applications where the test results were used to make short-term instructional decisions. For example, a student who scored at or above the level identified as mastery of a domain of content might be moved on to more complex content while the student scoring below the mastery cutscore would be given additional material that was of comparable complexity in the same content domain. This type of use was consistent with notions of learning hierarchies such as those described by Glaser and Nitko (1971). A greatly expanded use of some of the concepts of criterion-referenced testing appeared in the late 1980s and early 1990s under the umbrella of standards-based assessment. Genesis of the National Education Goals Panel (NEGP), announced by President G. H. W. Bush in his 1990 State of the Union Address, is described in the introductory chapter of this book. The NEGP played a leadership role in establishing and defining the standards-based reform movement (Vinovskis, 1999, p. 1).

Two types of standards, content standards and performance standards, are critical for standards-based reform. Content standards specify what teachers are supposed to teach and students are supposed to learn in specific content areas such as mathematics or English language arts. They also specify the material that should be included on assessments of student achievement.

Performance standards specify the level of student achievement that is expected. They identify performance criteria and cutscores on assessments that define adequate or exemplary levels of student achievement. In the words of an NEGP Technical Planning group:

> Performance standards are *not* the skills and modes of reasoning referred to in the content standards. Rather, they indicate both the nature of the evidence (such as an essay, mathematical proof, scientific experiment, project, exam, or combination of these) required to demonstrate that content standards have been met and the quality of student performance that will be deemed acceptable (what merits a passing or an A grade). (National Educational Goals Panel, Goals 3 and 4 Technical Planning Group on the Review of Education Standards, 1993, p. 22)

The standards movement received additional support during President Clinton's administrations. Content standards, student performance standards, and standards-based assessments were key ideas of the *Goals 2000: Educate America Act* signed into law by President Clinton in 1994. The standards-based approach to assessment and accountability was also a central feature of Title I evaluations mandated in the 1994 reauthorization of The Elementary and Secondary Education Act of 1965 (ESEA) by the Improving America's Schools Act (IASA) of 1994.

AMBITIOUS PERFORMANCE STANDARDS

The 1989 Governors' Charlottesville Education Summit and the NEGP encouraged the establishment of high performance standards. The emphasis on standards set at "world class" levels was also consistent with the stress in *A Nation at Risk* (National Commission on Excellence in Education, 1983) on the inadequacy of educational achievement in the United States. Hence it is not surprising that when performance standards, called achievement levels, were established in 1990 for the National Assessment of Educational Progress (NAEP), they were set at quite ambitious levels. In 1990, the first year that NAEP results were reported in terms of achievement levels, for example, the proficient level on the mathematics assessment corresponded to the 87th percentile for fourth grade students, the 85th percentile for eighth grade students, and 88th percentile for 12th grade students (see, for example, Braswell, Lutkus, Grigg, Santapau, Tay-Lim, & Johnson, 2001). Comparisons of NAEP to the Third International Mathematics and Science Study (TIMSS) Grade 8 mathematics results indicated that no country is anywhere close to having all of their students scoring at the proficient level or higher (Linn, 2000) thus providing another indication that the NAEP achievement levels are set at quite ambitious levels.

Improving America's Schools Act encouraged states to adopt content standards and set performance standards on their assessments. A number of states responded by adopting content standards, developing assessments based on those standards, and setting performance standards on their assessments during the 1990s. In keeping with the spirit of the times, the performance standards set by states, like the NAEP achievement levels, were set at quite high levels in many cases. During the 1990s, it was not unusual for a state to set its performance standards at the 70th percentile or even higher. Performance standards on NAEP and on many of the state assessments had no real consequences for students or schools and there was no requirement for actually achieving the lofty goal of the standards. Although reports that, say, only a third of the students are proficient may paint a negative picture for the public, many would argue that it is good to have ambitious goals even if they are never achieved. "If you reach for the stars, you may not quite get them, but you won't come up with a handful of mud either" (Leo Burnett, as quoted by Applewhite, Evans, and Frothingham, 1992, p. 22).

No Child Left Behind

The importance of performance *standards* was greatly increased when President George W. Bush signed the No Child Left Behind Act (NCLB) into law in January 2002. NCLB requires that all students achieve the proficient level or higher by 2013–2014 and schools that fall short of intermediate targets set by states to achieve the 100% proficiency goal in 2013–2014 are subject to sanctions. Under NCLB, high performance standards are no longer merely symbolic aspirations. Rather they have potentially serious consequences for schools, school administrators, and teachers. But what does proficient mean? According to NCLB states must set

> challenging academic achievement standards that (1) are aligned with the academic content standards; (2) describe two levels of high achievement (proficient and advanced) that determine how well children are mastering the material in the State academic content standards; and (3) describe a third level of achievement (basic) to provide complete information about the progress of lower-achieving children toward mastering the proficient and advanced levels of achievement. [NCLB, 2001, Part A, Subpart 1, Sec. 1111 (b) (D) (ii)]

The establishment of academic content standards and the setting of academic achievement standards corresponding to proficient, advanced, and basic levels of achievement are left to the states. The NCLB admonition that the academic achievement standards should be challenging is consistent with the earlier press for high performance standards. The major new wrinkle, however, is that failure to meet targets for the percentage of students who are proficient or above now has consequences for schools and school districts.

Taken at face value, the accountability system appears to support equity by emphasizing proficient performance for all students. Certainly it contrasts with earlier goals of maintaining or slightly improving a student's relative standing in comparison to a norm group. In practice, however, the target of proficient performance is so far away from the actual performance for some struggling students that it may appear to be beyond reach. It is important that improvement in performance of students who still fall short of the proficient standard be recognized.

STATE NAEP RESULTS

The movement toward reporting results in terms of student performance standards was led by NAEP and states frequently used the NAEP achievement levels as models for setting their own student performance standards. The distinctions made on NAEP between advanced, proficient, basic, and below basic performance were also made by a number of states, frequently using the same labels. National Assessment of Educational Progress provides a kind of benchmark that is frequently used to compare the standards and performance of students in different states.

States had been participating in state administrations of NAEP on a voluntary basis since 1990. Starting in 2003, NCLB mandated state participation in NAEP reading and mathematics assessments at Grades 4 and 8 every other year. Although NCLB does not specify how state NAEP results should be used, NAEP does provide a rough benchmark against which state results can be judged.

As was mentioned above, the NAEP performance standards (achievement levels) were set at ambitious levels that would surely satisfy the NCLB demand for challenging academic achievement standards. In fact, the requirement that all students achieve at the proficient level or higher in both mathematics and reading/English language arts is completely unrealistic for standards set at such high levels (Linn, 2003a). Setting a state's academic achievement standards at levels approximating NAEP would be setting schools up for failure by 2013–2014 or before.

There has been an improvement in the percentage of students achieving at the proficient level or above on NAEP since the achievement levels were first established. The increases for mathematics have been encouraging, especially at Grade 4. Increases in the percentage proficient or above for reading, on the other hand, have been discouragingly small. Tables 6.1 and 6.2 display the percentages of public school students in each of the 50 states who achieved at the proficient level or above on the 2005 NAEP reading assessments at Grades 4 and 8, respectively. Parallel percentages are displayed for the 2005 NAEP mathematics assessments at Grades 4 and 8 in Table 6.3 and 6.4, respectively.

For Grade 4 reading the percentage proficient or above ranged from a high of 44% in Massachusetts to a low of 18% in Mississippi. Thirty nine percent of the students in Connecticut and in New Hampshire were at the proficient level or above in reading at Grade 4 in 2005. Louisiana had the second lowest percentage (20%) proficient or above in reading at Grade 4. There are no big surprises in the relative ordering of the states in Table 6.1. Rather, the ordering is consistent with what might be expected from

Table 6.1. Percentage of Students at the Proficient Level or Above on the 2005 NAEP Grade 4 Reading Assessment by State

Percentage	Count	States
41–44	1	MA
36–40	10	CO, ME, MT, PA, VA, MN, NJ, VT, CT, NH
31–35	16	MI, MD, MO, IA, ID, KS, NE, SD, WI, NY, WY, DE, ND, OH, UT, WA
26–30	15	AK, GA, OK, SC, WV, TN, AR, TX, FL, IL, IN, KY, NC, OR, RI
21–25	6	NM, NV, AL, CA, HI, AZ
18–20	2	MS, LA
Total	50	

Source. Perie, Grigg, & Donahue (2005).

Table 6.2. Percentage of Students at the Proficient Level or Above on the 2005 NAEP Grade 8 Reading Assessment by State

Percentage	Count	States
41–44	1	MA
36–40	9	OH, PA, MN. MT, ND, NJ, VT, ME, NH
31–35	17	CO, DE, IL, KY, MO, ID, NY, OR, CT, IA, KS, WA, WI, NE, SD, VA, WY
26–30	10	AR, TN, TX, AK, NC, IN, MI, RI, UT, MD
21–25	9	CA, AL, NV, WV, AZ, GA, FL, OK, SC
18–20	4	HI, MS, NM, LA
Total	50	

Source. Perie, Grigg, & Donahue (2005).

other indicators of achievement and knowledge of state-to-state differences in student demographic characteristics.

Massachusetts showed some improvement in the percentage of fourth grade public school students who were proficient or above in reading from 2003 with 40% to 2005 with 44%. Assuming the average rate of increase of 2% a year could be maintained from 2005 to 2014; however, Massachusetts would have 62% proficient or above on NAEP Grade 4 reading, which would fall far short of the 100% target. The other two high performing states, Connecticut (which had a 4% decrease from 2003 to 2005) and New Hampshire (which had the same percentage in 2003 and 2005) would be even farther from the mark. Of course, the 100% target seems even more unrealistic for the low performing states such as Louisiana and Mississippi.

The 2005 Grade 8 reading results in Table 6.2 are reasonably similar to those for Grade 4. Massachusetts with 44% proficient or above ranks first, Maine and New Hampshire with 38% tie for second and Louisiana and Mississippi are among the four states with the lowest percentages. Increases in percentages from 2003 to 2005 are generally much smaller at Grade 8 than at Grade 4, making the 100% target by 2014 even more unrealistic at Grade 8 than at Grade 4.

The percentages of students who are proficient or above on the 2005 mathematics assessments at Grades 4 (Table 6.3) and 8 (Table 6.4) reveal differences among states that are similar to the differences for reading. At Grade 4, the percentage for the top states (49% for Massachusetts, and 47% for Kansas, Minnesota, and New Hampshire) is slightly higher for mathematics than reading. The gains in percentage proficient or above for Grade 4 mathematics from 2003 to 2005 are also larger for mathematics than reading (8% for Massachusetts, and 4%, 5%, and 6% for New Hampshire, Minnesota, and Kansas, respectively). If the 4% per year gain for Massachusetts could be sustained between 2005 and 2014, Massachusetts would still fall short of the 100% target, but only by 15%. No other state would come that close.

The Grade 8 mathematics results are less encouraging than the Grade 4 mathematics results because the highest percentages in 2005 are slightly lower and the increases from 2003 are somewhat smaller. Nonetheless, mathematics achievement at Grade 8 is more encouraging than the results for reading at Grade 8. As with the results shown in the earlier tables, no state is on a trajectory that would suggest the 100% proficiency target in 2014 is feasible.

Table 6.3. Percentage of Students at the Proficient Level or Above on the 2005 NAEP Grade 4 Mathematics Assessment by State

Percentage	*Count*	*States*
46 to 49	5	NJ, KS, MN, NH, MA
41 to 45	7	ID, PA, WA, WY, CT, VT, WY
36 to 40	19	DE, FL, NE, NY, SC, IA, MI, OR, UT, IN, MD, CO, ME, MT, NC, SD, TX, VA, WI
31 to 35	6	MO, RI, IL, OH, AK, AR
26 to 30	9	NV, WV, HI, KY, AZ, CA, OK, TN, GA
21 to 25	2	AL, LA
19 to 20	2	MS, NM
Total	50	

Source. Perie, Grigg, & Dion (2005).

STATE ASSESSMENT RESULTS

Results on state assessments, of course, rather than results on NAEP, determine whether a school reaches its adequate yearly progress target in a given year. Furthermore, the 100% proficiency by 2013–2014 applies to the proficient academic achievement standards on the state assessments. As was noted above, a number of states that set performance standards for their assessment in the 1990s modeled them after NAEP, and set rather high standards. Quite a few states had to set new performance standards after NCLB became law because they had to start assessing in grades where they did not assess students in mathematics or reading/English language arts in the past. Some other states that were not adding new grade levels to their assessment systems also reset their performance standards in light of the new consequences of NCLB. As a result, almost all states now have performance standards that are more lenient than NAEP. Some states have defined proficient performance at levels that are much less demanding than the NAEP proficient achievement level.

Olson (2005) reported the percentage of students who were proficient

Table 6.4. Percentage of Students at the Proficient Level or Above on the 2005 NAEP Grade 8 Mathematics Assessment by State

Percentage	Count	States
41–43	2	MA, MN
36–40	6	MT, NJ, SD, WA, WI, VT
31–35	14	NY, PA, TX, CO, NC, OR, VA, IA, KS, OH, CT, ND, NE, NH
26–30	14	AZ, FL, MO, IL, AK, WY, DE, ID, IN, MD, ME, MI, SC, UT
21–25	7	NV, TN, AR, CA, KY, GA, RI
16–20	4	LA, WV, HI, OK
13–15	3	MS, NM,. AL
Total	50	

Source. Perie, Grigg, & Dion (2005).

or above on state reading and on mathematics assessments at Grades 4 and 8 for 47 states.[1] The distributions of percentages of students proficient or above in reading at Grades 4 and 8 are displayed in Tables 6.5 and 6.6, respectively. As can be seen in those two tables, 16 of the 47 states reported that 81% or more of their students performed at least at the proficient level in reading at Grades 4 and 9 states reported that 81% or more of their students were at the proficient level or above on their Grade 8 reading assessments. Only two states, Missouri and South Carolina, had less than 40% of their students at the proficient level or above on their 2005 reading assessments at Grade 4.

The results in Tables 6.5 and 6.6 contrast sharply with those in Tables 6.1 and 6.2 in at least two respects. First, the percentages based on the state assessments in Tables 6.5 and 6.6 are generally much higher than the corresponding percentages for NAEP shown in Tables 6.1 and 6.2. Second, the ordering of states in terms of percentages of students who performed at the proficient level or above is markedly different for the state assessments than for NAEP. Mississippi, for example, had the lowest percentage of students at the proficient level or above on the 2005 NAEP Grade 4 reading assessment

Table 6.5. Percentage of Students at the Proficient Level or Above on 2005 State Grade 4 Reading Assessments

Percentage	Count	States
86–89	7	CO, OR, GA, ID, SD, TN, MS
81–85	9	MD, WI, WV, MI, NC,. NJ, AL, DE, NE
76–80	10	OH, VA, KS, MN, UT, AK, IA, OK, TX, WA
71–75	4	FL, IN, MT, ND
66–70	4	CT, IL, KY, NY
61–65	3	AZ, LA, PA
56–60	0	
51–55	4	AR, HI, NM, ME
46–50	3	CA, WY, MA
41–45	1	NV
36–40	1	SC
31–35	1	MO
Total	47	

Source. Olson (2005).
Note. The closest grade with a reading assessment was used for states that did not have a Grade 4 reading assessment in 2005. Within a row states are listed in ascending order of the percentage of students who are proficient or above.

(18%), but the highest percentage scoring at the proficient level or above on their 2005 Grade 4 state reading assessment (89%). A number of other large, albeit not quite as extreme, discrepancies between percentages students who were reported to have exceeded the proficient cutscore at both grades 4 and 8 according to either the state reading assessment or NAEP in 2005.

Tables 6.7 and 6.8 display the distributions of percentages of students in the 47 states with results reported by Olson (2005) who are proficient or above in 2005 according to the state mathematics assessments at Grades 4 and 8, respectively. As was true of reading, comparisons of the distributions for the 2005 state mathematics assessments in Tables 6.7 and 6.8 with

Table 6.6. Percentage of Students at the Proficient Level or Above on 2005 State Grade 8 Reading Assessments

Percentage	Count	States
86–88	4	CO, NE, TN, NC
81–85	5	OK, ID, GA, TX, WI
76–80	8	VA. KS, UT, DE, OH, SD, AK, WV
71–75	7	IA, ND, NJ, IL, MI, MN, CT
66–70	5	MA, MD, IN, AL, WA
61–65	5	KY, AZ, OR, MT, PA
56–60	2	AR, MS
51–55	2	NV, NM
46–50	2	NY, LA
41–45	2	FL, ME
36–40	3	HI, CA, WY
31–35	1	MO
29–30	1	SC
Total	47	

Source. Olson (2005).
Note. The closest grade with a reading assessment was used for states that did not have a Grade 8 reading assessment in 2005. Within a row states are listed in ascending order of the percentage of students who are proficient or above.

those for the 2005 NAEP mathematics assessments in Tables 6.3 and 6.4 reveal sharp contrasts in the ordering of states and in the magnitude of the percentages of students who are said to be proficient or above.

Means and standard deviations of the percentages of students who are reported to be proficient or above in reading and mathematics at Grades 4 and 8 according to the 47 2005 state assessments included in Olson's report and according to the 2005 NAEP assessments are listed in Table 6.9. The mean percentages are consistently higher on the state assessments than on the NAEP. There is also greater between-state variability in the percentages for the state assessments than there is for NAEP.

Table 6.7. Percentage of Students at the Proficient Level or Above on 2005 State Grade 4 Mathematics Assessments

Percentage	Count	States
91–92	1	NC
86–90	6	OR, TN, NE, VA, CO, ID
81–85	6	IA, TX, SD, OK, KS, NY
76–80	9	MD, AK, MN, CT, DE, IL, MS, ND, NJ
71–75	8	AZ, WI, AL, IN, MI, GA, UT, WV
66–70	2	OH, PA
61–65	3	LA, WA, FL
56–60	1	MT
51–55	1	NV
46–50	2	AR, CA
41–45	3	SC, MO, KY
36–40	4	ME, NM, WY, MA
31–35	0	
29–30	1	HI
Total	47	

Source. Olson (2005).
Note. The closest grade with a reading assessment was used for states that did not have a Grade 4 mathematics assessment in 2005. Within a row states are listed in ascending order of the percentage of students who are proficient or above.

Not only are the means higher and the standard deviations larger for the percentages based on state assessments than those based on NAEP, but the ordering of states is only weakly related for the two categories of assessments. The correlations of the percentages of students in the 47 states who were proficient or above according to the four state assessments and four NAEP assessments (reading and mathematics at Grades 4 and 8) are shown in Table 6.10. The four correlations of the state assessment percentages with the NAEP assessment percentages in the same grade and subject area (shown in bold in Table 6.10) range from a low of .14 for Grade 4 reading to a high

Table 6.8. Percentage of Students at the Proficient Level or Above on 2005 State Grade 8 Mathematics Assessments

Percentage	Count	States
86–87	1	TN
81–85	3	VA, NE, NC
76–80	3	CT, MN, OK
71–75	5	IN, WI, UT, CO, IA
66–70	5	KS, SD, GA, ID, WV
61–65	9	TX, AK, MI, NJ, AL, MT, PA, OR, ND
56–60	4	NY, AZ, FL, OH
51–55	6	LA, WA, MD, DE, MS, IL
46–50	1	NV
41–45	0	
36–40	4	KY, CA, WY, MA
31–35	1	AR
26–30	1	ME
21–25	3	HI, SC, NM
16–20	1	MO
Total	47	

Source. Olson (2005).
Note. The closest grade with a reading assessment was used for states that did not have a Grade 8 mathematics assessment in 2005. Within a row states are listed in ascending order of the percentage of students who are proficient or above.

of .33 for Grade 8 mathematics. Those correlations are much lower than the uniformly high correlations of the percentages across subjects and/or grades for either the state assessments or NAEP (shown in bold in Table 6.10).

There clearly is substantial variability between states in the percentages of students who are said to be proficient on state assessments. There also are large discrepancies between the percentages based on state assessment results and the percentages of students who perform at the proficient level or

Table 6.9. Means and Standard Deviations of Percentages of Students at the Proficient Level or Above on State Assessments and on NAEP in 2005 for the 47 States with Percentages Reported by Olson (2005) on State Assessments

Assessment	Mean	Standard Deviation
State Grade 4 Reading	71.5	14.7
NAEP Grade 4 Reading	30.7	5.7
State Grade 8 Reading	66.6	15.8
NAEP Grade 8 Reading	29.8	6.1
State Grade 4 Mathematics	69.3	17.1
NAEP Grade 4 Mathematics	35.4	7.4
State Grade 8 Mathematics	58.1	17.8
NAEP Grade 8 Mathematics	28.6	7.2

Note. State assessment results in the closest grade were used when a state did not have an assessment at Grade 4 or 8 in reading or mathematics.

Table 6.10. Correlations of Percentage Proficient or Above on 2005 State Assessments and on 2005 NAEP for 47 States with State Results Reported by Olson (2005)

Variable	SRG4	SRG8	SMG4	SMG8	NRG4	NRG8	NMG4	NMG8
SRG4	1.00							
SRG8	.82	1.00						
SMG4	.84	.78	1.00					
SMG8	.81	.83	.88	1.00				
NRG4	**.14**	.29	.14	.25	1.00			
NRG8	.13	**.25**	.15	.22	.93	1.00		
NMG4	.14	.27	**.22**	.28	.88	.83	1.00	
NMG8	19	.33	.27	**.33**	.87	.88	.92	1.00

Notes. (1) Closest grade was used when state did not test in Grade 4 or 8 reading or mathematics. (2) SRG4 = State Reading Assessment Grade 4, NRG4 = NAEP Reading Assessment Grade 4, etc.

above on NAEP. Moreover, the percentages based on state assessments are only weakly related to the percentages based on NAEP. In light of the large variability, the large discrepancies, and the low correlations of state and NAEP percentages, it would appear that proficient achievement is a concept that has so many definitions that it is almost devoid of meaning.

UNCERTAINTIES OF STANDARD SETTING

Standard setting is not precise or scientific undertaking. Rather it is an activity that has many uncertainties. Although standard setting has been the subject of considerable controversy in the measurement community, there is a broad consensus "among measurement specialists that standard setting is a judgmental process" (Jaeger, 1989, p. 492). A variety of methods have been used to translate the judgments of standard setters into cutscores on an assessment that determine whether a student has or has not met a particular performance standard. There is no agreed upon best method of setting performance standards. Rather, there is a general consensus among measurement specialists that "...there is NO true standard that the application of the right method, in the right way, with enough people will find" (Zieky, 1995, p. 29).

The standards that judges set depend on many factors. As is evident from the difference in stringency of performance standards set prior to and since the enactment of NCLB, it is clear that the context in which standards are set matters. Performance standards also depend on the judges who set the standards and the procedures that the judges use when setting standards. When judges attempt to set performance standards, "they disagree wildly" on the placement of the cutscore (Glass, 1978, p. 251). Of course, some variability is to be expected simply on the basis of sampling error, but there are also systematic differences among judges that influence to stringency of their recommended performance standards. Jaeger, Cole, Irwin, and Pratto (1980), for example, found that the characteristics of the judges that set the standards such as whether they were counselors, teachers, or parents, influenced the level at which standards are set (see also, Jaeger, 1989, p. 492).

There is considerable evidence that different methods of setting standards can yield widely discrepant standards. Jaeger (1989) reviewed studies that had compared different methods of setting performance standards. He was able to compile 32 comparisons of standards set by different methods. He computed the ratio of the largest recommended cutscore to the smallest recommended cutscore for the 32 comparisons. The ratios ranged from a low of 1.00, indicating the same recommended cutscore for the different methods, to a high of 42.0. The median ratio was 1.46. Thus, in roughly half the studies the cutscore for the more stringent method was nearly half and again as large as the cutscore for the more lenient method. The practical implications of the differences due to the method are more apparent in comparisons of the percentages of students who would fail according to the methods that were compared. The failure percentage ratio was computable for 18 of the 32 comparisons reviewed by Jaeger. For those 18 comparisons the failure ratio was 1.00 for one comparison, indicating the same failure rate for the different methods being compared. For the remaining 17 comparisons, however, the ratio ranged from 1.16 to 29.75. That is, in the worst case, nearly 30 times as many test takers would fail if the more stringent recommended cutscore were used than would fail if the more lenient cutscore were used. The median percentage failure ratio was 2.74. Clearly, the "choice of a standard setting method is critical" (Jaeger, 1989, p. 500).

Although several authors (see Hambleton, 1980; Jaeger, 1989; Koffler, 1980; and Shepard, 1980, 1984) have suggested that it would be wise to use multiple methods when setting standards and bring other considerations to bear when recommending a performance standard, in practice that is rarely done because of the cost involved and the challenges of synthesizing diverse results to determine the standard. Recently, however, Kentucky undertook a major standard setting effort in which three quite distinct standard setting methods were used to set performance standards on 18 different assessments—6 content areas with assessments at the elementary, middle, and high school levels (Green, Trimble, & Lewis, 2003; see also, CTB/McGraw-Hill, 2001; and Kentucky Department of Education, 2001, for more detailed descriptions). The bookmark (Lewis, Green, Mitzel, Baum, & Patz, 1998; Mitzel, Lewis, Patz, & Green 2001), the contrasting groups (Livingston & Zieky, 1982), and the Jaeger-Mills (Jaeger & Mills, 2001) methods were used. Recommendations based on each of the three methods were reviewed by synthesis panels that then provided a single set of recommendations to the State Board of Education.

The percentage of Kentucky students who would have been proficient or above using the recommendations of the different methods was quite variable. The difference in the percentage of students scoring at the proficient level or above, between the most stringent method and the least stringent, ranged from a low of 8.2% to a high of 50.5% across the 18 different assessments. The median difference was 25.7% and the average difference was 25.1%. The contrasting groups method resulted in the most lenient recommended proficient standard for 7 of the assessments, the most stringent for 1 assessment, and an intermediate value for the other 10. The bookmark was the most lenient method for 11 assessments, tied for most stringent for 1 assessment, was intermediate for the other 6. While the Jaeger-Mills method was generally the most stringent, there were 2 exceptions (Linn, 2003b). Thus, one cannot be sure that the use of any one of the three methods included in the Kentucky standard setting would yield relatively lenient or relatively stringent performance standards.

A complaint about norm-referenced interpretations of scores is that they highlight individual differences that may lead to invidious comparisons among students rather than fostering equity. Use of criterion-referenced assessments as a tool in improving learning, appear to be more compatible with the goal of equity. Enthusiasm for standards-based interpretations of criterion-referenced measures needs to be tempered, however, by the recognition that there is considerable uncertainty and subjectivity associated with the standard-setting process.

ARE PERFORMANCE STANDARDS NECESSARY?

There are uses of assessments for which a standard of performance is essential. In many instances assessments are used to make dichotomous decisions. If a law requires that a student must pass a test in order to graduate from high school, for example, it is obvious that a minimum passing score must be set. Similarly, a cutscore must be set for tests used for licensure or certification. Cutscores are an integral part of the use of assessment results to make dichotomous decisions.

As stated by Mehrens and Cizek (2001): "It seems tautological to suggest that we set standards because we wish to make dichotomous (categorical) decisions. There is simply no way to escape making such decisions" (p. 478). Performance standards clearly will be required as long as assessments are used to determine who will be certified to practice a profession or who will graduate from high school. This is so despite the uncertainties associated with any standard setting method.

Although performance standards are clearly essential in some uses of assessment results, they are now being imposed in many situations where they are not essential. The NAEP achievement levels were introduced in an attempt to specify levels of performance that were deemed adequate or exemplary with the hope that they would help with the interpretation of NAEP results. For NAEP's primary purpose of monitoring trends in achievement over time, however, scale score means and distributional statistics such as percentile ranks are at least as effective as monitoring changes in the percentage of student at or above fixed achievement levels.

The NCLB requirement that schools be held accountable for meeting targets for the percentage of students who are proficient or above has some intuitive appeal. Certainly it would be desirable for all students to meet some minimum level of performance called proficient. As was noted above, however, *proficient* has so many different definitions that it has become a meaningless concept. Furthermore, performance targets can be set in other ways that do not require the setting of performance standards.

The use of arbitrary performance standards to make high-stakes decisions about schools has a number of drawbacks. The determination of whether a school makes adequate yearly progress (AYP) by a comparison of the percentage of students who perform at the proficient level or above to a fixed annual target places schools serving initially low performing students at a substantial disadvantage in comparison to schools that have student bodies that are high performing before they enter school or start the school year. It is also harder for large schools with heterogeneous student bodies to make AYP than it is for small schools or schools with homogeneous student bodies (Kim & Sunderman, 2005; Linn, 2005). This is because of the NCLB requirement that schools with substantial numbers of students in subgroups defined by race/ethnicity, economic status, student disability status, and English language proficiency meet AYP targets each year for each subgroup as well as for the student body as a whole.

One alternative approach that has considerable precedent in statistical analysis would be to compare student performance across time by using effect size statistics. That is, the mean assessment score in a baseline year, say 2002, would be subtracted from the mean for a current year, for example, 2006, and the difference would be divided by the standard deviation of the scores in the baseline year. Effect size statistics could also be used to monitor the performance of subgroups and the closing of the achievement gap.

For example, if school A had an average score of 250 and a standard deviation of 50 on the 2002 state assessment while 4 years later the average score for the school was 265, the school would have a 2006 effect size of 0.3. A target effect size might be established for all schools to equal the average increase of s subset of schools that had consistent increases over several years. If the average effect size for that subset of schools was 0.05 per year, the 2006 target would be set at 0.2 for all schools and school A would make its AYP target in 2006. On the other hand, school B, though higher achieving than school A in both 2002 and 2006 could fail to make AYP, if, for example, it had a standard deviation of 50 in 2002 and average scores of 265 and 270 in 2002 and 2006, respectively, because it would have an effect size of 2006 of only 0.1, well below the 2006 target for all schools of 0.2.

Another approach would be to compare cumulative distribution functions from one year to the next and for different subgroups (see, for example, Holland, 2002). Changes in student performance at various points throughout the range of assessment scores can be evaluated by comparisons of cumulative distribution functions. The difference in the percentage of students exceeding various score levels can be determined rather than focusing on a single cutscore that corresponds to the proficient standard. Comparisons of cumulative distribution functions also can be used for comparing the achievement of subgroups and to monitor the closing of the gap at various points in the range of scores.

Yet another approach that does not require the setting of arbitrary performance standards that lack common meaning across states, is to compare performance in the current year to norms established for a baseline year. The percentage of students in any given year who scored above the median in the 2002 baseline year, would provide a clear indication of the amount of improvement in student achievement. Targets might be established for purposes of AYP that are based on empirical evidence of the gains achieved by, say, the 10% or 20% of schools that showed the largest gains over the previous 3 or 4 years. This would set ambitious performance targets, but ones that, unlike the 100% proficient target, there was reason to believe might be obtainable with sufficient effort.

To track progress in terms of the percentage of students scoring above a fixed cutscore, sometimes referred to as *percent above cut* (PAC), it would be better to pick the cutscore based on norms in a baseline year than basing it on an arbitrary definition of proficient performance that bears little similarity to the definition of proficient performance in another state. The median or some other percentile rank in a baseline year would be a clearly defined cutscore. It would provide a consistent meaning that does not seem possible to achieve for the proficient performance standard.

The use of arbitrary and often unrealistic definitions of proficient performance together with a requirement of 100% proficiency by 2014 puts schools serving poor students, minority students, and students with disabilities or limited English proficiency at a substantial disadvantage, because those students often start school with relatively low achievement. Thus, even if the students in those schools show substantial gains in achievement, the schools are apt to fall short of the fixed achievement targets established by the requirements of NCLB. The NCLB system may therefore be considered unfair to those schools and because the goal is so far out of reach is likely to do more to demoralize teachers than to motivate them to work harder to enhance student achievement.

CHAPTER 7

Rethinking No Child Left Behind Using Critical Race Theory

Jori N. Hall
Laurence Parker

University of Illinois at Urbana-Champaign

Despite decades of education reform efforts and the most recent federal education policy, the No Child Left Behind Act (NCLB) of 2001, the academic achievement gap between low-income and minority students and their counterparts remains significant (Lee, 2006). We argue that, in large part, the uneven achievement persists because the current external accountability measures emphasize the deficiencies of schools and students, while deemphasizing collaborative and proactive interventions at the school level. This chapter suggests educational initiatives are needed that counter deficit thinking, investigate and understand the social, economic, and political contexts that can negatively impact academic achievement, and assist in engaging those inside and outside schools to collectively and meaningfully serve low-income and minority students.

From this perspective, the purposes of this chapter are to bring attention to how the deficit thinking model and compensatory programs are connected; to suggest critical race theory (CRT) as a lens to challenge and expose societal inequities related to deficit thinking and discourse in NCLB's external accountability model; and to explore alternative educational initiatives that counter deficit thinking. The first part of the chapter will discuss cultural deficit theory and its link to compensatory education and the external accountability framework of NCLB. The next part will briefly review key components of CRT and apply them broadly to NCLB to uncover the inherent inequities and deficit thinking embedded in the law and its implementation. The final part of the chapter will highlight educational initiatives that have sought to counter the ideology of deficit thinking in federal education policy programs for low-income and minority students at the local school level.

CULTURAL DEFICIT THEORY AND COMPENSATORY EDUCATION

Cultural deficit theory perpetuates a detrimental cycle in our nation's education system, which holds minority and low-income students and their families primarily responsible for academic failure. The cultural deficit thinking paradigm, as a whole, suggests that students who fail in school do so because they come from a deficit home environment (Tozer, Violas, & Senese, 2002). The theory suggests low-income and racial minority students have social, cultural, intellectual and motivational deficiencies as compared to their middle-class White peers, and that remedial or preventative services are needed to *compensate* for what they are not supposedly getting in their home environment. Guided by the cultural deficit theory and as a product of the War on Poverty and the Elementary and Secondary Education Act (ESEA) of 1965, compensatory educational reform strongly influenced educational services. To be sure, Stein (2004) argues, based on a cultural analysis of educational policy, the federal compensatory education programs of the 1960s were predicated by their very nature on a deficit perspective based on negative assumptions about the effects of race and social class on student achievement. It should be noted that the effective implementation of early compensatory programs funded by Title I of the ESEA did result in academic gains in reading and math achievement outcomes during the 1970s and 1980s, largely among low-income and African American students; however, the benefits of these programs began to fade during the late 1980s (Borman, 2002/2003).

Yet, despite these gains, after almost three decades, some researchers (Pugach, 1995; Wang, Reynolds, & Walberg, 1995) suggest Title I programs were, for the most part, "fragmented, uncoordinated, and ineffective" (as cited in Waxman, Padron, & Arnold, 2001, p. 137). Part of this criticism was related to research that documented the stigmatizing impact of pull out programs on students (Rutherford, 2001) and the deficit oriented curriculum and pedagogy of students placed at risk in Title I programs. For the most part, Title I programs tended to focus on basic skills remediation which raised concerns with respect to the likelihood low-income and minority students would be given opportunities to learn the core curriculum and be held to high standards (Wong & Meyer, 2001). For instance, when students who have poor academic success were placed in remedial or pull-out Title I programs that were undergirded with deficit thinking, they typically received what Haberman (1991) characterizes as a *pedagogy of poverty*. This form of pedagogy, he argued, emphasizes direct instruction and student compliance.

Haberman's argument mirrors a review of studies that examined classroom instruction of high poverty Title I schools that found main features of classroom instruction to include teacher control, remediation, lectures, and worksheets, with students typically assuming a passive, minimally engaged role (Waxman, Pardon, & Arnold, 2001). When students who received this type of instruction failed to meet desired outcomes, they were often blamed for their failure. Riester, Pursch, and Skrla (2002) capture the practice of the deficit model in schools succinctly when they state:

> The deficit-thinking model is a theory that blames the victims of school failure for their own lack of success in a system that was designed to serve the interests of the wealthy and powerful. This theory is consistent with historical documentation of the ways in which many students from low-income homes fail academically and then are grouped, tested, labeled, and/or categorized, which significantly affects the academic knowledge they receive. (p. 282)

Given the pedagogical and curricular concerns regarding the implementation of Title I pull-out and remedial programs, in the mid-1990s policy makers focused on more comprehensive forms of school reform. For example, in 1994, the Improving America's Schools Act (IASA) expanded the implementation of whole school reform efforts. This meant that instead of using Title I funds to serve only disadvantaged students, schools could use the funds for all students. Overall, despite the potential of IASA to increase cohesive and collaborative school improvement and reduce fragmented, deficit-oriented instruction, significant patterns of failure for high poverty students have not been reversed in Title I schools (Waxman, Pardon, & Arnold, 2001) which implies external federal policies alone are insufficient to meaningfully and substantially shape school and classroom practices.

In sum, past concerns related to Title I programs indicate that the organizational and instructional practices of schools have major implications related to the education of low-income and minority students. In order to effectively address the underachievement of students placed at risk, collective organizational and instructional practices need to be in place that address high expectations and engage student learning and teaching in ways that are culturally and linguistically sensitive (Waxman, Pardon, & Arnold, 2001). However, despite what we understand with respect to the limitations of external federal policies to change schools and the concerns surrounding the deficit model, these practices have come to be reflected in the most recent federal educational policy, the No Child Left Behind Act (NCLB) of 2001.

As a recent reauthorization of the Elementary and Secondary Act (ESEA), NCLB uses annual high-stakes testing to hold states accountable for the academic achievement of their students. Disadvantaged students who attend schools that fail to make annual yearly progress (AYP) for 3 consecutive years may use Title I funds to transfer to a higher-performing public or private school, or they can receive supplemental educational services from a provider of choice. Schools that fail to make AYP over time can get a reduction in federal funds, be restructured, be converted into charter schools, or be taken over by their district or state (U.S. Department of Education, 2004). A critical theory lens is useful for examining NCLB in relationship to educational equity and excellence, particularly as it relates to low-income and minority students.

CRITICAL RACE THEORY AND ITS RELEVANCE TO UNDERSTANDING NO CHILD LEFT BEHIND

A number of different sources have utilized Critical Race Theory (CRT) and its connection to the analysis of racial group identity and conflict in order to critique societal conditions related to justifying cultural deficit ideology in terms of how race and racism profoundly affect the lives of students of color in the U.S. education system (see Delgado, 2003; Delgado Bernal, 2002; Ladson-Billings & Tate, 1995: Lynn, 1999; Solórzano, 1998; Tate, 1997; Villalpando, 2003; and Yosso, 2005). Since the inception of CRT as an interpretive lens in education policy, a central theme was built on the work of Harris (1993) and her landmark article entitled "Whiteness as Property" to make the connection between race and property as a central construct toward understanding the "property functions of whiteness" in relation to schooling (pp. 58-59). Critical Race Theory in education portrays U.S. racism as a persistent historical and ideological construct that could account for inequalities such as dropout rates and school suspension rates for Blacks, Latinos, American Indians, and Asian American/Pacific Island groups. Critical Race Theory also makes important links between property values in the U.S. and the quality of schools by illustrating how poverty and low social status is racialized with Blacks and other people of color routinely having access to property with low value. This, in turn, affects the inherent value of the schools attended by those students, which includes intellectual property such as curriculum and pedagogy in schools that service students of color.

This notion of property has been extended in more recent CRT scholarship by Roithmayr (2004) and her use of *locked-in* inequality as a particular Critical Race Theory lens to analyze how certain institutions have developed monopolistic means of effectively limiting any form of social justice equity because of the ways in which racial and social class advantages have been established for White European Americans over Blacks and other racial groups. Roithmayr argues that in the pre-Brown era of de jure segregation, White European Americans used Jim Crow laws of segregation in the south, and tracking in public schools, housing segregation and job discrimination in the North and West, to effectively and severely restrict the life chances of African Americans and Latinos. The generational effect of this type of discrimination has been that now, even though current laws such as NCLB on its face seemingly grant equality of opportunity in terms of holding all public schools accountable for student academic progress, institutional racism has the effect of locking-in inequalities that may not indeed be overcome. So, for example, because neighborhoods are currently highly segregated in the United States along race and social class lines, White students and their families have social and physical capital advantages that they can pass on in ways that Black and Latino families cannot readily do (Conley, 1999). In addition, school finance equalization efforts, while well intended, fall short of true equity because the neighborhoods and schools that wealthy Whites have always fought for gives them access to advantages that Blacks and other minority groups lack, regardless of class.

One of the key features of new scholarship in CRT is using it to trace generational disparities in educational resources and discriminatory practice. For example, using critical race methodology and critical race policy analysis frameworks for content analysis purposes, Gill, Parker, Cain and Lynn (2006) sought to gain an understanding of African American ideas about schooling in their local communities of east central Illinois; how African American students in this setting actually obtain their education; and how parents and families over generations after the post-desegregation era have tried to implement their educational expectations; and the barriers they have faced in schools over time. In this way, the study hoped to uncover any recurring policy patterns and trends surrounding desegregation and racial inequity.

The project gathered interview data (and descriptive statistics from school district equity audits) from senior African American community members who were involved in the original racial desegregation efforts in an east central Illinois community during the 1950s and 1960s and subsequent generations of families who went through desegregation in this community in the 1970s and 1980s, to the current generation of African American middle school and high school students. The initial interviews, conducted in 2002 with these senior African American community members, revealed that many of them thought they were striving for a noble goal of desegregation in the hope for a better education for their children and the children of the Black community. Now, well after the 50th anniversary of the Brown decision, many of them reflect on how things have changed in terms of the progress of desegregation. However, they also pointed out the problems plaguing the low achievement of African American students have, in some cases, worsened due to the implementation of policies harmful to minority students. This issue has also contributed to the racial hostility and antagonism that has been a part of this community in east central Illinois.

USING CRT TO EXPOSE AND CHALLENGE
THE RACIALIZED DEFICIT THINKING OF NCLB

Conservatives have trumpeted a new call for equality through legislation such as NCLB, but they have been loathe to attach significant spending dollars that would address the historical and generational effects of racism and social class divisions that have an impact on achievement in many U.S. schools both in urban and rural areas. The late Senator Paul Wellstone (D-Minnesota) voiced one of the few dissenting opinions on NCLB as it was being debated on the floor of the Senate (C-Span U.S. Senate debate, 2001). He basically argued that NCLB played a cruel joke on public schools as another unfunded federal mandate that appears to call for equality of opportunity for all students regardless of race, social class, language minority or special education status. In reality, due to the lack of federal funding for K–12 education at all levels, true equity would be an elusive dream for schools. His prediction was that the majority of school teachers who worked with low income and minority students on a daily basis would be angry at the federal government for imposing NCLB on them. Senator Edward Kennedy (D-Massachusetts) echoed the same concerns about NCLB on the Senate floor when he questioned: "Where is the funding? You can't find it!. . . You can't get this by with a tin cup budget. . . . The funding isn't there for this legislation, but the need is there for these children, and these children have needs that will not be met by this legislation unless there is adequate funding from the federal government" (C-Span U.S. Senate debate, 2001).

The arguments made on the floor of the U.S. Senate by Wellstone and Kennedy in the spring of 2001 have proven prophetic now when we see how their predictions have rung true. NCLB has been the greatest piece of federal legislation that has had an impact on all public schools in the United States However, federal funds covered only 1 year of this legislation and states have had to bear the majority share of NCLB implementation costs, which in turn put more emphasis on covering testing, and assessment costs rather than other state-supported student educational services (Thomas & Brady, 2005).

A CRT analysis of NCLB shows that this major legislative policy has come up short with respect to resource allocation, and as a result has a deleterious impact on students, especially low-income students of color in high poverty districts. This has been especially problematic for students whose primary language is not English. Many states have made the argument that the 3-year time limit initially imposed on states to transition limited English speaking students to English only classrooms was too rigid and would have a harmful effect on the educational progress of certain groups of students, particularly recent immigrants from Southeast Asia and the Pacific Islands if they are attending impoverished schools in low-income districts (Louie, 2005; Thomas & Brady, 2005).

We need to ask why the racial achievement gap has been defined in a public policy crisis mode, particularly with the NCLB legislation. Critical Race Theory helps us understand this policy discourse around race and school achievement. From a CRT perspective, race still very much explains public policy discourse. For example, the roots of the racial divide on education and achievement started with the first term (1980–1984) of Ronald Reagan and his campaign on school vouchers, tuition tax credits, and making an appeal to traditional values taught in schools that would appeal to not only Whites in the suburbs but also some working class Black and Latino parents who were unhappy with the urban public schools (Lugg, 1996). Part of the Reagan agenda during this period was to implement a political strategy and ideology that would question the value of government sponsored social programs that extended benefits to persons of color, from welfare, to compensatory programs and to affirmative action.

It is through this historical policy lens that CRT illuminates the pros and cons of the research on the achievement gap for minority students and how it became a *racialized* problem. Black, Latino, American Indian and Asian-American Pacific Islander students have been normed vis-à-vis the success of White students as the model of academic achievement. No Child Left Behind thereby becomes the standard of success in order to judge AYP standards and schools serving these students of color. Therefore, students of color are still viewed as deficient; further, a political agenda is set to disengage support for public education and build support for choice policies for parents as consumers. This helps the lucky families of color in urban areas who can take advantage of other public and private school options but leaves the hard to educate students behind in the public schools that the NCLB legislation was intended to help.

From a CRT perspective, high standards and high-stakes testing is appealing to policy makers in the sense that they serve to draw attention away from the social, economic and political deficits embedded our nation's education system and "set high expectations for all" (Linn, 2005, p. 15), particularly for low-income and minority students. However, the focus on accountability through state testing and AYP is insufficient. To be sure, the standards and testing, as reflected in NCLB, are not premised on a growth model that acknowledges students' past performance and fails to address the unequal quality of schools. Ryan's (2004) legal analysis of the effects of NCLB suggests that shedding light on the deficiencies of low performing students and schools does not give us enough insight as to how much progress some schools made given their previous performance, and that federal resources should be rewarded to schools in terms of their overall progress as opposed to seemingly unreachable AYP standards.

Furthermore, from a CRT perspective, we need to hold NCLB accountable for what the policy was intended to do. NCLB's intent was to push states through test-driven accountability to achieve results in reducing the achievement gap between White students and Black and Latino students. It was trumpeted as the legislation that was going to finally push states and schools to provide equal educational opportunity that would lead to measured gains and results in achievement for all students, particularly those low-income and racial minority students who had been previously left behind. While the rhetoric of the policy has reflected this orientation, the recent data prove that NCLB as implemented has not resulted in marked gains for Black and Latino students.

Lee (2006) recently tracked the achievement gains in math and reading during the time of NCLB implementation. Overall, the gaps have persisted and in some states have grown when one applies the NAEP (National Assessment of Educational Progress) test data to the analysis of this gap. The federal government has provided $412 million a year to help pay for the testing requirements to meet accountability standards. Yet, according to Lee:

> the racial achievement gap in national public schools persists after NCLB. The White-Black and White-Hispanic gaps among 4th and 8th graders did not narrow significantly between 2002 and 2005 in reading and between 2003 and 2005 in math. The racial gap in reading remained about the same between 2002 and 2005 at both grade 4 and grade 8; the one-point change was not only statistically insignificant but also it is much smaller than the 5 point reduction of the gap made during the 2000–2002 period. The White-Black and White-Hispanic reading gaps at grade 4 increased in the early 1990s and then decreased in the late 1990s and by 2002 (prior to NCLB). The discrepancies between NAEP and state assessment results are the largest for Black and Hispanic and poor students and these findings are consistent across grades in both reading and math. (pp. 26, 49)

If NCLB was intended to end or significantly narrow the achievement gap, so far the policy has not worked, and from a CRT standpoint the Bush Administration needs to be held accountable for the failure of the policy to deliver.

No Child Left Behind accountability measures are also objectionable as they overlook the personal commitment to the education of low-income and minority students. No Child Left Behind does not hold educators *personally* responsible for meeting the individual needs of each student; instead educators are held accountable for following standard *procedures*, with an emphasis on high-stakes testing, and student achievement defined as the level of performance on a single test. Basically, educators can comply with policy mandates without a personal commitment to decisions made in the classroom on behalf of minority and low-income students. Therefore, as long as they meet the requirements of NCLB, educators have technically done their job. It is within this context of NCLB's accountability measures that educators are held accountable to test scores—not students.

In addition, NCLB's use of traditional supplemental programs neglects the wide range of social and emotional needs of low-income students and students of color. Even NCLB's charge that supplemental services use "effective methods and instructional strategies that are grounded in scientifically based research" does not address the range of needs of low-income and minority students (U.S. Department of Education, 2004, p. 13). For instance, more resources, counselors and English as a Second Language (ESL) teachers would be needed to address the various needs of different immigrant students, the context to which they came to the United States and their progress in schools if they are to truly succeed under NCLB. Given the current political backlash against certain immigrant groups (e.g., Mexicans, and others from Central America), this would be an important way for schools to take a progressive leadership stance as opposed to a defensive position against immigration and educational accountability.

Also, in some high schools, school administrators have pushed teachers to teach to the accountability test to simply meet AYP standards, rather than teach to foster more engaged learning and critical thinking. For instance, when faced with the pressures of meeting AYP goals, some school use supplemental programs to focus on the tested subjects of NCLB through test drill and preparation. This practice has major implications for African Americans and Latinos, as they are typically enrolled in underperforming schools and therefore, more than likely subjected to habitual basic skills and test preparation practices (Lipman, 2004). Furthermore, the external accountability of NCLB assumes all schools have the capacity to respond effectively to the policy and does not provide the information schools need about what to do or how to improve education and student learning (Ryan, 2002). Rather, the educational accountability of NCLB labels schools as failing. This method of holding schools accountable places some schools in a position to function from a deficit orientation (Lipman, 2004). That is, under the stigma of failing, some schools focus on deficiencies or which students did not meet desired outcomes of tested subject areas.

This stigma can foster a culture within schools that can be characterized as functioning in compliance mode, meaning these schools operate in way that primarily addresses the policy mandate and not the instructional needs of students (DeBray, Parson, & Avila, 2003). When schools try to simply survive the policy, this gives some schools, particularly those schools that serve poverty stricken or diverse groups who are supposedly deficient—low-income students, students with disabilities, immigrants, or second language learners—a greater incentive to narrow curriculum by focusing on tested subject areas and to push out students who are failing (Meier & Woods, 2004). Moreover, students placed at-risk of failing have an extra burden, as some high schools, school districts such as Chicago, and states such as California, link graduation or promotion to the next grade to testing. Therefore, high-stakes testing and placing low-income and minority students in supplemental programs is insufficient.

In short, through using CRT as one lens of analysis, we attempted to expose some of the effects of deficit thinking in our country's current educational programs for students of color and low-income students. Our analysis suggests educational reform is needed to address finance equalization, the promise of students and schools, generation disparities, culturally relevant instructional practices, and a personal commitment to educate low-income and minority students beyond the tested subjects of NCLB. This exposure can hopefully foster policy discussion on what needs to be reformed regarding the challenge to deficit thinking.

RETHINKING EDUCATIONAL REFORM

The hope and challenge comes in using CRT in educational policy analysis as an interpretive research agenda-setting framework that can probe more deeply into a teaching and learning process that truly values the success of all students of color, not only in terms of short-term test accountability gains, but in terms of the teachers', principals', and school communities' interest in these students as unique learners over time. This requires a conceptualization of school reform as complex and multifaceted. Boykin (2000) articulates this point well:

> School reform connotes changing why we school; what goes on at school; how schools are structured, governed, and administered; and how to conceive of the learner and the learning process. It connects what gets taught, changing how it gets taught, the role the teacher plays in the schooling process, the relationship between a given school, the families served, and the surrounding community. It connotes changes in the organizational culture of the schooling process. (p. 4)

Boykin's statements imply rethinking school reform in terms of what it means to effectively and meaningfully change schools. Accordingly, effective reform efforts for low income and minority students should go beyond NCLB's preoccupation with deficiencies and the privileging of performance outcomes to consider the community, the culture of the school and what happens *inside* classrooms. One school reform effort that attempts to address these issues by utilizing a social justice agenda of encouraging schools and students to be collectively proactive, think critically about how to best improve learning while cultivating a culture of caring is the High Performance for All Student Success Schools (HiPass) model. Embedded in the HiPass model are five core beliefs (Scheurich, 1998).

The first core belief of the HiPass model is that *All Children Can Succeed at High Academic Levels*. Educators don't just pay lip service; they show commitment to this belief through their actions. This belief emphasizes high expectations for all students without exception. The second core belief is *Learner-Centered Schools*. This focuses on a pedagogy that is child centered. That is, all aspects of the school (community, staff development, school structure, and so forth) are geared toward providing a safe, effective, learning environment. The third core belief, *All Children Must be Treated with Love, Appreciation, Care, and Respect*, reinforces the humanistic approach of the HiPass model. The attitude embedded in this belief is at the heart of the model as it cultivates a culture of care in the school. In a way, it is a sense of family and an attitude of we're in this together coupled with shared experiences between educators and students of similar backgrounds that foster meaningful relationships. The model suggests that school staff who have similar ethnic backgrounds with students share a historical solidarity.

The fourth core belief, *The Racial Culture, Including the First Language, of the Child is Always Highly Valued*, values the culture students bring to the school setting rather than focusing on perceived cultural deficits. Incorporated into this belief is what Ladson-Billings (1994) characterizes as "culturally relevant teaching." Specifically, culturally relevant teaching is a "pedagogy that empowers students intellectually, socially, emotionally, and politically by using cultural referents to impart knowledge, skills, and attitudes" (pp. 17–18).

The last belief of the HiPass model suggests that the school exists for and serves the community. The principle central to this belief is that the school and community are not separate but interrelated. This perspective promotes a proactive stance by schools to identify alternative methods of involving the community. Educators and parents are viewed as collaborators in the education of students. Also incorporated into the HiPass model is the use of testing. However, tests are mostly used to modify instructional goals, as opposed to the punitive focus of high-stakes accountability as implemented by NCLB.

Taken together, the HiPass model of educational reform focuses on high expectations, student-centered learning, use of test scores to inform instruction, and culturally relevant teaching. In this way, meaningful interactions and relationships amongst all stakeholders (students, teachers, schools, and the community) can be fostered that hold them *personally* responsible for academic success.

The implementation of the HiPass model or other school level initiatives that attempt to counterbalance the deficiency focus and policy demands of NCLB can be exceptionally daunting, particularly given the increased pressure for schools to meet AYP goals. However, some of the changes outlined by the HiPass model can still occur given the inequalities embedded in current social, economic, and political contexts. For example, one elementary school that serves majority minority students mandated a scripted reading program that challenges instructional methods that are antideficit. As part of the reading program, teachers present students with *fluency petals* every 6 weeks to reflect how many words per minute students read, which add up to *fluency flowers* posted in the classroom (Miner, 2005/2006). One teacher's response to the mandated posting of fluency flowers demonstrates the problems that can arise in classrooms where schools are implementing mandated classroom practices. As Miner explained, "The kids who pass the fluency benchmark, yeah, they'll feel great. But the kid who doesn't, they're going to feel terrible. And there's all sorts of research showing that making kids feel bad is not going to motivate them." Rather than displaying fluency flowers and making less successful students feel bad, this teacher shows each student his or her flower privately, thereby maintaining the dignity of students while making them aware of their reading progress (Miner, 2005/2006). The comments of this teacher represent similar struggles that are experienced in classrooms that serve low-income and minority student elsewhere.

Low-income and minority students need teachers who think critically about instructional practices as well as respond proactively to ensure that all students receive a more equitable education. This is no easy task, particularly given the current external accountability pressures of NCLB. Ultimately, addressing the education of low-income and minority students cannot be done by teachers or government policy alone. Addressing these needs demands a multifaceted vision of school reform that requires *both* those outside and within school walls to work collectively and proactively to confront issues of school inequality.

CONCLUSION

Essentially, educational policy and programs designed to increase the level of academic success of low-income and minority students must go beyond the rhetoric of leaving no child behind. Indeed, there must be a culture-collective responsibility created in a school that is firmly grounded in the belief that low-income and minority students can learn. From this perspective, we offer CRT as one of several interpretive lenses to critique federal education policy. We propose CRT as a way to better understand the societal inequities that breed educational inequities and disrupt deficit thinking. CRT in education policy can be used to provide more informed perspectives that lead to action against the high rates of school suspensions and other seemingly neutral school policies and practices that have a deleterious impact on students of color. Dixson and Rousseau (2005) call for using CRT's grounding in the law and its untapped potential in educational research to build more complex understandings of the operationalization of the origins and impact of racism in educational settings.

From our perspective, federal and state accountability systems would do well to abandon the deficit model and seek earnest, alternative methods and measures that promote educational equity. Critical Race Theory has a potential future for education policy action on the continuum of raising critical issues of race and social class to the center of the debate to push for change in policy legislation such as NCLB. Given the ways in which NCLB has not served racial minority children, CRT scholarship can provide a critical race perspective as to why, and point to alternatives that truly seek to improve educational equity for students of color.

CHAPTER 8

Accountability, Standards, and Race Inequity in the United Kingdom: Small Steps on the Road of Progress or the Defence of White Supremacy?

David Gillborn

Institute of Education, London

> *Many schools in our country are places of hope and opportunity ....*
> *Unfortunately, too many schools in America have failed in that mission.*
> *The harm has been greatest in the poor and minority communities. Those*
> *kids have been hurt the worst because people have failed to challenge the*
> *soft bigotry of low expectations. Over the years, parents across America*
> *have heard a lot of excuses—that's a reality—and oftentimes have seen*
> *little change. One year ago today, the time for excuse-making has come*
> *to an end. With the No Child Left Behind Act, we have committed the*
> *nation to higher standards for every single public school. And we've*
> *committed the resources to help the students achieve those standards. We*
> *affirm the right of parents to have better information about the schools,*
> *and to make crucial decisions about their children's future. Accountability*
> *of results is no longer just a hope of parents. Accountability for results is*
> *now the law of the land.*
>
> —President George W. Bush, January 8, 2003

Accountability has become one of the watchwords of contemporary education policy. Policy makers in both the United States and the United Kingdom have asserted that many of the problems of the education system can be blamed on teachers and administrators who were not held to account for their actions. Politicians and media commentators frequently present education policy as a series of incremental steps, each building on the last and moving toward a position of greater overall attainment (higher standards) and simultaneously addressing existing social inequities. This link is clearly asserted in President Bush's statement that "The harm has been greatest in the poor and minority communities" where children have "been hurt the worst because people have failed to challenge the soft bigotry of low expectations" (Bush, 2003). Even the most cursory glance at the statistics of educational inequity, on either side of the Atlantic, confirms that many minoritized groups, and especially Black students, have certainly not shared equally in the fruits of public schooling.[1] However, can we be sure that these problems will be remedied by greater "accountability" and the related reforms? Indeed, could these changes actually make the situation worse?

In this chapter I draw on evidence from England to examine this issue. The English case is especially significant because many measures that are now enshrined in U.S. education policy were first enacted through a series of policy changes in England that stretch back to the late 1980s. These include the increasing reliance on high-stakes testing, the use of published school and district report cards, and a growing discourse that presents public schools as uniformly low quality in comparison to the assumed excellence of the private sector. In this sense the English experience serves as a form of natural experiment where some of the U.S. policies, and their likely consequences, can be studied in advance of their application across the States and throughout K–12 education. Before sifting the evidence, however, it is useful to clarify the conceptual tools that underpin the analysis.

WHAT DOES RACISM REALLY LOOK LIKE IN EDUCATION?

The concept of racism is constantly contested and debated, both formally (through academic work and in the law) and more informally (for example, through the media). This has been especially true in the United Kingdom since 1999, when the report of the Stephen Lawrence Inquiry briefly catapulted the notion of "institutional racism" to the top of the political and news agendas alike.

Stephen Lawrence was 18 years old when, as he waited for a London bus, he was attacked and stabbed to death by a group of White youths. The police inquiry generated no arrests. Stephen's parents, Doreen and Neville, were treated more like troublemakers than grieving parents. They became convinced that the case was being mishandled because Stephen's death was not a sufficient priority for the investigating officers nor the Metropolitan Police Force as a whole, since Stephen was a young Black man. After years of campaigning the Lawrences' demands for a public inquiry were finally met by an incoming Labour government in 1997. *The Stephen Lawrence Inquiry*

Report (Macpherson, 1999), and the consequent public debates, provided the closest British parallel yet to the kinds of national furor over racism that were sparked in the United States by the Rodney King affair and the O.J. Simpson trials. The Inquiry Report stated categorically that "institutional racism" was a routine and pervasive factor in many of the key agencies of society, including the police, education and the health service. The Report stated that "racism, institutional or otherwise, is not the prerogative of the Police Service. It is clear that other agencies including for example those dealing with housing and education also suffer from the disease" (p. 33).

One of the most significant aspects of the report concerned an attempt to move beyond the superficial notion of racism that had previously characterized policy debate (in education and beyond). Public authorities and commentators tend to work with a view of racism as encompassing only the more obvious and deliberate forms of race hatred: as if "racism is restricted to a few 'rotten apples' in a basket that is basically sound" (Rizvi, 1993, p. 7, after Henriques, 1984, p. 62). Remarkably, for a report that began with a racist murder (surely the most crude and vicious form of racism), the Stephen Lawrence Inquiry insisted on a broad reworking of the term *institutional racism,* that explicitly included unintended and thoughtless acts that have the *effect* of discriminating (regardless of their intent):

> [Institutional racism consists of the] collective failure of an organisation to provide an appropriate and professional service to people because of their colour, culture, or ethnic origin. It can be seen or detected in processes, attitudes and behaviour which amount to discrimination through unwitting prejudice, ignorance, thoughtlessness and racist stereotyping which disadvantage minority ethnic people. (Macpherson, 1999, p. 28)

Needless to say, this definition has been subject to endless scrutiny and debate. It is by no means a simple paraphrasing of previous approaches and it is not without its problems; nevertheless, one thing that is common to this perspective and longer established definitions is its fundamental challenge to complacency about the realities of contemporary racial politics and inequities. As Stokely Carmichael and Charles V. Hamilton observed 40 years ago, institutional racism "is less overt, far more subtle, less identifiable in terms of *specific* individuals committing the acts. But it is no less destructive of human life. [It] originates in the operation of established and respected forces in the society, and thus receives far less public condemnation. . ." (Carmichael & Hamilton, 1967, original emphasis, reprinted in Cashmore & Jennings, 2001, p. 112).

The Lawrence definition of institutional racism currently occupies a contradictory position in British politics: on one hand, the definition has been officially accepted and underlies recent extensions to equity legislation: on the other hand, in practice the race equity legislation in education is almost completely ignored and right-wing commentators have waged a campaign to rubbish the definition: "One can't be an unwitting racist any more than one can be an unwitting burglar and to pretend otherwise is to put back the cause of multi-culturalism for years" (Steven, 1999, p. 35).

Despite the continuing controversy, the Lawrence definition has proven especially valuable to antiracists, who have long argued that if the effects of an action or policy are discriminatory (that is, they disproportionately disadvantage one or more minoritized groups) then they are racist in their consequences regardless of their conscious intent. This viewpoint echoes the racial realism advocated by Derrick Bell (1992), a leading African American legal scholar, who seeks to break free of the limiting formal conceptions of equality that limit analyses to only the most superficial and obvious forms of discrimination. Bell is one of the founding authors in Critical Race Theory (CRT), a movement of radical legal scholars that is now being taken up and used by increasing numbers of critical theorists in education (see Dixson & Rousseau, 2005; Ladson-Billings & Tate, 1995; Parker, Deghler, & Villenas, 1999). Critical Race Theory offers a new and challenging perspective, as Richard Delgado and Jean Stefancic (2000) have argued:

> Critical Race Theory begins with a number of basic insights. One is that racism is normal, not aberrant, in American society. Because racism is an ingrained feature of our landscape, it looks ordinary and natural to persons in the culture. Formal equal opportunity—rules and laws that insist on treating blacks and whites (for example) alike—can thus remedy only the more extreme and shocking forms of injustice, the ones that do stand out. It can do little about the business-as-usual forms of racism that people of color confront every day and that account for much misery, alienation, and despair. (p. xvi)

Before further considering the utility of a critical race perspective, perhaps it is best to consider the evidence. The next section of this chapter, therefore, looks at some basic facts about the shape and outcomes of contemporary education policy.

WHO AND WHAT IS EDUCATION POLICY FOR?

Public debate about education policy has become increasingly couched within an economistic language of efficiency and effectiveness. Quantitative approaches have often been adopted in an attempt to judge the value for money that schools offer. In the process, concerns with social justice can become lost or, worse still, assumed to be part of old failed approaches (Morley & Rassool, 1999).[2] In this context, policies that proclaim a central concern with accountability and higher standards often take for granted that *all* students and communities will share in the promised improvements. Indeed, as Thrupp and Willmott (2003) argue, there is a growing cadre of textual apologists (commentators and self-proclaimed experts) only too ready to support the view that educational inequities can be erased by freeing the market, empowering school principals and ensuring the dominance of managerial theory. As each new policy is unveiled, however, it is easy to be blinded by the discourse and confused by the supposed complexity of the arguments and mechanisms that are at work. Indeed, when considering educational policies and their consequences, I believe that it is instructive to begin with some deceptively simple and blunt questions.

In view of the restrictions of available space, I want to ask three questions that directly address the material consequences of education policy. These are by no means the only relevant tests of equity and policy but they are among the most revealing and fundamental because they go beyond the expressed intent of policy makers and practitioners to examine how policy works in the real world. First, the question of priorities: who or what is driving education policy? Second, the question of beneficiaries: who wins and who loses as a result of education policy priorities? And finally, the question of outcomes: what are the effects of policy? I will address each question in turn.

Priorities

As several studies have shown, over the last half-century issues of racism, race relations and race equity have featured differently in education policy. From early postwar ignorance and neglect (Lynch, 1986), through periods of overt assimilationist policies (Mullard, 1982; Tomlinson, 1977 & 2005), it has been clear that, although the particular measures meant to address ethnic diversity have changed from time to time, one constant feature has been a place on the margins of education policy. Superficially there have been significant changes. For example, during much of the 1980s and 1990s successive Conservative administrations—reflecting Margaret Thatcher's infamous assertion that there is "no such thing as society" (Thatcher, 1993: 626)—insisted that the only fair approach was a "colour-blind" perspective that denied any legitimacy to group-based analyses and claims. John Major, who succeeded Thatcher as Prime Minister, asserted:

> Life is lived, people join in, people belong. Darkness, lightness—that's a difference losing significance with every day crossed off the calendar. ... Few things would inflame racial tension more than trying to bias systems in favour of one colour— a reverse discrimination that fuels resentment. An artificial bias would damage the harmony we treasure. Equality under the law—yes; equality of opportunity and reward—yes. These promote harmony. Policy must be colour blind—it must

just tackle disadvantage. Faced by British citizens, whatever their background might be. (Major, 1997, pp. 6–7)

The assumption of constant incremental progress "with every day crossed off the calendar" is clear in this quotation. Major's determination to refuse the significance of raced inequity (reducing race and racism to a question of "darkness" and "lightness") was highly significant. The subtext of his attack on "[a]n artificial bias" would seem to suggest an acceptance of some form of nonartificial (natural?) bias.

In a stark reversal of this language, Tony Blair's incoming "New Labour" administration of 1997 openly named race inequity as an unacceptable feature of the education system and even quoted critical research that had raised questions about teachers' role in producing raced inequities in school (DfEE, 1997). Unfortunately, the tangible outcomes of this approach have mostly concerned granting funding to a handful of minority ethnic schools on the basis of a distinctive religious identity, for example, creating the first state-funded Muslim schools (see Figueroa, 2004; Gillborn, 1998 & 2001).

A particularly stark indicator of the place of race equity in contemporary English education policy is provided by the Department for Education's five-year strategy published amid a flurry of publicity in the summer of 2004. Running to more than 100 pages, the document set out Labour's proposals for the next 5 years of education policy. Minority ethnic pupils are granted a single mention in the text; in a 25-word paragraph headed *low achieving minority ethnic groups* (DfES, 2004). The word *racism* does not appear at all; neither do the more sanitized concepts of *prejudice* and *discrimination*. In contrast, *business* and *businesses* appear 36 times, and *standards* appears on 65 separate occasions: the latter equates to an average reiteration of *standards* once every page and a half. Clearly, the 5-year strategy prioritized an official version of *standards* in education, but one could legitimately ask: standards for whom?

The first step toward enacting the plans that had been laid out in the strategy document was an official Education White Paper (a statement of detailed policy intent) published in late 2005. Interestingly, the document includes several references to minority ethnic children and their parents. Unfortunately, each reference follows a disturbing pattern whereby minoritized groups are portrayed as somehow deficient, and programs to support them are presented as an optional extra, divorced from the main thrust of policy and lacking any mandatory force, so that schools are free to ignore the issue if they choose. For example, the White Paper proclaims the success of the Aiming High program, a small pilot project that targeted support to a group of 30 schools in order to focus on the attainment of Black/African Caribbean students (DfES, 2005b). Notwithstanding the fact that the project's formal evaluation was not completed until 2006, the policy document confidently announced the success of the program but simultaneously failed to require any formal response from schools. Rather than extend the program nationally, for example, the White Paper merely stated a commitment to offer "advice and support to meet the aspirations of BME [Black & Minority Ethnic] parents and pupils" (DfES, 2005b, p. 58). Later in the same document, minoritized parents are mentioned within a deficit framework that stresses a negative view rather than valuing the strong support that is a known quality of these communities: "for those from poorer and minority ethnic backgrounds ... these parents may feel less confident to come forward and ask for support, especially if they do not speak English fluently" (DfES, 2005b, p. 71).

Regardless of the political persuasion of the incumbent political party, therefore, race equity has constantly to fight for legitimacy as a significant topic for education policy makers. Education policy in England has, at best, paid limited attention to race as a marginal issue not worthy of significant attention; at worst, it is an issue that is completely absent when new policies are formulated.

Beneficiaries

Since 1988, when the first major legislative changes to the postwar system were announced, education policy in England (under both Conservative and Labour governments) has been driven by the assertion that standards are too low and must be raised. The dominant measure of standards has been crude quantitative data, in particular, students' performance in high-stakes tests conducted at the end of their primary and secondary education. These data are published nationally in tabular form and provide a misleading, but easily reproduced, guide to school standards.[3] The reforms have fundamentally altered how schools operate, placing a premium on those subjects that will count in the school tests[4] and leading to increased selection and separation of students who are thought to be academic in secondary schools.

A good performance in the official statistics is extremely important for schools: continual underperformance can trigger a range of sanctions including, ultimately, school closure. Not surprisingly, therefore, the proportion of 16-year-olds attaining the requisite five higher grade passes in their high-stakes examinations has consistently risen since the late 1980s. However, students of color have not always shared equally in these gains.[5] In fact, of the principal race/census categories monitored continuously since the late 1980s, only one group—Whites—have enjoyed consistent year-on-year improvement. The proportion of Whites attaining the benchmark level (at least *five* higher grade passes) has risen from 30% in 1989 to 55% in 2004 (DfES 2005a). Each of the other groups counted in official statistics have experienced periods where their rate of success has held constant (as in the case of Indian students between 2000 and 2002) or even where their success rate has *fallen back*—for example, Black students between 1992 and 1994, and between 2000 and 2004; Pakistani students between 1992 and 1996, and between 2002 and 2004; and Bangladeshi students between 1998 and 2000 (DfES, 2005a).

On the whole, therefore, minoritized students have not shared equally in the improved attainments associated with the recent reforms. In particular, Black students find themselves even further behind their White counterparts than they were in the 1980s: in 1989, 30% of White students achieved five or more higher grade passes, compared with 18% of Black students (an inequity of 12 percentage points); in 2004, however, the gap was 20 percentage points (with the benchmark being attained by 55% of White students and 35% of their Black peers: DfES, 2005a). Similarly, Pakistani students (who were 11 percentage points behind Whites in 1992) have experienced widening inequities of attainment in recent years: in 2004, 37% of Pakistani students reached the required level, that is, a gap of 18 percentage points behind Whites.

A great deal of official attention focuses on pupils categorized as of Indian ethnic heritage. This group was first recognized separately in official statistics in 1992, when 38% attained the benchmark level of success. Since then, Indian students have generally enjoyed *greater* success than the White group: with 72% achieving at least five higher grade passes in the most recent survey (17 percentage points ahead of the White group). This level of attainment is often given special prominence by the government: for example, a statistical press release was entitled "Minority Ethnic Pupils Make Further Progress at GCSE" (DfES, 2005d). Indeed, the attainment of Indian pupils (along with certain other Asian peers) is frequently cited as evidence that the system rewards effort and that, consequently, any race inequities can have nothing to do with racism in the system (neither overt nor unintended). The following opinion, for example, was confidently expressed by a columnist in *The Sunday Times:* "I'm no educationist, but if you examine the statistics it is certainly difficult to conclude that our schools discriminate against ethnic minorities, even unwittingly. Chinese and some other Asian pupils excel, easily outperforming the whites" (Liddle, 2005).

Much has been written in the United States about how certain groups have come to be seen as model minorities. This stereotype of hard work and success harms both the group itself (by ignoring their experience of racist harassment and obscuring other disadvantages, such as higher rates of unemployment) and, by implication, other less successful groups (whose failure it is reasoned, must surely be their own fault): see Min (2004) and Takaki (1993).

This literature is less well developed in the United Kingdom but qualitative research has already established that racism in schools works differently for different ethnic groups (see Youdell, 2000; 2003). A more detailed examination of Indian and Chinese attainments is beyond the scope of the present chapter; suffice it to say that their relative success in high-stakes tests evidences nothing about an absence of racism in their school experiences (see Archer & Francis 2005a & b; Bhatti 2004). Furthermore, their relative success should not distract from the much less positive picture that emerges for the other minoritized groups counted in official data.

Outcomes

A major reason for the different patterns of improvement shown by some groups lies in the ways that schools have responded to the pressure to raise standards. Anecdotal evidence, for example, suggests that some schools have sought to limit the proportion of minoritized students they admit and to expel disproportionate numbers of Black students. By their very nature, such practices elude official documentation and scrutiny, but it is certainly the case that Black students continue to be significantly more likely to be expelled from school than their White peers (as they have ever since records began: DfES, 2002) and that Black students are frequently treated more harshly than Whites accused of similar offences—a pattern long established in British qualitative research (Blair, 2001; Connolly, 1998; Figueroa, 1991; Gillborn ,1990; Gillborn & Youdell, 2000; Mac an Ghaill, 1988; Mirza, 1992 & 1999; Nehaul, 1996; Sewell, 1997; Wright, 1987 & 1992; Wright, Weekes, & McGlaughlin, 2000), and now even identified in official school inspection data.

A report by the official body that inspects schools (Office for Standards in Education[Ofsted]) noted that "the lengths of fixed-period exclusions varied considerably in some schools between black and white pupils for what were described as the same or similar incidents" (Ofsted, 2001, p. 23). These comments must be read within a context where Ofsted itself has been criticised for failing to take a sufficiently active role in combating race inequity (Osler & Morrison, 2000). Indeed, a research report funded and published by the Department for Education has noted that "Ofsted school inspections rarely comment on disproportionality in exclusions" (Parsons, Godfrey, Annan, Cornwall, Dussart, Hepburn, Howlett, & Wennerstrom, 2004: 1). The study noted that even where evidence of over-representation was contained within reports, it usually went unremarked: "None of the seven Ofsted inspection reports published on secondary schools [in the sample] commented on disproportionality of minority ethnic exclusions, which was evident in the tables published in six of them" (p. 50).

It is also clear that schools are increasingly using "setting by ability" and other forms of internal selection to separate children into hierarchical teaching groups. *Setting* is an approach to pupil grouping whereby, in certain subjects (especially mathematics, science and modern foreign languages), students are placed in hierarchical teaching groups (taught by different teachers in separate classrooms). In theory it is possible for a student to be in a high ranked set for one subject but a lower ranked group for another. In practice, however, there is a strong tendency for the same students to be placed in the sets at either end of the spectrum (Gillborn & Youdell, 2000).

This kind of development is openly advocated by government. For example, the Labour Party's 1997 election manifesto claimed that setting benefits both high- and low-achieving students (Labour Party, 1997), something that is directly contradicted by the international research evidence.[6] Despite the lack of supporting evidence, however, both the Labour and Conservative parties have pledged to extend the use of setting in all schools and in a greater number of subject areas (Conservative Party, 2006; DfES, 2005b)

Additional policies have further extended this principle of selection and separation, for example, first, by creating advantaged pathways for those designated as gifted and talented, and second, by increasing the number of specialist schools, each with increased provision to choose pupils according to aptitude and/or ability (see Edwards & Tomlinson, 2002). Wholly predictably, in view of previous research on the raced nature of selection to gifted programs, evidence is already emerging that certain minoritized groups, especially Black students, are markedly under-represented in the advantaged provision for the so-called gifted and talented (Ofsted, 2004).

Despite the clearest evidence of current race inequity, however, the policies continue to be pursued. In January 2005, for example, the Department for Education published the first ever official analysis of the racial profile of students benefiting from the national gifted and talented scheme: 10% of Whites were identified for inclusion compared with 6% of Indian students, 5% of Pakistani students, 4% of Black students identifying their family heritage in the Caribbean, and just 2% of Black students identifying their ethnic heritage as African (DfES, 2005c). Nevertheless, in October of the same year, the latest round of reforms was presented and an extension of the Gifted and Talented provision was announced (establishing a national register) but, once again, no mandatory safeguards for race equity were mentioned (DfES, 2005b).

Policy makers' failure to protect the rights of people of color in selective processes is a particularly striking example of how apparently color-blind approaches can have pronounced and predictable negative, racial consequences. One of the most consistent findings in research on school-based selection processes is that, when asked to judge the potential, attitude and/or motivation of their students, White teachers tend to place disproportionate numbers of Black students in low ranked groups (Commissions for Racial Equality [CRE], 1992; Gillborn & Gipps, 1996; Hallam & Toutounji, 1996;

Sukhnandan & Lee, 1998). These decisions frequently have a cumulative effect whereby the initial decision compounds inequity upon inequity until success can become, literally, impossible. For example, when students are placed in low ranked teaching groups they frequently cover a restricted curriculum; their teachers have systematically lower expectations of them; and, in many high-stakes tests in England, they are entered for low tiered examinations where only a limited number of grades are available. In the lowest mathematics paper, for example, the best available grade is D: that is, *less* than the C grade that is commonly accepted as the minimum necessary for entry into the professions or further dedicated study at advanced level.

In a study of these decisions in London secondary schools, it was Black students who were most likely to be placed in this situation: two thirds of Black students in the schools under study (Gillborn & Youdell, 2000). It is difficult to think of a clearer example of institutional racism than a test, disproportionately taken by Black students, in which the highest possible grade is commonly judged to be a failure. We have to ask whether such discriminatory processes would be permitted if their victims were White, and especially, middle class Whites. Ernest R. House (1999) has noted an identical situation in the United States in relation to the practice of retaining students, that is, holding them back a year:

> Americans will support policies that are harmful to minorities that they would not tolerate if those same policies were applied to majority populations. In education, for example, Americans are strongly in favor of retention—retaining students at the same grade level for another year—even though the research evidence overwhelmingly shows strong negative effects. ... Retention programs are applied massively to minorities in large cities, but not to majority populations. (p. 2)

In relation to the three tests I set out earlier, therefore, the English education system appears to be a clear case where the routine assumptions that structure the system encode a deep privileging of White students and, in particular, the legitimization, defense and extension of Black inequity. In terms of policy priorities, race equity has been at best a marginal concern, at worst nonexistent. In relation to beneficiaries the picture is more complex than usually recognized: although some minoritized groups do relatively well, the most consistent beneficiaries are White students and, in key respects, Black students' position is no better than it was when the whole reform movement began in the late 1980s. Finally, an examination of outcomes clearly shows that central reform strategies (such as the use of selection and hierarchical teaching groups) are known to work against racial justice but are nevertheless promoted as best practice for all. These reforms are known to discriminate in practice (regardless of intent) and are, therefore, racist in their consequences. But how are we to understand the wider significance of these facts? In the following section I reflect on the utility of a critical race perspective and consider the deeper questions raised by such an analysis.

MAKING SENSE OF THE EVIDENCE: ACCOUNTABILITY FOR ALL OR WHITE SUPREMACY BY STEALTH?

> As I write, I try to remember when the word racism ceased to be the term which best expressed for me exploitation of black people and other people of color in this society and when I began to understand that the most useful term was white supremacy. (hooks, 1989, p. 112)

"White supremacy" is a term usually reserved for individuals, organizations and/or philosophies that are overtly and self-consciously racist in the most crude and obvious way: organizations that not only claim a distinctiveness for White-identified people, but add a social Darwinist element to argue for intellectual and/or cultural superiority, frequently based on a supposedly fixed genetic inheritance. Even after the genocide of the Nazi era in the previous century, such perspectives continue to be openly preached by some, although they remain firmly outside the political mainstream in the United States and the United Kingdom.

Critical work on race has moved beyond the "commonsense" superficial readings of White supremacy as solely the preserve of obviously extreme racialized politics. Some scholars have penetrated even further the façade of contemporary politics, to argue that mainstream political parties, and the functioning of agencies like the education system itself, are actively implicated in maintaining and extending the grip that White people have on the major sources of power in Western capitalist societies. As Frances Lee Ansley (1997) has argued:

> [By] "white supremacy" I do not mean to allude only to the self-conscious racism of white supremacist hate groups. I refer instead to a political, economic, and cultural system in which whites overwhelmingly control power and material resources, conscious and unconscious ideas of white superiority and entitlement are widespread, and relations of white dominance and non-white subordination are daily re-enacted across a broad array of institutions and social settings. (p. 592)

Of course, this is not to argue that White people are uniformly powerful, as Noel Ignatiev (1997) has argued in relation to poverty among Whites: "whiteness does not exempt people from exploitation, it reconciles them to it. It is for those who have nothing else" (p. 1). The growing influence of critical race theory has supported this line of analysis but it is a perspective that was present before the advent of CRT in education (see Sleeter, 1993) and is by no means limited to those who identify with a CRT perspective (see Doane & Bonilla-Silva, 2003). For example, I began this section with a quotation from bell hooks who, writing in the late 1980s, used the term to explicitly critique a central and extensive form of racism that evades the simplistic definitions of liberal discourse. In particular, hooks (1989) identifies White supremacy as a deeply rooted exercise of power that remains untouched by moves to address the more obvious forms of overt discrimination:

> When liberal whites fail to understand how they can and/or do embody white-supremacist values and beliefs even though they may not embrace racism as prejudice or domination (especially domination that involves coercive control), they cannot recognize the ways their actions support and affirm the very structure of racist domination and oppression that they profess to wish to see eradicated. (p. 113)

Recent years have seen something of an explosion in writing about Whiteness but, as several authors have noted, far from unmasking the dynamics of racial domination, much of this literature threatens to obscure and indulge the operation of White power (e.g., see the critiques by Apple, 1998; Bush, 2004; Howard, 2004; Sheets, 2000). Zeus Leonardo (2004) is especially critical of tendencies in the literature on White *privilege* that fall into the trap of treating a lack of conscious intent as if it equates to an absence of malice or an innocence on the part of Whites:

> the theme of privilege obscures the subject of domination, or the agent of actions, because the situation is described as happening almost without the knowledge of whites. It conjures up images of domination happening behind the backs of whites, rather than on the backs of people of color. The study of white privilege begins to take on an image of domination without agents. (p. 138)

Leonardo's analysis is especially pertinent to understanding the role of education policy and the racial effects of the twin discourses of accountability and standards.

CONCLUSION

Earlier in this chapter I examined some basic but vital questions about education policy: its drivers, beneficiaries and material outcomes. The evidence (both qualitative and quantitative, much of it distilled from official analyses and reports) suggests that, despite a rhetoric of public accountability and standards for all, education policy in England is actively involved in the defense, legitimation and extension of White supremacy. People of color, especially Black students, are markedly disadvantaged by the very processes that are championed in the name of raising attainment and inclusion for all. These effects were the predictable outcomes of processes that are known to discriminate: Nevertheless, these processes are given centre stage in the continuing reforms of public education. The assumptions that feed, and are strengthened by, this regime are not overtly discriminatory but their effects are empirically verifiable and materially real in every meaningful sense. After the Stephen Lawrence Inquiry, and the official acceptance of its findings, these effects amount to institutional racism of a most damaging and revealing kind. The lack of conscious intent is not an accidental characteristic of the current situation, an unfortunate oversight by policy makers too busy to realize what they doing (as if the voices of community activists, Black parents and radical scholars had somehow fallen silent), this pseudo-innocence is, in fact, further evidence of the size of the task facing those of us who struggle for race equity in education. As Charles W. Mills (2003) has commented, White supremacy has "characteristic and pervasive patterns of not-seeing and not knowing—structured white ignorance, motivated inattention, self-deception, and moral rationalization—that people of color, for their own survival, have to learn to become familiar with" (p. 46). Shaped by long established cultural, economic and historical structures of racial domination, the continued promotion (in the name of accountability and standards) of policies and practices that are known to be racially divisive testifies to exactly the kind of structured White ignorance and motivated inattention that Charles Mills identifies.

Acknowledgments. This chapter is a revised and updated treatment of ideas that I have presented elsewhere, notably in a Presidential session organized by Professor James A. Banks for the annual meeting of the American Educational Research Association (Montreal, 2005) and in the pages of the *Journal of Education Policy* (vol. 20, no. 4). My thanks to the numerous friends and colleagues who have supported, and constructively critiqued, this work.

CHAPTER 9

NCLB, U.S. Education, and the World Bank: Neoliberalism Comes Home

Lois Weiner

New Jersey City University

With overwhelming support from both Democrats and Republicans, the Bush administration rewrote the Elementary and Secondary Education Act (ESEA) in 2001, drastically changing public education. One of the key initiatives of the Johnson-era war on poverty, ESEA has been the main source of federal aid to schools serving children in poverty. Employing the rhetoric of equity, the legislative package called No Child Left Behind (NCLB) has made federal aid dependent on schools' accepting new regulations on a host of policies, from teacher qualifications, to instructional content and methods permissible for reading instruction, to the privatization of school services, like tutoring. Although there is much else in the package that affects all public schools that accept ESEA funds, testing and score reporting are NCLB's elements that are most hotly debated, in part because they affect all schools, everywhere, and not just those that are assumed to be failing (e.g., city schools with high concentrations of poor, minority children).

No Child Left Behind's supporters argue that its requirements for testing, reporting test results, and sanctions will finally hold public schools throughout the nation accountable for their failure to educate poor and working class Hispanic and African American students. I suggest that rhetoric of increasing educational opportunity masks another purpose: creating a privatized, fragmented system of public education that has a narrow, vocationalized curriculum enforced through use of standardized tests. The purpose of this chapter[1] is to illuminate how the intended and actual outcomes of NCLB's major components relate to the educational reforms that the World Bank has enacted elsewhere in the world, in particular privatization of services, fragmentation of control, vocationalization of curriculum through use of standardized testing, and deskilling of teaching and teacher education.

NCLB AS A FAUSTIAN BARGAIN

No Child Left Behind both perpetuates and significantly deepens bipartisan policies begun under President G. H. W. Bush and continued by the Democrats and President Clinton. Both parties supported the 1989 National Education Summit, which Natriello (1996) noted, diverted attention away from many pressing problems in the U.S. economy and its schools in a policy statement presenting high academic standards as a panacea. For example, describing the marketization of education in North Carolina, Bartlett and colleagues (2002) identified intensified race and class stratification that resulted from policies implemented in the Clinton administration, tracing Clinton's reliance on corporate allies for direction in setting educational policy to his vigorous support for Bush's National Goals 2000, including its emphasis on national standards enforced through standardized testing.

No Child Left Behind sharply divided the weakened traditional labor-liberal coalition that generally works together to win increases in school funding. The Council of Chief State School Officers, the Council of Great City Schools, and one teachers union—the American Federation of Teachers (AFT), which represents teachers in most cities—supported the rationale that holding schools to high standards enforced through yearly standardized tests, with severe penalties for poor performance, would force schools to shape up. The National Education Association (NEA) led the opposition to NCLB, arguing that its punitive sanctions, the absence of significant new funding, and the testing mandates were dangerous and destructive to public schools. In its opposition to NCLB, the NEA was joined by the American Association of School Administrators, which represents some 14,000 superintendents and local administrators, major civil rights organizations including the NAACP, as well as most progressive advocacy groups.

But NCLB's rhetoric and its provisions that require reporting disaggregated test scores are enormously seductive to parents and low-income communities whose children attend poorly funded, poorly functioning schools. Schools in predominately Hispanic and African American neighborhoods are often incapable of providing children with more than the rudiments of literacy and numeracy—if that. Often these schools cannot recruit and retain sufficient numbers of teachers to staff classrooms. City and rural schools that enroll large concentrations of recent immigrants are frequently so underfunded and overwhelmed by the sheer numbers of students that bathrooms and closets are pressed into use as classrooms (see, for example, Gándara, Rumberger, Maxwell-Jolly, & Callahan, 2003). Even in better-funded school districts in which African American and Hispanic youth are a demographic minority, these youth are frequently tracked into classes that offer a diet of low-level materials and poor instruction, robbed of the opportunity to take college preparatory work (Oakes, Wells, Jones, & Datnow, 1997; Yonezawa, Wells, & Serna, 2002). African American boys are placed into special education in numbers vastly disproportionate to their presence in the school population, and once students are labeled as having special needs they rarely move into regular programs, although this is the presumed rationale for identifying their problems and grouping them together (Losen & Orfield, 2002).

Although for many years previously, schools and school districts' test scores, graduation rates, and other statistical indicators commonly used to measure achievement have been made public, in many states such as New York, reports of test scores did not break down the achievement for different groups of children. So, inequality of achievement was often masked. Given school practices and conditions that allow millions of minority children to be undereducated, NCLB's requirements for disaggregated test reports and for getting tough on schools that fail to help minority youth pass standardized tests are attractive to many parents, especially those who feel powerless to make institutions that are publicly funded serve their children adequately.

Critical to understanding the reasons for NCLB's passage is the history of the civil rights movement's reforms to equalize educational opportunity. No Child Left Behind's stated goal to "leave no child behind" would have far less popular resonance if schools presently served poor children of color reasonably well. No Child Left Behind's use—or "hijacking," as its sharpest critics contend—of the rhetoric of progressive educational reform would not be possible had the civil rights movement's efforts to improve schooling been fully actualized. Instead, a radical vision of improved schooling for all children was lost in what could be considered a Faustian bargain negotiated by legislators and government officials, embodied in the legislation creating ESEA.

As Bastian and colleagues (1986) explain, under ESEA relatively small infusions of public funds were given to schools and targeted at specific students—those presumed to need extra help based on their family income, or in the case of bilingual education, their native language. The funding's efficacy was measured by standardized tests, given at the beginning and end of each school year to students enrolled in classes that had materials and teachers paid for by ESEA monies. These compensatory programs ushered in the first widespread use of standardized test scores to measure teaching and learning, initiating their acceptance as valid measures of whether public funds for education were being well spent. As Parker and Hall argue in Chapter 7 of this volume, the "compensatory" model assumed that poor, minority children were not achieving because they and their families were deficient. Historically, public education in this country has coped with demands to equalize educational outcomes by blaming lack of achievement on students' individual problems, labeling their deficiencies, and then grouping them in separate programs that "meet their needs" (Deschenes, Cuban, & Tyack, 2001). Our present policies for classifying students as having various sorts of educational disabilities differ primarily in nomenclature from those developed at the turn of the 19th century, when working class students disinterested in school would be assigned to categories like *anemic* or *phlegmatic* and shunted into separate classes or schools (Franklin, 1994).

No Child Left Behind definitively breaks this pattern by presuming that if children are not succeeding in school, responsibility rests with the school, and not the children. But the way it does so destroys the structure and organization of a publicly funded and presumably publicly controlled system of education begun more than a century ago (Tyack, 1974). To be successful, a program to advance educational opportunity should be part of a larger project of attacking inequality with other social policies, including policies designed to end de facto school segregation. At the same time, recognizing that schools have a limited capacity to ameliorate economic and social inequality does not diminish the moral or political importance of working to improve education. Any progressive movement deserving of the name will demand that public schools provide all students with an education that will allow them to be well-rounded, productive citizens, which includes the ability to compete for whatever well-paying jobs exist. Improving schools that serve poor and working class youth can make a difference in the lives of some, and for that reason alone, progressive school reform deserves our attention. Moreover, struggling to improve schools for all children has a critical political significance because it demands that American society make good on its democratic ideals, its pledge of equality.

But public education can only challenge the tyranny of the labor market—it cannot eliminate it (Bastian, Fruchter, Gittell, Grier, & Haskins, 1986). Especially as free market policies tighten their grip on governments, schooling becomes an ever weaker lever for improving the economic well-being of individuals, even while it remains a critical arena for political struggle (Anyon, 2005b). The heart of any agenda for progressive social change, which includes improving education, must address what historian David Hogan (1996) terms "the silent compulsion of economic relations" (p. 243), the nexus of racial segregation in schools and housing, combined with dependence on local property taxes for school funding. Progressives who argue against NCLB without making the case that racial segregation, school funding, and school quality are inextricably connected to one another lack persuasive power. Segregation in housing has become the pretext for abandoning the challenge of racially integrating schools, and school segregation has seriously weakened the forces challenging funding inequities. Some African American activists and researchers advocate dropping the demand for integrating schools, arguing that the society has turned its back on its commitments to educate African American children, who would be better served in segregated schools staffed by African American teachers. Although the despair that underlies desertion of the goal of integration is understandable, romanticizing segregated schooling ignores the reality that racially segregated schools and school systems are more isolated politically, and, thus, more vulnerable in funding battles in state legislatures. The urgency of making segregated schools better is undeniable, but so is the necessity of mounting a political and legal challenge both to the de facto segregation of schools and the use of local property taxes for schooling. Activists who lived through the busing battles of the 1970s, even those who have read about them, do not want to take up an issue that can incite vicious racism. But, as racism underlies much of the opposition to funding schools serving poor, minority students adequately, it must be confronted.

While NCLB's passage results partly from the Right's heightened political presence generally, its allure is also attributable to public confusion about defending a system of public education that seems to be unreformable. The argument of both Democrats and Republicans that Americans must scale back their expectations about governmental responsibility for concerns now portrayed as individual and personal, like housing and health care, signals that U.S. society cannot fulfill its promise of providing equal educational opportunity. Ralph Nader (n.d.) points out that NCLB's passage is an indication of the degree of popular disorientation about the role of education in a democracy and the contradiction of having this essential civic function privatized.

NCLB AND THE BIPARTISAN NEOLIBERAL AGENDA FOR EDUCATION

No Child Left Behind contains much that contradicts basic premises of liberal capitalism in the past 50 years, including new inroads into separation of church and state by allowing religious organizations to provide after-school services and requiring that classes in sex education focus on abstinence. Bipartisan endorsement of a legislative package that contains such disparate, and for liberals, historically unacceptable provisions, deserves closer scrutiny. Moderates and conservatives in both parties were joined by many liberal Democrats in embracing NCLB, with Bush identifying Senator Ted Kennedy for special praise for his assistance with its passage (Broder, 2002).

According to the Constitution, education is a responsibility of the states, and in theory states could refuse to comply with NCLB by refusing ESEA funds. States have been reluctant to do so, however, because schools in revenue-poor districts, which also have students who are the most expensive to educate, would be financially devastated. State governments would be obliged to craft a rescue. As is obvious from the protracted legal battles in many states to equalize school funding, there is little political will in the states for this (Wenglinsky, 1997).

Why, then, were liberals and moderates in both parties so willing to support a legislative package with regressive provisions? To address this question, we need to look beyond domestic politics, to shared ideological assumptions about the global transformation of the economy, and with it education's character and role.

NCLB, GLOBAL ECONOMIC RESTRUCTURING, AND THE WORLD BANK

No Child Left Behind enacts a program for education that economists and governments have pursued internationally, a set of ideas and policies that are often termed *neoliberal*. U.S. pundits and politicians tend to frame political differences as between liberals and conservatives; as a result, neoliberal is seldom used to describe either policies or ideas. Given that global relationships increasingly drive national policies, to grasp the underpinnings of NCLB, we need to examine the neoliberal philosophy that undergirds it.

Neoliberalism is a form of political conservatism that draws on tenets of 19th-century liberalism (hence the *neo* in its name). To paraphrase a definition used by Robertson and Dale (2003), neoliberalism is a political and economic program that aims to contain public spending for social services, integrate economies in a world trading system based on rules established by international finance organizations, like the World Bank and International Monetary Fund, and privatize social services, providing modest compensatory programs when its other programs exacerbate inequality. It is important to understand a few ways that neoliberal premises differ from conservative principles. In contrast to conservatives, neoliberals adopt an internationalist stance and advocate reducing the power of the nation state. They argue for making capitalism a *global* economic system, creating global markets unfettered by local or national regulations. Unlike conservatives, neoliberals adopt the rhetoric of social progress, a discourse previously associated with progressive social movements and the social goals they advanced, for example equalizing educational opportunity. Also, neoliberals reject the social pact negotiated with trade unions after World War II that made governments responsible for maintaining a safety net of social services, including free public education (Willis, 2003).

In both industrialized nations and the developing world, neoliberal reforms are promoted as making delivery of social services more efficient and more equal. Education is seen as critical in this process so international finance agencies like the World Bank demand curricular and structural change in education when it provides loans. The neoliberal wish list of how education should be restructured throughout the world is apparent in a draft report of "World Development Report 2004: Making Services Work for Poor People" (Devarajan & Reinikka, 2002; *WDR 2004*). Although the report focuses on the particular challenges posed in developing countries, its economic and political assumptions are stated in universal terms. The report describes education's purpose solely as preparing workers for jobs in a global economy. Reformed educational systems will allow transnational capitalism to move jobs whenever and wherever it wishes, that is, to the country with the working conditions and salaries that are worst for workers and best for profits.

The draft was later modified in negotiations with governments and nongovernmental organizations, and published under the same title (World Bank, 2003); but the unvarnished political attack on education in the draft version makes visible neoliberalism's intention to eliminate free pubic education and independent teachers unions. Public education remains the largest realm of public expenditures throughout the world that is unionized and not yet privatized, and the draft report identifies unions, especially teachers unions, as one of the greatest threats to global prosperity in poor countries. The draft argues that unions in poor countries have "captured" governments and resources, holding poor people hostage to demands for more pay. It combines sharp attacks on teachers and teachers unions, including a suggestion that teachers should be fired en masse when they strike or otherwise resist demands for reduced pay. The draft calls for privatized services, greatly reduced public funding, devolved control of schools to neighborhoods, and increased user fees.

The World Bank has already implemented many elements of the program outlined in the draft report in its loans and aid in developing countries. Loans were made contingent on restructuring, that is, essentially eliminating publicly funded, publicly controlled education systems. The results, including reduced literacy rates, have been devastating, as University of Buenos Aires Professor Adriana Puiggros (2004) describes in her report contrasting the reality of implementation in Argentina with the World Bank's rhetoric of equality.

A key element of the program is limiting access to higher education through the imposition of higher tuition and reduced government support to institutions and individual students. Limiting access to higher education means that lower education is charged primarily with preparing students for work, namely for jobs requiring basic skills that multinationals aim to move from one country to another. Schools that train most workers for jobs requiring limited literacy and numeracy, which *WDR 2004* explains is all we can realistically expect for poor people in poor countries, do not require teachers who are themselves well-educated or skilled. In fact, teachers who have a significant amount of education are a liability because they are costly to employ; teacher salaries are the largest expense of any school system.

In many ways, NCLB mirrors recommendations in *WDR 2004*. Paradoxically, NCLB's definition of a highly qualified teacher actually deskills teaching because it assumes that all one needs to teach well is content knowledge in selected disciplines in the liberal arts. There is no question that teachers are more successful when they have deep knowledge of the subjects they teach. But widely varying school conditions and students' characteristics require teachers to be prepared in programs that take into account the social contexts of schools and communities (Lee, 2001; Weiner, 1993, 2006). Defining a highly qualified teacher as one who has knowledge only of the content to be taught and not of the contexts in which schools function or of students' characteristics as learners, parallels the neoliberal stance that teaching can be defined as the transmission of content and that schools have no social or political responsibilities beyond providing an education that is de facto vocational training. If teaching consists solely of transmission of content that is identified in standardized tests, then teacher education also has little value. Seen in this light, *all* of the disciplines that now make an elementary teacher highly qualified are problematic because one's qualifications for teaching inhere solely in mastery of subject matter knowledge. In several states K–12 teachers are considered highly qualified by presenting a B.A. in a core subject and a passing score for an online exam of teaching (Au, 2004). Officials in the Bush administration have been quite open about the explicit linkage between a deskilled teaching force and a narrow curriculum. The Bush administration has advanced arguments of the Abell and Fordham Foundations and the American Enterprise Institute, neoliberal think tanks, that teacher education is little more than an impediment to qualified individuals entering the occupation, a charge that has been consistently rebutted by Darling-Hammond (2002; Darling-Hammond, Holtzman, Gatlin, & Heilig, 2005).

A corollary to the argument that further investment in research in teacher education is unnecessary is that teachers need to know only what is in scripted materials. Yet this linkage is not publicized by Democratic supporters of the legislation. Because neoliberalism considers substantial public investment in research about teacher education as unnecessary because the government is required to provide only a basic education that will prepare students for entry-level jobs, government funds are better spent creating materials for teaching basic skills that teachers with little or no expertise in teaching can use. This is precisely the strategy promoted in *WDR 2004*, which lauds projects that replace a stable (and often unionized) teacher population with young girls who receive minimal training in literacy and then work in rural villages.

One way to limit access to education is to charge fees and tuition to attend school, in both lower and higher education. This strategy has been implemented in underdeveloped countries, where families often must pay for schooling that was once available for free. In fact, a World Bank policy prohibited provision of free education as a requirement for loans, until a movement by liberals in the U.S. Congress, informed and inspired by global justice activists, challenged this measure.

Access to learning is also limited by narrowing what is taught. Larry Kuehn (1999), research director of the British Columbia Teachers Federation, has traced this process, beginning the trail in Washington in 1987, when the Reagan administration promoted development of education indicators to guide curricula and testing at the Organization for Economic Cooperation and Development (OECD), an organization of the 29 most industrialized countries and some rapidly industrializing nations, like South Korea and Mexico. In these early discussions, the OECD planned how to develop uniform curricula with culture-free materials, appropriate for the new information economy. Kuehn's research illuminates not only the anti-intellectual and antihumanistic assumptions of these curricula, but also how existing expectations about what students should know had to be downscaled. The National Assessment of Educational Progress (NAEP), a federal agency that monitors academic achievement, works with the OECD. In the United States the NAEP has traditionally assessed students' achievements in three sorts of reading: reading for literary experience, reading to be informed, and reading to perform a task. The OECD determined that only "reading to perform a task," as measured by reading a computer manual, would be used in international assessments of student learning. The ability to read for literary experience was rejected as being too difficult to assess because of cross-cultural differences. The decision to limit the reading assessment to "reading to perform a task" and the example of reading a computer manual illustrate transnational capitalism's push to redefine education as vocational training (Kuehn, 1999).

Most of NCLB's elements for reorganizing education in the United States are found in the draft report for *WDR 2004*.

- Privatization, accomplished mainly through vouchers, which would create a collection of schools paid for, though—not controlled or overseen—by the public sector. Other provisions that advance privatization allow corporations to provide services previously regarded as the responsibility of the public school system, like tutoring and professional development.
- Fragmentation of control over schooling, accomplished by the creation of charter schools. Each charter school is in essence its own small school system; the regulatory functions previously exercised by

a community's school board, are given over to each school.

- The deskilling of teaching, which is defined as transmission of content that is assessed with new testing requirements and increasingly punitive measures for low test scores.
- Teacher education, including in-service professional development, is linked to testing and provided by corporations that create the standardized tests and textbook packages.
- Pay and professional development are tied to testing, undercutting salary schedules based on levels of education negotiated by teachers unions. Professional development for teachers tied to raising test scores undercuts union influence and membership.

INTERNATIONAL RESISTANCE TO NEOLIBERAL REFORMS

Teachers unions, when organized globally, have power to lead resistance to NCLB and, more broadly, the neoliberal program for reorganizing education. However, such global organizing requires development of a critical political consciousness among teachers, particularly those in the United States As Puiggros (2004) observes in her description of education's restructuring in Latin America, resistance has been led by teachers unions. Teachers union activists in Latin America have paid a hefty price: firings, beatings, even assassination. While both the American Federation of Teachers (AFT) and the National Education Association (NEA) have offered statements of support to Latin American unionists, such statements are undercut and contradicted by political allegiances and ideological beliefs that reinforce much of the neoliberal program (Weiner, 2005, 2006). The AFT and NEA differ in important ways that I analyze below, but the starting point for understanding their response to the neoliberal assault is that they see the world in a U. S.-centric view. Or more specifically, their vision of the world is refracted through the eyes of U.S. capitalism, which dominates the World Bank.

Although Albert Shanker, AFT's longtime chief, died in 1997, his policies and politics were continued by his replacement, Sandra Feldman, until her resignation due to poor health in 2004. Classroom teachers' opinions about NCLB and testing are not necessarily reflected in national AFT policies, because Shanker masterfully exploited the post of AFT president to promote his political views, using his control of the massive New York City local to leverage control of the state and national organizations (Weiner, 1998). Shanker (1997) made visible similarities between his vision for school reform, which because of his ironclad control of the union were de facto those of the organization, and the neoliberal program manifested in NCLB.

Shanker contended that U.S. schools are far worse than those in OECD nations because we offer too many students access to higher education, because we do not put students into tracks that prepare them for either college or vocational careers at an early age. Shanker criticized the absence of penalties for students' failure to pass tests, the absence of mandatory national curriculum standards, and the presence of far too much tolerance for student misconduct. Shanker faulted the laxity of the pre-NCLB curriculum standards, which were additionally problematic for being left to the states to execute. Shanker's argument that some standards can be too vague—for example, "Learn to appreciate literature" resonates with the Organization for Economic Cooperation and Development's (OECD) rejection of international assessment in reading for literary experience.

The NEA generally can be counted on to adopt liberal positions on the important political issues of the day. But, while it is better positioned than the AFT to lead a struggle in this country for progressive school reform, the NEA is hampered by its own diffused bureaucratic structure and its roots as a professional organization controlled by school administrators: It moved to become a collective bargaining agent only after the AFT's stunning successes in organizing city teachers into unions in the 1960s and 1970s forced it to do so (Urban, 2000). The NEA is willing to be openly critical of the use of U.S. military and political force to safeguard capitalism in a way that the AFT is not. On the other hand, perhaps in part because of its roots as a professional organization, the NEA lacks the ideological sophistication of other progressive unions in the United States and its counterparts in Europe. The NEA leadership appears to be trying to make ideological sense of the global attack against teacher unionism and public education, searching unsuccessfully for a vocabulary—and lever—for resistance. Confusion about the intention and international scope of neoliberalism's project has prevented the NEA from actively linking with progressive unions elsewhere in the world, a development that would encourage formation of the broad, popular movement needed to derail NCLB in this country and the neoliberal agenda for education throughout the world (Weiner, 2005, 2006).

NEA and AFT are by far the biggest member organizations in the Educational International (EI), the international confederation of teacher sunions, which works with other international organizations of unions. The EI seems to agree to disagree, that is, not take a position or action on issues on which its most powerful members, the AFT and NEA, dissent—either with one another or with the other delegates, especially those from developing countries who are feeling the brunt of the neoliberal policies formulated and pressed by the United States (Weiner, 2005). Furthermore, the EI itself suffers from a lack of grassroots involvement. An outgoing officer noted:

> Most classroom teachers in the North have never heard of EI, and that is a bit worrisome. We run the risk of becoming a club of union leaders and their international secretaries. . . . But we must, I believe, find ways to open our gates to your members and enable them, where possible, to take part in our work. Teachers are world citizens by nature; they are among the most active members of organizations like Amnesty, Greenpeace and other NGOs. Why not find ways to get them involved in their own organization? (van Leeuwen, 2001)

Although the EI and its work are invisible to members of its constituent organizations, like the AFT and NEA, the EI is in the midst of a promising transformation, marked by election of a new president from South Africa. It conducts important campaigns in defense of public education unionists who have been jailed, kidnapped, and tortured by governments. However, the EI's advocacy of teacher unionists who are victimized by their governments needs to be linked to a broader campaign to build an international social movement that challenges neoliberalism's demands for privatization, defunding, and fragmentation of educational services.

The enormous potential of teachers unions in organizing resistance to reforms that are destroying public education was apparent in the Global Campaign for Education, a broad alliance of NGOs, child rights activists, and teachers' organizations active in more than 150 countries that challenged the *WDR 2004*'s draft analysis and conclusions, tapping the vitality and language of the global justice movement. (A recent report on EI collaborative advocacy can be found at http://www.ei-ie.org/en/news/20050603.htm.) The Global Campaign succeeded in tempering the *WDR 2004* draft report, compelling World Bank officials to acknowledge teachers' concerns.

The stark contrast between how U.S. teachers and those elsewhere in the world see neoliberalism's program for education was apparent at a panel of educational researchers at the American Educational Research Association's (AERA) annual meeting in April 2004. Mary Hatwood Futrell, the immediate past president of the EI and a past president of NEA, spoke, as did Hugo Aboites, a well-known Mexican researcher working with teacher unionists in his country. Futrell described the dismay of EI officials when they saw the *WDR 2004* draft report; they immediately called the World Bank president, who denied knowledge of the report and said its viewpoint had not been officially sanctioned. I asked Futrell how she understood this series of events and she fell silent, unable to answer. Hugo Aboites answered that he did not know of this particular report but was familiar with the policies. Teacher unionists in Mexico are experiencing horrible attacks on their jobs, their unions, and their bodies when they resist, all under the watchful eye of the government—and the World Bank. Mexican teachers have already learned where the World Bank program of privatization and fragmentation of education lead. They understand much better than U.S. teachers about what we can anticipate from World Bank policies that have come to this country in provisions of NCLB.

CONCLUSION

Until recently, teachers in the United States have not experienced directly the heaviest blows of neoliberalism's global assault on education. With NCLB, teachers and teacher educators in the United States are now being subjected, albeit in a protected version, to the neoliberal program that is wreaking devastation elsewhere. On September 11, 2001 the illusion that physical distance protects us was shattered. With NCLB another illusion has been challenged: that teachers unions can deliver the bottom line of maintaining teachers' wages, benefits, and jobs without allying themselves with social movements that challenge the status quo. Yet, still missing in the work of teachers unions, their leaders and their ranks, is an understanding that to defend public education in this country, teachers and their unions must help develop an international response to neoliberalism, one that puts justice and equity at the forefront of the union's program for education, one that develops alliances that span national borders.

The history of the neoliberal reforms in the rest of the world provides compelling evidence that NCLB cannot be doctored and should not be better funded. Rather, it needs to be replaced with a different paradigm for school reform (Anyon, 2005b); one that takes up globalization and the economic and political changes that have accompanied school reforms (Lipman, 2004). Such a paradigm would embed school improvement in a network of policies to address political, economic, and social inequality. The federal government would provide the economic and legal supports necessary to promote equality of educational opportunity by assuming full responsibility for school funding, vigorously pursuing legal interventions to integrate schools, across school districts if necessary, and protecting teachers' and students' civil rights.

We can see the elements of the sort of struggle that's needed to put this new paradigm before the public—in the work of advocacy groups that fought NCLB; in teachers unions' mobilization of community groups and parents to resist World Bank policies throughout Latin America and Africa; in EI's campaign with advocacy and global justice organizations to challenge the draft report of *WDR 2004*. In the United States we need most immediately to recognize NCLB's origins and aims in the neoliberal project—and combat the project in its entirety. That requires overcoming the determination of both political parties to maintain a system of education that makes children needs and democracy subservient to transnational corporations' race for global profits.

CHAPTER 10

Ruthless Assessment in a Post-Welfare U.K. Society

Sally Tomlinson

University of Oxford

A meritocracy where no one can remember what the moral bases for merit were, but where it can be ruthlessly assessed nonetheless, promises a competitive dynamism that few nation states could match today.

—Bobbitt, 2002, p. 231

Consider the case of Louis, an 11-year-old English boy, reported recently in a Sunday United Kingdom newspaper:

The horrendous process of getting Louis into a preferred local secondary school began that September. The fight for places in the local city technology college soured the atmosphere in the primary school and put a strain on friendships among children and parents. There were 2000 applications for 200 places. The college relied on aptitude tests and application forms, Louis's sister went there and his father, Steve, was confident he would get in. Louis was rejected. "I felt dreadful," said Steve. Father and son had been given no information why Louis was rejected by his local school. "It was a completely secret admissions system, they seemed to take the brightest and best-off children." It was a harrowing experience for Steve and Louis, "It is not the parents who chose the school, it is the school which chooses the pupils, and they call this parental choice." (Asthana, 2006a, p.19)

Louis and his father were experiencing an education system that has moved from its position as a pillar of a welfare state, with a promise of free local public education, to one which supports a post-welfare society dominated by competitive markets and private enterprise (Tomlinson, 2005). From 1945 to 1979 education policy in England was largely based on a social democratic consensus that governments should regulate and resource education to achieve some measure of social justice and provide equal opportunities for all. (Scotland, Wales and Northern Ireland, since devolution in 1999, largely have control of their own education systems, and are not the subject of this chapter.) Although up to the 1960s it was a selective system that separated children by testing at age 11—the academic grammar schools being dominated by the children of the middle classes, and the rich and influential attending private schools—there was an optimistic feeling that there was a real intention to educate all young people to higher levels than ever before. This was encouraged by an expanding economy and relatively full employment. With the partial ending of selective testing and the development of comprehensive education from the 1960s, there were hopes of an end to education as a vehicle for perpetuating social class divisions and beliefs that the talents of the whole population could be put to social and economic use, including the children of recent immigrants from former colonial countries.

From 1979, however, a radical restructuring of public welfare provision in the UK began to take place. Reforms of all public services, especially education, were undertaken by the Conservative governments of Margaret Thatcher and John Major, and continued from 1997 under the New Labour government of Tony Blair. Young people, continuously assessed from the age of 4 in preschool, and defined as human capital, were required to invest in themselves in a process of lifelong learning, in order to find or retain any kind of job. As in the United States, a standards agenda came to dominate education. Teachers were gradually stripped of their professionalism, expected to deliver a regulated curriculum, assess children by preset national tests, and policed by new and expanding inspection regimes. Low-achieving school students were blamed for their individual deficits, but schools, teachers, and local authorities were also increasingly held responsible for students who failed to achieve well, and a new notion of whole schools failing was introduced. The roles and responsibilities of local authorities were diminished, and the role of private contractors and business entrepreneurs expanded. A language and practice of managerialism, assessment, testing, targets, accountability and inspection took over, legislated for by some 30 Education Acts between 1980 and 2006. As the reality of a competitive global economy and resulting job insecurity became apparent, debate about the purpose of education beyond preparation for the economy disappeared. There was little discussion about what Sennett (2006) has called "the culture of the new capitalism," or any questioning as to whether the unequal possession of economic, cultural, and social capital gave different social classes and ethnic groups unequal chances in the competition for high level credentials and jobs. Moving into the 21st century, optimistic feelings about education were replaced by anxiety and uncertainty among growing numbers of parents and educators. Almost every aspect of the education system had been reformed and schooling had become a market commodity, with a good education a prize to be competitively sought, not a democratic right.

This chapter provides a description of the changing English school system, with its emphasis on choice and diversity of provision, the penalties for falling into the failing school category, and the complex assessment for a competitive meritocracy. It then moves on to analyze why welfare states that held out a promise of care for all citizens are being transformed into entrepreneurial market states (Bobbitt, 2002), in which education has become a competitive commodity, with schools increasingly handed over to business and religious influence. The dominant rationale for reform, as in the United States, is that educational standards are too low and schools are failing to provide workers who can compete in a competitive global economy. Schools and universities are now predominantly about jobs, business, enterprise, and competition, with staff held accountable for the success of their students in preparation for the market. This chapter leads readers through an examination of school transformation in the context of an economic transformation that has resulted in an increasingly narrow meritocracy.

A DIVERSITY OF SCHOOLS

From 1945 all children were guaranteed 6 years of nonselective primary schooling, and then at 11 were selected for grammar schools, or the few technical schools, with the majority relegated to secondary modern schools with a formal leaving age of 15 or 16 from 1973. Belief in meritocracy, by all the political parties, supported the principle of selection, and sanctioned the differential treatment of the supposedly able, less able and disabled. By the 1960s, in common with governments around the world, there was a recognition of a need for expanded education for all, and at secondary level nonselective comprehensive schools developed, although considerable selection by tracking and setting continued within most schools. By the later 1980s over 85% of secondary students in England were in comprehensive schools, although the curriculum remained largely academic, with vocational courses underdeveloped and for lower achievers, the rest were in some form of selective, private, or special schooling. Both primary and secondary sectors incorporated religious schools, funded by the state as voluntary aided or controlled. State funding of various faith schools had an historical antecedent, as schooling in England in the 19th century was originally provided by various religious faiths. In the early 2000s around 23% of school students were educated in state-funded religious schools. These were mainly Church of England, Roman Catholic, and a small number of Jewish schools, with Muslim, Hindu, Greek Orthodox and other faiths given the right to claim state funding in 1997.

Rightwing Conservatives, including Mrs. Thatcher, retained beliefs in selective schooling as an underpinning for an hierarchical social structure. Indeed, in 1984 one of her civil servants reported to a researcher that, "we are creating aspirations we cannot match . . . so we must select, ration the educational opportunities. People must be educated once more to know their place" (Ranson, 1984, p. 241).

In 1988, a Conservative Education Reform Act set up a framework for reintroducing selection of students within a more complex diversity of schools, a process that was continued by the New Labour government of Tony Blair. This act introduced parental choice of schools, and also gave secondary schools the right to opt out of local authority regulation, with funding coming directly from central government. Although less than a third of schools chose this option these schools could control their own admissions of students, which meant that they could choose students when the school had too many applications. Choice was in reality only the right to express a preference for a school, and as money followed pupils, schools were now in competition with each other for students. The intention was that weaker, unpopular schools would close. English choice policies were admired by American choice enthusiasts Chubb and Moe (1990). Although some poor families were enabled to avoid what they saw as bad schools, choice meant more middle class and white flight, leaving open schools that took in working-class students, ethnic minorities, second language learners and students with special needs. Choice policies were fueled by the media publication, from 1992 of *league tables* of examination results. Copying football league table results published in sports pages, newspapers took advantage of the requirement that all secondary schools publish the results obtained by students in their General Certificate of Secondary Education (GCSE) school examinations taken at age 16, to put all schools in order of results obtained. Eventually, as all examination results were required to be published the league tables expanded to pull-out newspaper supplements on results obtained by children at all levels, even the test scores by school for children as young as 7. Parents eagerly study these tables, which on raw score results, tend to show the social class area of the school more than anything else.[1]

The 1988 Act was also the first Act to formally attempt to bring private business money into the state education system. Entrepreneurs were to be encouraged to set up city technology colleges, which would supposedly concentrate on communications and information and other technologies. As it happened, business was not interested and only fifteen of these were set up, largely funded by taxpayers. Nevertheless, the idea of business putting money into the state education had been introduced, and from 1993 a sponsored specialist schools program began. Schools could raise private sponsorship money (£50,000) to be matched by central government, and, despite a national curriculum, specialize in technology, business, sports, arts, music, and other curriculum areas.[2]

The New Labour government, in a 1998 School Standards and Framework Act, gave secondary schools the right to call themselves foundation, voluntary aided (religious) or community school, with the first two kinds largely controlling their own admission of students. The specialist schools program was expanded, and by 2005 it covered over two thirds of all these secondary schools, and was described as a way of modernizing the comprehensive principle, with specialist schools allowed to give tests of aptitude for their specialism. In 2001 a White paper explained that the specialist schools program would lead to "a diverse system where schools differ markedly from each other but are equally excellent in giving their pupils a broad curriculum" (DfES, 2001, p. 38).

In support of specialist schools the government quoted contentious research in an effort to prove that exam results were better in specialist schools (Edwards & Tomlinson, 2006). Successful schools were given extra money as beacon schools or advanced specialist, and school uniforms to distinguish students provided business for textile companies. The Trudex Textile Company reported that sports schools, largely in urban areas and attended by minorities, tended to choose sweatshirts, rather than the blazers and ties favored by arts schools. On the question of specialist schools and their permitted admission of 10% of students on the basis of aptitude tests, a House of Commons Committee noted in 2003 that "we are not satisfied that any meaningful distinction between ability and aptitude has been made and we have found no justification for reliance on a distinction between them" (House of Commons Education and Skills Committee, 2003, p. 139).

Further diversity was provided by the retention of 164 grammar schools in 36 English local authorities, with fifteen retaining complete selection after an 11+ examination. These highly selective schools, oversubscribed by intensively tutored children, continued to educate middle class students, including those from some Indian and Chinese families with small numbers of African-Caribbean and other Asian children (Abbas, 2004). The government encouraged philanthropic schemes based on the idea of escape from poorer schools, but a survey of parents in 2004 found that parents favored local schools taking local children, with selection of any kind less popular than selection by lottery (Shaw, 2004). Some 7% of students continued to be educated in private schools, deemed to be "independent," and these provided some 26% of students taking the A level examinations at age 18, required for university entry. The private schools continued to provide over half the undergraduate intake of Oxford and Cambridge universities, and Prince Charles's sons both attended the prestigious Eton College, which is a private, fee-paying school.[3] No member of the Royal family in England has yet sent any of their children to a state-maintained school.

PRIVATIZING DIVERSITY

A policy which combined several agendas—providing more diversity of schools including more faith schools, reducing the powers of local authorities and bringing in private money—was encapsulated in the creation of *academies*.

These were announced in 2000 and the first three opened in 2002. Academies were to be independent semiprivatized schools sponsored by business, faith, or voluntary bodies and were partly modeled on the charter schools in the United States (Miron, 2001). They were set up as limited companies with charitable status, in effect private schools publicly funded, as sponsors only had to contribute £2 million, in cash or kind, with the taxpayer contributing £25 million in cash. The sponsors were then given control of school staffing, admissions, and curriculum. Twenty-two of the planned academies were in the control of Christian organizations, including evangelical sponsors. By 2006, 39 academies were open or planned, with a goal of 200 by 2010. Prime Minister Blair was heavily committed to the academies program, hosting breakfasts in Downing Street for potential sponsors, including American investment bankers, and by 2006 sponsors included bankers, shipping magnates, football clubs and sports agencies, private school head teachers, and several religions, including a creationist believer, whose money had been made in second-hand car dealing. The Prime Minister's advisor who promoted the academies program, Andrew Adonis, was made a Lord and, although unelected, a government education Minister. Academies have not been part of the education system long enough for any meaningful research to indicate whether these very expensive schools could boost exam results, although they were claimed to be replacements for struggling schools. One of the first Academies to open did enhance its exam results by excluding three times the number of so-called difficult students than other local schools (see Tomlinson, 2005, p. 127).

In 2004 the Education Department produced a 5-year strategic plan for education (DfES, 2004), which included a proposal to create *independent specialist schools* in place of the *traditional comprehensive*, with local authority powers further reduced. By 2005 legislation required the authorities to hold competitions if new schools were required, with religious, parental, or business groups able to promote a school. There was a voluntary code of practice on admissions, which schools could ignore[4] and many schools continued to set admissions tests, interview parents, and discourage undesirable children. In 2006 a further Education Act was introduced, this time causing considerable antagonism among Labour members of Parliament and party supporters. This Act gave all schools, primary, secondary, and special, powers to remove themselves completely from local control and become self-governing charitable Trusts or Foundations, backed by business, charity, faith, or other groups, with unelected governing bodies. Although it currently seems unlikely that many schools will take advantage of this, most still preferring to have contact with their local authority, the possibility exists for state-owned schools to be run by private interests. The act also allowed successful schools to expand and take more students, and federate with neighboring schools. The role of local authorities was again reduced, although it was proclaimed that they would be champions of children, and they now required the permission of the Secretary of State to open a new community school. Although a new Code of Practice on school admissions was introduced that banned interviewing for school placements, the authority had few powers to ensure schools complied, and selective tests for ability and aptitude could continue to be used. The act was intended to bring private business into a commanding position in schools where the Governors voted to make themselves independent of local authority control. But even before the act was passed a DfES document was circulated on setting up trusts— a term not used in the Act itself—quoting as an example Monkseaton school in Tyneside, which already had a specialism in languages, as one where Bill Gates's global Microsoft company was "interested in developing their existing links into a trust to... drive innovation" (DfES, 2006a, p. 3). Global businesses running state schools in England and assessing students for "aptitudes" for school places may be against all welfare state notions of locally provided broad and balanced education for all, but may fit well into the kind of market-state described below.

By 2006 parents and students did indeed theoretically have a choice of schools, of which many were now removed from local control, sponsored or influenced by business, religious and other groups, and with the possibility of schools now being run by these organizations. The experience of Louis noted above indicated that in fact, schools were able to select their students in a variety of overt and covert ways (West & Hind, 2003; West, 2006). Choice was also a nonsense in most rural areas where there was only one local school, and in urban areas depended, if preferences were honored, on children traveling long distances to schools. The contradictions between funding policies which forced schools to compete for students while urging cooperation by federation and sharing best practice was obvious. The role of elected local authorities had given way to central control and the larger input of private business, religious, and other groups.

FAILING SCHOOLS

In England, as in other developed countries up until the early 1970s, most urban schools were neither designed nor resourced to educate students to high levels, and as a consequence failed many young people. In England educational opportunities were deliberately limited from 1945 on. The first postwar Labour government reduced the number of grammar school places, prevented the 80% of pupils who attended the secondary modem schools from taking public examinations and openly stated that these schools were for "children who will not require any measure of technical skill or knowledge" (Ministry of Education, 1945, p. 13). Since a workforce was desperately needed for economic reconstruction it made sense to hurry as many working class students through an education to age 15 and into waiting jobs. In 1953 the Labour leader Gaitskill was reported as "still wanting an educated elite learning Latin verse," while the rest attended what turned out to be poorly resourced schools with less-well qualified teachers (Benn, 1994). From the 1970s a rise in oil prices and a recession affected the employment of young people, as did a growing realization that it made economic sense to educate more young people to higher levels. The school-leaving age was raised to 16 in 1973, and all students were permitted to take the same public examinations from the mid-1980s. An education system which had been regarded as adequate while there were unskilled and semiskilled jobs to fill, was from the 1970s, condemned as inadequate by politicians of all parties (see Tomlinson, 2005, pp. 25–27).

In England from the 1980s, although comprehensive schools developed, no political party was committed to developing the democratic egalitarian ideals that were inherent in extended secondary education in common schools, with an equalizing of opportunities and resources, and there were no coherent plans for educating working class children to higher levels nor preparing a modern workforce. Researchers on both sides of the Atlantic concentrated on inequalities of attainment among individuals and debated how far exam results could be predicted by family background or schools (Coleman, 1966; Jencks, 1972). Eventually the notion that schools could make a difference replaced what became known as the *Jencks pessimism,* and research concentrated on factors which made schools more effective for all students (Purkey & Smith, 1983; Rutter, 1983; Smith & Tomlinson, 1989). The subsequent school effectiveness and school improvement movements of the 1990s and 2000s did encourage schools to examine their organization, management, and practices, and there was some help and much pressure on weaker urban schools, but the government in England seized on school effectiveness research to proclaim that poverty was no excuse for schools in deprived areas obtaining low examination scores, and created a blame and shame culture. Smith and Tomlinson, publishing a 5-year study in 1989, were concerned to find their research quoted in support of the no excuse slogan (Smith & Tomlinson, 1989). While there was increasing bitterness among working class, and especially Black and other minority parents, that schools were not educating their children well and preparing them for higher education or good jobs, politicians persisted in blaming schools for failure to overcome what were increasing social and economic disadvantages, pretending that schools in class societies in which general inequalities were widening could be a major force in reducing rather than reproducing disadvantage.

By the end of the 1990s the notion of the failing school was entrenched in legislation, despite a history that showed most of these schools were former urban secondary modern schools which had never had sufficient resources to compete with suburban schools and were largely attended by poor pupils. Failing schools in England became demonized institutions whose head, teachers, governors, and sometimes parents, were held personally responsible for the underperformance of its students. Schools where students performed badly in public examinations and lowered league table performance were castigated as failing whole communities and weakening the whole educational structure (see Tomlinson, 1997a; O'Connor, Hales, Davies, & Tomlinson, 1999). The failing schools legislation was set out in Education Acts and circulars in 1992 and 1993, whereby schools could be declared in need of special measures, later schools requiring significant improvement. Press coverage of failing schools was derisory—journalists regularly discovering the worst school in Britain and approaching general elections politicians competed to demonstrate their zero tolerance of school failure, and willingly named and shamed individual schools.

Characteristics of failing schools were that they served areas of deprivation, had high numbers of settled minorities, recent immigrant and refugee children, second-language speaking students, and students with special educational needs not wanted in other schools. Indeed, a report in 2006 from the government National Audit Office confirmed that schools most likely to be categorized as failing were those attended by poor children receiving free school meals and by children with special educational needs (NAO, 2006). Whereas previously schools were never expected to succeed in credentialing all children to higher levels, now market forces were helping to create failing schools. Urban schools, as in the United States, continued to lose middle class students, others excluded the troublesome and some made themselves vulnerable by accepting those with learning and behaviour difficulties, with no recognition for this. One head of an inner city school, serving a largely poor, Black intake, noted bitterly that "we have had a Herculean task to improve in a climate of hostility" (Gardiner, 1997, p. 7). Some attempts were made to mitigate the historical and newly created deficiencies of inner city schools where parents could not move away. An *Excellence in Cities* program was initiated in 1999, which promised "an improvement in parental confidence in the capacity of city schools to cater for ambitious and high-achieving pupils" (DfEE, 1999, p. 1). The policy included programs for the gifted and talented, separating the low-achieving and disruptive into learning support centres, providing learning mentors, more setting (tracking) in schools, and the introduction of so-called world class tests. Early evidence indicated that Black students were the least likely to be selected as gifted and talented. While all students have improved their test and examination performance considerably over the past 20 years the evidence seems to show that creating more balanced social and ability intakes, providing good, well-qualified teaching staff with good leadership, resourcing more equally and involving parents continually in the life of the school, has helped raise standards more than blame and shame measures.

Where schools have been regarded as failing, the academies program was promoted as a solution although a minister later admitted that none of the academies had replaced schools actually designated as failing. All this was similar to the well-documented controversies following the U.S. No Child Left Behind legislation (Gotbaum, 2002; Hursh, 2005; Lipman, 2004). Hursh (2005) linked the legislation that allowed schools that did not improve their aggregated test scores year after year to be designated as failing, to a privatizing agenda.

> One reason the NCLB is allowed to label thousands of schools as failing, restrict what schools may do to improve student learning, and reduces funding to so-called failing schools may be because the federal government is interested in replacing rather than improving public schools. (p. 617)

In England local education authorities could also be designated as failing and be taken over by private companies. Islington LEA in London, despite being the former home area of Prime Minister Blair, became the first LEA to have its day-to-day running taken over by a private firm, Cambridge Education Associates. This firm was eventually penalized by the DfES for failing to meet agreed targets on student performance, and ran the school system no better than the elected LEA. Leeds LEA was taken over in 2001 by the private company Capita. This IT company was awarded hundreds of millions of pounds for educational and other public service contracts, and was appointed by the DfES to run a national individual learning accounts scheme for those taking vocational courses, a scheme which collapsed with some cost to the taxpayer after fraud investigations. In 2006 the founder and current chair of Capita resigned after it emerged that he had loaned £1 million to the New Labour Party to help the Prime Minister win a third term (Brown, 2006). Southwark LEA was forced to transfer its education services to a private engineering company W. S. Atkins, but by 2003 Atkins performance was considered to be "shambolic" (Centre for Public Services, 2003). The numbers of schools in special measures had increased and even the company that franked the mail was unpaid. Certainly evidence that private involvement in schools and local administrations actually increased efficiency or improved educational achievements for all students was conspicuously lacking in the early 21st century in England, as was evidence that private involvement had actually reduced state spending on education. Nevertheless, attention continued to focus on the failings of students and schools rather than on the failings of government policies or private companies.

ASSESSMENT FOR A MERITOCRACY

From the later 1980s assessment of children became more extensive and ruthless. Preschool children were subject to baseline assessment, originally designed as developmental measures to aid teachers, but inevitably becoming an early judgment on children's ability, with parents asking whether their child had passed the baseline assessment. National tests (SATs—standard assessment tasks) given to all children at key stages 7, 11, and 14 years— were followed by preparation for the GCSE, subject-centred examinations taken at age 16, the official school leaving age. The benchmark for a successful school became the percentages of students attaining A to C grades in this public examination, with results by school published in league tables in the media. Attempts to create vocational qualifications in schools continued from the 1980s (Tomlinson, 1997b; Hayward, 2004) and eventually vocational GCSEs were introduced. Success in the Advanced A level examinations were also published in league tables to indicate school success, as were advanced supplementary (A/S) examinations developed in 2001. These examinations were intended to expand the number of subjects studied after age 16, most students previously taking only three or four subjects to advanced level at age 18 (in contrast to students in U.S. high schools who continue to study a wide range of subjects after age 16). The introduction of these examinations meant that students in England now take public examinations at ages 16, 17, and 18 or over, an unprecedented examination overload.

Gillborn and Youdell (2000) documented the refinements to public testing introduced by New Labour, and also the tiering practices at GCSE, which prevented many working class and Black pupils from achieving well. An academic expert on testing, Dylan Wiliam, who later left to work in the United States, declared in 2002 that national tests at 7, 11, and 14 were useless as measures of progress and rising scores reflected little more than teachers ability to teach to the tests (see Tomlinson, 2005, p. 138). There were problems during the introduction of the A/S level, with faulty grading in 2002 causing the resignation of both the chairman of the Qualifications and Curriculum Authority, and the secretary of State for Education herself. Undeterred, New Labour continued to create more public examinations, with fourteen vocational diplomas to be introduced into schools by 2010 (DfES, 2006b), the development of these diplomas being led by business-dominated Sector Skills Councils. Katharina Tomasevski (2005), a Swedish Professor of International law and former reporter to the UN Convention of the Rights of the Child, has claimed that the British government is in breach of Article 29 of the UN Convention on Children's Rights by its extensive testing regimes, and has argued that the system has been designed to serve political objectives rather than student needs.

By 2006 even the chief executive of the Qualifications and Curriculum Authority, the body responsible for testing, was voicing doubts about the excessive amount of assessment students faced in schools. However, his solution was to ensure tests were made more difficult. "We have got 22% of people at A level getting a grade A, it may be time to add a few inches at the top," and the DfES was quick to reiterate that "tests were here to stay" (Asthana, 2006b, p.1).

The public parading of school and individual children's test scores, and the consequences for schools of low scores, while offered in the name of public accountability and school improvement, demonstrates a ruthlessness with no precedent in English education. While a rhetoric of raising standards, reducing inequalities, encouraging accountability and improvement were employed, the reality was that students continued to be sorted into schools and tracks, and schools continued to be identified within hierarchies of different quality and perceived worth, in which familiar patterns of inequality by social class and ethnicity were recreated. The structural situation in the UK in the early 21st century, as in other developed countries, was that there were expanded and diverse middle and aspirant classes whose needs took precedence in any competitive struggle for positional advantages in society. In England, the political reality was that these groups, whose votes governments depended on, were catered to by the educational policies put in place from the 1980s, which created and recreated social exclusions on a daily basis. Social class remained a powerful predictor of life chances. While by 2003 some 72% of young people with parents in the higher social classes obtained the five A-C GCSEs, which allowed them to move into higher education, only 29% of routine manual workers' children obtained these. While the new Labour government had put in place some ameliorative policies to improve the prospects of the poor, in 2003 some 4 million children were reported as living in low-income households and attending the poorest schools (Social Trends, 2003. p. 109). These households disproportionately included families with origins in the Caribbean, Pakistan, and Bangladesh. Families with origins in India, and those who were expelled from East African countries during the late 1960s and early 1970s, and who had higher levels of education, were more likely to be economically successful, and less likely to be categorised as poor. Their children were also more likely to perform well in school examinations. The situation of Black children with African and African Caribbean origins in the English education system remained an area of bitter anxiety for parents (Richardson, 2006). Policies to aid the disadvantaged had little effect on the middle classes, apart from ensuring that more than ever before, the future status and security of their children would be a primary aim, educating them as far as possible, apart from the poor.

The rationale for English education policies has continued to be the ideology of meritocracy, an ideology embraced by most western capitalist countries during the 20th century. Belief in both the economic and moral rightness of advancement by merit, rather than by birth, wealth, nepotism, bribery, or patronage, was espoused by Labour intellectuals over 100 years ago (Lawton, 2005) and continued as a central tenet of Blair's New Labour government. As Blair remarked in 1999 the New Labour government wished to create ladders of opportunity for all "with no more ceilings that prevent people achieving the success they merit."

But success must be earned. A central ideal in a modern meritocracy is that all members of the society have a duty to invest in their own human capital, which will in turn, improve national economic productivity in a global market. Since all cannot acquire the desirable jobs in a high-skills economy, there must be meritocratic competition between individuals who have different abilities and aptitudes, softened in government publications to the language of different needs and aspirations. In this scenario, the government will provide the ladders of opportunity, there will be equal opportunity for all to climb, unhindered by social class, gender, ethnicity, or disability. In these meritocratic terms it makes sense that beliefs in educating all young people together in equally resourced schools, without prior and ongoing selection for unequal and differential provision, has to be jettisoned. The notion of a diverse school system creating a stratified workforce that corresponds to economic and business needs is very attractive to governments. A report produced for the European Commission in 1996 unambiguously asserted that "education systems are required to function as an hierarchical talent filter" (Reiffers, 1996, p. 2). Selection, diversity and inequality of provision make sense if education is seen primarily as a means by which young people are prepared for work at different levels in a flexible labor force, with a curriculum increasingly influenced by economic interests.

There are, of course, considerable problems associated with the concept of meritocracy itself. In the early 20th century Max Weber (1947) pointed out that dominant groups always need a theoretical legitimation for their own privileges, and during the whole of the 20th century mental testing movements, with ever increasing refinements to tests of intelligence, ability, aptitudes, and competences provided a "theodicy of privilege" for those who believed their success due solely to merit (p. 132). In reality, as Goldthorpe (1997), reviewing the history of the concept, demonstrated, throughout the twentieth century the working classes have always had to demonstrate considerably more merit than others to achieve desirable positions, and that attempts to provide the structures of inequality in modern societies with meritocratic legitimation are not convincing. The history of sponsoring able meritorious poor children into private or selective education has been one persistent attempt to legitimate a system geared to social inequality, and the ways in which already privileged groups find ways of reproducing their children in privileged positions via education has been well documented, particularly in the writings of Bourdieu (see Reed-Danahay, 2005).

In England Michael Young produced a satire on meritocracy in 1958 in which he described the creation of a new social class that believed their privileges and superior status arose purely from their own merits, with clever children progressively separated from the dull who remained or were demoted to lower social classes. The process was derailed by the dull children of lords not happy to be demoted, women who were not keen on producing an IQ card before marriage and "envious egalitarians" who eventually challenged the meritocracy in violent confrontation (Young, 1958). This cautionary tale has not been widely read and the sad situation of dull demoted lords was never a reality, but Young's point was that a meritocracy can harden into a self-regarding group with no room in it for others. The rich and powerful are encouraged to think their advancement comes from merit, those judged without merit can feel demoralized and resentful. Again, the story of Louis at the beginning of the chapter illustrates this.

THE POST-WELFARE MARKET STATE

Education was central to post-Second World War reconstruction in England after 1945, and the English welfare state, with recognized social security benefits for all, a free National Health Service, and free primary and secondary education for all young people, became well known around the world. However, over the years, the principles of a welfare state that cared for all its citizens has been eroded. The country could now be described as a post-welfare market society, and there had been a fragmentation of social welfare programs via the introduction of market principles. Education, subject to these principles, had by 2006 become a competitive enterprise and a commodity, rather than a preparation for a democratic society. While traditionally it was Conservative policy to support a selective and differentiated school and higher education system to create a stratified workforce and to support privatization and competitive market principles, the New Labour government after 1997 changed the welfare state into a market state "pushing marketization and privatization as zealously as the Conservatives did" (Marquand, 2004 p.118).

Both political parties justified their policies by the need for higher standards of education in a competitive global economy, and by assertions of a meritocratic ideal. All young people were to have equal opportunities to rise to the top. Belief in meritocracy, with its associated need for continuous assessment to help identify winners and losers, is a necessary component of a market state. It notionally fills the posts for which higher education and high-level skills are required with the most talented. Whether this is true or not, in the global economy there is an increasing divide between those who are part of the high-skills knowledge economy, and those whose supposed lesser talents or lack of merit leads to jobs with lower income and status or unemployment. Assessment in education is fast becoming the major legitimation for the unequal treatment of a majority of people in a ruthless market society.

New Labour policies in England have changed the idea of a welfare state that undertook to improve the welfare of all citizens into an entrepreneurial market state. In this state government promises to maximize opportunities for all citizens, including minorities, providing they enter into meritocratic competition with each other, continually upgrade their human capital, and accept the winner and loser mentality, which translates into widening income and status inequalities. It also means accepting that a competitive education system must have further measures to control the reluctant, disaffected or those whose special needs or disabilities might interfere with the prescribed education, assessing, and sorting of the majority.

Market states supposedly encourage meritocracy. Eventually, no one remembers the moral basis for assessing merit, but assumes that it can be "ruthlessly assessed and measured" (Bobbitt, 2002, p. 232). Market states must maximize opportunities by encouraging competition; providing incentive structures and also draconian penalties, especially the threats of demotion in schooling, unemployment and loss of job; income; and status. Because multinational companies evaluate countries for their workforce capabilities and other attractions for capital, market states must educate and train their young but are not in the business of redistribution of jobs or money and will no longer guarantee the welfare of all citizens, despite the knowledge that the same companies can easily move their business and create unemployment. Sennett (2006), in a perceptive account of how the search for meritocratic talent in the *new Capitalism* is developing, notes the "spectre of uselessness" which hangs over both the less well-educated and the older well-educated worker. Sennett pointed out that upward mobility through education is an inadequate solution to lack of jobs or rewarding work. It may assist some individuals to escape to a better life but is no answer to general well being. A skills society may only need a relatively small number of the highly educated and talented. High-tech societies can function with smaller educated elites. If the society does not require large numbers of workers in order to be globally profitable "what will it offer people who are cast aside?" (Sennett, 2006, p. 99). Even the rush to create new types of vocational qualifications will not necessarily secure employment for the recipients. While in England the government continues to exhort more and more people to obtain more and more qualifications, and to sort people into hierarchies of supposed worth by elaborate testing and assessment, the links between education and national and global economies are ill understood. Brown and Lauder (2006) have suggested that middle class families in both the United Kingdom and the United States have abandoned any lingering commitment to meritocratic competition in education. As elite credentials are now essential for high level and even second level jobs, ruthless strategies, which need economic, cultural, and social capital, must be deployed.

The market state notion of a social contract—that governments exist only to maximize opportunities for individuals, and partly do this through their beliefs in the filtering of merit via complex assessment systems—is a dismal one for those who believe in democratic ideals and a common good. Examination of the beneficiaries of high quality education, however it is defined and assessed, indicate that this kind of education has always been confined to higher socioeconomic groups, with some concession to social mobility of lower class gifted individuals. Assessment and testing restricts access to certain forms of education, and this restriction acts as a major form of social exclusion. In England, as in other countries around the world, the government is attempting to deal with a situation in which more and more people are engaged in competitive attempts to gain qualifications and good employment, with large numbers excluded from entering the competition on equal terms, and others, driven by heightened insecurities, desperately attempting to gain or retain positional advantages.

In the minimizing of a welfare state, a major casualty has been the abolition of a collective voice for those who believed that a common educational experience equally resourced and based on shared values, was a democratic right. For governments to assert they are no longer in the business of caring for all citizens is an affront to democracy. Jobs, business, enterprise, and competition are tools of capitalist societies, but governments exist to regulate and mix the harsher attributes of markets capitalism with democratic rights. In England by the early 21st century a ruthless (and demonstrably unfair) competition between groups and individuals for social and economic advancement, with the endless assessment of young people that accompanies this, had developed. This situation is not likely to contribute to civic vitality and a common good.

Afterword

James A. Banks

University of Washington Seattle

The incisive and thoughtful chapters in this book present a myriad of informative perspectives, data, and insights on democracy, equity, and standardization at a time when democracy is seriously threatened in U. S. schools and in society writ large. However, as the chapters by Gillborn and Tomlinson indicate, the push for standardization and the privatization of the public schools reach beyond the borders of the United States. It is movement in Western nations around the world.

In my comments, I describe mixed results from the movement for high standards and accountability, the need for total school reform in order for students from diverse groups to meet high academic standards and have equal opportunities to learn, and the need to transform the canon used to determine the knowledge and skills taught in the curriculum and to construct tests and assessments. If the knowledge and skills taught in the curriculum and the assessments used to determine whether students have acquired them are not transformed, tests and accountability efforts will often reinforce and perpetuate the racial, ethnic, and class stratification within U. S. society.

MIXED RESULTS OF THE QUEST FOR STANDARDS AND ACCOUNTABILITY

The national focus on creating high academic standards and holding educators accountable for student achievement is having mixed results in U. S. schools. The mantra that all children can learn—which is a central tenet of multicultural education—is a positive outcome of the standards movement. Some of the objectives and test items that have been developed to measure student learning—such as the Essential Academic Learning Requirements for the state of Washington (EALRs, 2006)—determine whether students have acquired higher level knowledge, concepts, and principles. This learning goal from the EALRs is an example: "The student applies the methods of social science investigation to compare and contrast interpretations of historical events."

Some researchers and educational leaders view the reforms required by the No Child Left Behind Act (NCLB) Act as promising. A study by Roderick, Jacob, and Bryk (2002) indicates that performance improved in low-performing schools after the implementation of standards-based reform. Some school leaders in high-minority, low-achieving schools have applauded the NCLB Act because it requires school districts and states to disaggregate achievement data by social class, race, ethnicity, disability, and English proficiency. These administrators believe that the disaggregation of achievement data has helped to focus attention on the academic achievement gap between Whites and students of color such as African Americans, Mexican Americans, and Native Americans.

As the chapters in this book deftly document, the standards movement also has many negative outcomes. Students who have very different and unequal opportunities to learn are compared on standardized tests and assessments. Students from low-income and under-resourced schools are often the victims of punitive consequences when they do not perform well on standardized achievement tests. Teachers in low-income and under-resourced schools are frequently not provided the resources they need to teach students who require extra help to meet high academic standards. Yet they are held accountable and may experience punitive measures even though they have worked very hard to help their students experience academic growth. The knowledge and skills of their students may have greatly increased during the school year, but may not have reached the mark when compared to the assessment standards or with the achievement of students in more affluent and highly resourced communities and schools.

Michael Knapp (personal communication, October 17, 2006), my colleague at the University of Washington, has stated that educators often confuse and conflate *standards, assessment,* and *accountability*. Standards consist of the benchmarks or goals for student achievement. Assessment comprises the measures that are used to determine whether students have attained the standards. Accountability describes who is responsible for providing the learning opportunities needed for students to attain the standards that have been set for them and assigns consequences for success or failure to fulfill these responsibilities. These three concepts need to be distinguished in both theory and practice. Some teachers may work very hard with students in under-resourced and low-income schools and help them to greatly increase their knowledge and skills. However, because of the initial wide gap between the knowledge and skills of their students and the standards that have been formulated by the state department of education, the test scores of their students at the end of the year might miss state and national goals by a wide mark.

The NCLB Act and related reforms have evoked a chorus of criticism from some researchers and school reformers (Meier & Wood, 2005). The critics of the Act argue that standards-based reforms driven by the NCLB Act have had many negative consequences on the curriculum and on school life. They contend that these reforms have forced many teachers to focus on narrow literacy and numeracy skills rather than on critical thinking and the broad goals of schooling in a democratic society, have led to an overemphasis on testing and less focus on teaching, and have deskilled (Giroux, 1988) and deprofessionalized teachers. Amrein and Berliner (2002) analyzed 18 states to determine how high-stakes tests were affecting student learning. They concluded that in all but one of their analyses student learning was indeterminate, remained at the same level before high-stakes testing was implemented, or went down when high states testing policies were initiated.

NATIONAL STANDARDS AND SCHOOL REFORM

Diane Ravitch (1995), one of the leading proponents of national standards, writes in her book *National Standards in American Education: A Citizen's Guide*:

> National standards and assessments will accomplish little by themselves. Unless they are accomplished by better teaching, a better school environment, better instructional materials (including new technology), and more highly motivated students, student achievement will not improve. (pp. 24–25)

Although Ravitch (1995) is an influential proponent of national standards and I am not, I agree with her statement above. I am not opposed to the idea of state and national standards, but am deeply concerned about the inequitable, punitive, and politicized ways in which they are often implemented. I am concerned that we might again end up blaming the victims for their failures when they and their teachers have not been provided the resources and support needed to meet state and national standards.

We can help all students to meet high academic standards by reforming the schools in substantial ways so that students from diverse racial, cultural, ethnic, and language groups become personally involved in learning and motivated to learn. Students learn best when what they are taught has personal meanings for them. Also, students learn best when they are aware of themselves as learners. Brandt (1998) points out that "people learn what they want to learn" (p. 5). Students also "need to understand what it means to learn, who they are as learners, and how to go about planning, monitoring, and revising, to reflect upon their learning and that of others, and to determine for themselves if they understand" (Bransford, Brown, & Cocking, 1999, p. xiv).

To make learning meaningful for students from diverse racial, ethnic, cultural, and language groups, to teach conceptually, and to make learners mindful of themselves as learners, we need to reform the school as an organization and transform the curriculum, pedagogy, and assessments. Comprehensive multicultural education should be implemented, which consists of the five dimensions of multicultural education that I have identified and described (Banks, 2004b): content integration, the knowledge construction process, prejudice reduction, an equity pedagogy, and an empowering school culture and social structure.

THE CURRICULUM AND ASSESSMENT CANON: THE NEED FOR REFORM

In the push for academic standards and accountability, lists of knowledge and skills are often formulated without the input of scholars and educators from diverse racial, ethnic, cultural, and language groups. Consequently, these lists often reinforce the dominant and mainstream knowledge within schools, colleges, and universities and within society writ large. If students master mainstream knowledge without gaining the commitment, knowledge, and skills to question the knowledge they have attained or practices within society that perpetuated inequality, they will be unable to take action to increase equity and social justice within society (Baldwin, 1985). An important goal of citizenship education is to help students to acquire the knowledge, skills, and commitment needed to question mainstream institutions within society that perpetuate inequality and to develop the knowledge, attitudes, and skills needed to take action to make society more just (Banks, 1997).

Most of the tests and assessments used in the standardization movement are based on the Western-centric mainstream canon. A canon is a "norm, criterion, model or standard used for evaluating or criticizing." It is also "a basic general principle or rule commonly accepted as true, valid and fundamental" (*Webster's Third International Dictionary*, 1986, p. 328). A specific and identifiable canon is used to define, select, and test knowledge in the school and university curriculum in the United States and in nations around the world (Kornhaber, 2004). This canon is rarely explicitly defined or discussed. It is taken for granted, unquestioned, and internalized by writers, researchers, teachers, professors, and students. It is European-centric and male-dominated, often marginalizing the experiences of people of color, Third World nations and cultures, and the perspectives and histories of women.

African American scholars such as George Washington Williams (Franklin, 1985), Carter G. Woodson (1921), and W.E.B. DuBois (1935/1962) challenged the established canon in social science and history in the nineteenth and twentieth centuries. Their scholarship was influential in the African American academic community. However, it was largely ignored by the White world. The ethnic studies movement, which grew out of the civil rights movement of the 1960s and 1970s, seriously challenged the European-centric canon that dominates the school and university curricula. Later, scholars in women's studies also challenged the established canon (Schmitz, Butler, Guy-Sheftall, & Rosenfelt, 2004). The ethnic and women's studies movements are forcing an examination of the canon used to select and judge knowledge in the school and university curricula. The insights and perspectives from these movements are also needed to critically examine and reform the tests and assessments that are now driving the curriculum in U. S. schools (Kornhaber, 2004).

Women and people are color are trying to get their voices included into the school and university curriculum and their important historical and cultural works canonized. They feel that their voices have been silenced and their experiences have been marginalized in the existing curriculum. The struggle over the inclusion of ethnic content and content about women in the school and university curriculum and in assessments can best be understood as a battle over who will participate in or control the formulation of the canon or standard used to determine what constitutes a liberal education in a multicultural democratic society. The guardians and defenders of the traditional, established canon believe that it best serves their interests and consequently the interests of the society and the nation-state (Schlesinger, 1991; Stotsky, 1999). They also view it as consistent with their experiences, perspectives, and visions of the future. Those who criticize the established canon, such as many ethnic and feminist scholars, believe that it marginalizes their experiences and voices and results in a curriculum that largely ignores their histories and cultures.

A struggle for voice has emerged because the resistance to multicultural studies and curriculum transformation has been strengthened by the national quest for standards and testing (Stotsky, 1999). Many of the arguments against multicultural education and for testing and standardization are the expression of a conservative political agenda designed to promote the interests of a small elite rather than the interests of the nation or the public interest (Ladson-Billings & Tate, 2006). Many of the consequences of the standardization movement are also serving the interests of the mainstream elite. Yet, their interests are described as if they were universal and in the common good. A dominant elite describing its interest as being the same as the public interest marginalizes the experiences of structurally excluded groups such as women, people of color, and low-income citizens.

SPECIAL INTERESTS AND THE PUBLIC INTEREST

The individuals and groups that now determine and formulate the school curriculum canon, tests, and assessments often call the perspectives and priorities of people of color and women "special interests" (Schlesinger, 1991; Stotsky, 1999). *Webster's Ninth New Collegiate Dictionary* (1984) defines special interest as a "person or group seeking to influence policy often narrowly defined." *Special interest* implies an interest that is particularistic and inconsistent with the overarching goals and needs of the nation-state or commonwealth. To be in the public good, interests must extend beyond the needs of a unique or particular group (Ladson-Billings & Tate, 2006).

An important issue in today's public discourse about diversity and standardization is who formulates the criteria for determining what is a "special interest." Powerful groups that have already shaped the curriculum, the standards, assessments, institutions, and structures in their images and interests determine what is a special interest. The dominant group views its interests not as special but as identical with the common good. Special interests, in the view of those who control the curriculum, the assessments, and other institutions within society, are therefore any interest that challenges their power, ideologies, and paradigms, particularly if the interest group demands that the canon, assumptions, and values of institutions be transformed. History is replete with examples of dominant groups that defined their own interests as the public interest.

An important way in which those in power marginalize and disempower those who are structurally excluded from the mainstream is by labeling their visions, histories, goals, and struggles "special interests." This type of marginalization denies the legitimacy and validity of groups that are excluded from full participation in society and its institutions.

Only curricula and assessments that reflect the experiences and interests of a wide range of groups in the United States and the world is in the national interest and is consistent with the public good. Any other kind of curriculum reflects a special interest and is inconsistent with the needs of a nation that must survive in a pluralistic and highly interdependent global community. Special interests curricula and assessments—such as history, literature, and tests that emphasize the primacy of the West and the history of European American males—is detrimental to the public good because it will not help students to acquire the knowledge, skills, and attitudes essential for survival in the global community of the 21st century (Banks et al., 2005).

The ethnic studies and women studies movements do not push for special interests; their major aims are to transform curricula and assessments so that they will be more truthful and inclusive, and will reflect the histories, cultures, experiences, hopes, and dreams of the diverse groups in the United States and around the world. These movements contribute to the democratization of the school, the curricula, and assessments. They contribute to the public good rather than to the strengthening of special interests.

For a variety of complex reasons—including the need to enhance the survival of the United States in a period in which it is experiencing serious economic and social problems as well as a lack of moral authority around the world—educators need to rethink such concepts as *special interests, the national interest,* and *the public good.* Educators need to identify which groups are using these terms and for what purposes, and to evaluate their use in the context of a nation and world that is rapidly changing. Powerless and excluded groups accurately perceive efforts to label their visions and experiences as special interests as an attempt to marginalize them and to make their voices silent and their experiences invisible.

KNOWLEDGE AS A SOCIAL CONSTRUCTION PROCESS

The knowledge construction process is an important dimension of multicultural education (Banks, 2006). It describes the ways in which teachers help students to understand, investigate, and determine how implicit cultural assumptions, frames of references, perspectives, and biases within a discipline influence how knowledge is created. This process teaches students that knowledge reflects the social, political, and economic context in which it is created. The knowledge created by elite and powerless groups within the same society also tend to differ in significant ways.

Our concept of knowledge and cultural literacy should be broader than the one presented by Hirsch (1996) in his books. Hirsch writes as if knowledge is neutral and static. His books contains lists of important facts that he believes students should master in order to become culturally literate. Knowledge is dynamic, changing, and constructed within a social context, rather than neutral and static as Hirsch implies. Hirsch recommends transmitting knowledge in a largely uncritical way. When we help students to attain knowledge, we should help them to recognize that knowledge reflects the social and political context in which it is created and that it has normative and value assumptions.

Students can analyze the knowledge construction process in science by studying how racism has been perpetuated by genetic theories of intelligence, Darwinism, and eugenics. In his important book, *The Mismeasurement of Man*, Gould (1996) describes how scientific racism developed and was influential in the 19th and 20th centuries. Scientific racism has also had a significant influence on the interpretations of mental ability tests in the United States (Kornhaber, 2004). When students are examining how science has supported racist practices and ideologies, they should also examine how science has contributed to human justice and equality. Biological theories about the traits and characteristics that human groups share, as well as anthropological theories that challenged racist beliefs during the post World War II period—especially the writings of Franz Boas (1910) and Ruth Benedict (1947)—are important examples of how science and scientists have helped to eradicate racist beliefs, ideologies, and practices. Students should learn how science, like other disciplines, has been both a supporter and eradicator of racist beliefs and practices.

Students can examine the knowledge construction process in the social sciences and humanities when they study such units and topics as "The European Discovery of America" and "The Westward Movement." The students can discuss the latent political messages contained in these concepts and how they are used to justify the destruction of Native American cultures and civilizations and the taking of Indian lands by the European American settlers in the West.

The teacher can ask the students why the Americas are called the *New World*, and why the people from England are often called *settlers* and *pioneers* in textbooks, while people from other lands are usually called *immigrants*. The teacher can also ask the students to think of words that might have been used by the Lakota Sioux to describe the same people that the textbook call settlers and pioneers. The students may think of such words as *invaders*, *conquerors*, and *foreigners*. The goal of this lesson is not to teach students that the Anglo immigrants who went West were invaders. Rather, the goal is to help students to view them from the point of view of both the Anglos and the Lakota Sioux. Another important goal of both teaching and assessment should be to help students develop empathy for both groups and to give voice to all participants in United States history and culture. Students will be able to gain a thorough understanding of the settlement of the West, as well as other events, only when they are able to view them from diverse ethnic and cultural perspectives and to construct their own versions of the past and present.

When studying the Westward movement, the teacher can ask the students, "Whose point of view does this concept (Westward movement) reflect, the European Americans or the Lakota Sioux?" "Who was moving West?" "How might a Lakota Sioux historian describe this period in United States history?" "What are other ways of thinking about and describing the Westward Movement?" The *West* wasn't the West for the Sioux; it was the center of the universe. For people living in Japan, it was the East. The teacher should also help the students to view the Westward movement from the point of view of people who lived in Mexico and in Alaska. The West was North for the Mexicans and South for the Alaskans. By helping the students to view the concept of the Westward movement from the perspectives of different groups and cultures, teachers can help students to understand why knowledge is a social construction that reflect people's cultural, economic, and power position within a society. Tests and assessments should also be constructed to determine whether students are able to view events, concepts, and situations from diverse ethnic and cultural perspectives and whether they understand that knowledge is a social construction.

TEACHING STUDENTS TO KNOW, TO CARE, AND TO ACT

Major goals of a curriculum that fosters multicultural literacy and multicultural assessments should be to help students *to know, to care, and to act* in ways that will develop and foster a democratic and just society in which all groups experience cultural democracy and cultural empowerment. Knowledge is an essential part of multicultural literacy but it is not sufficient. Knowledge alone will not help students to develop empathy, caring, and a commitment to humane and democratic change. To help our nation and world become more culturally democratic, students must also develop a commitment to personal, social, and civic action, and the knowledge and skills needed to participate in effective civic action.

Although knowledge, caring, and action are conceptually distinct, in the classroom they are highly interrelated. In my multicultural classes for teacher education students, I use historical and sociological knowledge about the experiences of different ethnic and racial groups to inform as well as to enable the students to examine and clarify their personal attitudes about ethnic diversity. These knowledge experiences are also a vehicle that enables the students to think of action they can take to actualize their feelings and moral commitments.

Knowledge experiences that I use to help students to examine their value commitments and to think of ways to act include the reading of *Balm in Gilead: Journey of a Healer*, Sara Lawrence Lightfoot's (1988) powerful biography of her mother, one of the nation's first Black child psychiatrists; the historical overviews of various U.S. ethnic groups in my book, *Teaching Strategies for Ethnic* Studies (Banks, 2003) and several video and film presentations, including selected segments from *Eyes on the Prize II,* the award-winning history of the civil rights movement produced by Henry Hampton. To enable the students to analyze and clarify their values regarding these readings and video experiences, I ask them questions such as, "How did the book or film make you feel?" "Why do you think you feel that way?" To enable them to think about ways to act on their feelings, I ask such questions as, "How interracial are your own personal experiences?" "Would you like to live a more interracial life?" "What are some books that you can read or popular films that you can see that will enable you to act on your commitment to live a more racially and ethnically integrated life?" The power of these kinds of experiences are often revealed in student papers, as is illustrated by this excerpt from a paper written by a student after he had viewed several segments of *Eyes on the Prize II:*

> I feel that my teaching will now necessarily be a little bit different forever simply because I myself have changed. . . . I am no longer quite the same person I was before I viewed the presentations—my horizons are a little wider, perspectives a little broader, insights a little deeper. That is what I gained from *Eyes on the Prize.* (Muir, 1990)

The most meaningful and effective way to prepare teachers to involve students in multicultural experiences that will enable students to know, to care, and to participate in democratic action, is to involve teachers in multicultural experiences that focus on these goals. When teachers have gained knowledge about cultural and ethnic diversity themselves, looked at that knowledge from different ethnic and cultural perspectives, and taken action to make their own lives and communities more culturally sensitive and diverse, they will have the knowledge and skills needed to help transform the curriculum canon as well the hearts and minds of their students. Only when the curriculum canon, tests, and assessments are transformed to reflect cultural diversity and social justice will students be able to attain the knowledge, skills, and perspectives needed to become reflective and active citizens who can advance democracy and equity in the United States and around the world.

Acknowledgment. Parts of this article are adapted, with the permission of Pi Lamda Theta, from: Banks, J. A. (1991). Multicultural literacy and curriculum reform. *Educational Horizons,* 69 (3), pp. 135–140.

Notes

Chapter 1

1. In New Zealand, Alton-Lee (2003) has synthesized research that connects teaching with student-learning outcomes in order to use the best evidence available showing quality teaching for diverse students. Her synthesis supports practices recommended in the literature cited here.

Chapter 2

1. This project is funded by the William and Flora Hewlett Foundation and focuses on four successful districts located in Texas, North Carolina, and Ohio that serve large populations of racially and economically diverse students. Education production functions utilizing state demographic data, U.S. census data, and student performance data in each of the three states were used to select study sites. Field research in the districts is ongoing. Research team members include the three authors of this chapter, Gary Sykes and Susan Printy of Michigan State University, Charles Thompson of East Carolina University, and Darleen Opfer of Cambridge University.

Chapter 3

1. The research that is summarized in the APA *Principles* derives from many fields, including psychology, education, sociology, and brain research. Research documentation can be found in Alexander & Murphy (1998); Combs, Miser, & Whitaker (1999); Kanfer & McCombs (2000); Lambert & McCombs (1998); McCombs (2000, 2001, 2004); McCombs & Miller (2006); McCombs & Whisler (1997); and Perry and Weinstein (1999). Copies of the *Principles* may be downloaded from education@apa.org.

2. Michael Beyerlein & Susan Beyerlein, University of North Texas; Jill Nemiro, Cal Poly Pomona; Marty Bink & Ann Rinn, Western Kentucky University; Barbara McCombs, University of Denver.

Chapter 4

This chapter is based on a more extensive discussion of Benjamin Franklin High

School in Banks, CAM. (2005). *Improving Multicultural Education: Lessons From the Intergroup Education Movement.* New York: Teachers College Press.

1. For more information on how to structure intergroup contacts see Allport's (1954) original work on the Contact Hypothesis, Pettigrew's (1998) expansion of Allport's work, and Stephan's (1999) discussion that and other related work.

2. Columbus Day was an important holiday for Italian Americans in East Harlem. It was a day when the entire city celebrated and recognized a person of Italian descent. It is important to note, however, that Columbus Day is not a time of celebration for many Native Americans. It is a day that reminds many of them of pain, loss, and a lack of recognition of their historic presence in this land. Teachers can use the Columbus Day incident at BFHS to help students think deeply about how cultural icons and celebrations can have different meaning to different groups, how a group's marginal status does not necessarily result in solidarity with other marginal groups, and why it is important to ask questions about who benefits and who loses even when it appears, as in the Columbus Day celebration, that everyone is a winner.

Chapter 5

1. The Interstate New Teacher Assessment and Support Consortium (INTASC) is a consortium of more than 30 states that has developed standards and performance assessments for beginning teacher licensing.

2. This section draws from Elmore and Burney (1999).

3. This section draws from Snyder (1999).

Chapter 6

1. For states that did not have a reading or mathematics assessment at Grade 4 or 8, Olson reported the percentage of students proficient or above for the closest grade in that subject.

Chapter 8

1. In common with current conventions in the United Kingdom, I use the word "Black" as a collective term for people who self-identify as of Black Caribbean, Black African and/or other Black ethnic origins, including Black British. Although flawed in numerous respects, this usage does at least correspond to the terms used most frequently by the people so labelled (see Mason, 2000).

2. The Office for Standards in Education (Ofsted) is the official body that inspects schools in England. Ofsted publishes reports on individual schools and local districts and offers advice and comment on the state of the system nationally. One of Ofsted's core functions is to make judgments on the "value for money" of the services they inspect (Case, Case, & Catling, 2000).

3. The annually published data are frequently retabulated by national newspapers and given headlines that describe them as a guide to the top schools, those with the highest failure rate and bottom of the league (Gillborn & Youdell, 2000).

4. An official survey, for the Qualifications & Curriculum Authority (QCA), found that 10- and 11-year-olds were spending 49% of their classroom time on just two subjects (English and maths). Coincidentally, it is these subjects that provide the basis for the national tests upon which primary schools are judged (Mansell & Clark, 2003).

5. The best guide to students' performance over this time period is the Youth Cohort Study (YCS), a survey of school-leavers' achievements and experiences that has been conducted at least every 2 years since the late 1980s. The YCS has the advantage of using large, nationally representative samples but it is far from perfect: Subsamples can become quite small, especially when trying to simultaneously examine several elements (such as gender, race, and socioeconomic background). Nevertheless, it does offer a unique snapshot of how certain minoritized groups have performed over time.

6. See, for example, the reviews offered by Hallam (2002) and Wiliam & Bartholomew (2001).

Chapter 9

1. This chapter is based on research that appeared in *New Politics*, Winter 2005, Volume 10, 2. Online: http://www.wpunj.edu/~newpol/issue38/Weiner38.htm.

Chapter 10

1. There has been a variety of statistical attempts to produce value-added league tables, which take into account prior attainment, but parents continue to study league tables of raw scores which demonstrate the social class of the area more than anything else.

2. By 2003 almost a thousand schools had developed a specialism after raising sponsorship money. A majority specialized in technology, arts, languages, and sport, with fewer specialising in business and enterprise, science, maths, computing, and engineering. By 2004 Music and humanities were added to the list. By 2006 two thirds of English secondary schools had a specialism of some kind.

3. In a court case in 2004 a member of the royal household produced a hand-written note from the Prince of Wales reading: "What is wrong with people now, Why do they think they are qualified to do things beyond their capabilities? This is all to do with the learning culture in schools. It is the consequence of a child-centred education system which tells people they can become pop stars, high court judges, TV presenters or competent heads of state without putting in the necessary work or having the natural ability." A number of commentators pointed out that the Prince had not had to pass exams to achieve his position (see Smithers & Yafai, 2004).

4. The Oratory School in London, attended by Prime Minister Blair's children, famously announced that it had "had regard," to the Code of Practice, that is, it had looked at the Code, and had decided to ignore it. The decision was upheld by the Secretary of State for education (Millar, 2004).

References

Abbas, T. (2004). *The education of British South Asians*. Basingstoke: Palgrave/
MacMillan.

Abrams, L. (2004). *Teachers' views on high-stakes testing: Implications for the
classroom*. Tempe: Educational Policy Studies Laboratory, Arizona State
University.

Achinstein, B., & Ogawa, R. T. (2006). (In)fidelity: What the resistance of new
teachers reveals about professional principles and prescriptive educational
policies. *Harvard Educational Review 67*(1), 30–63.

Ainley, P. (2004). The new market-state and education. *Journal of Education
Policy*19(4), 497–514.

Alexander, P.A., & Murphy, P. K. (1998). The research base for APA's learner-
centered psychological principles. In N. Lambert & B.L. McCombs (Eds.),
How students learn: Reforming schools through learner-centered education
(pp. 35–60). Washington, DC: American Psychological Association.

Allington, R. L., & McGill-Franzen, A. (1992). Unintended effects of educational
reform in New York. *Educational Policy 6*(4), 397–414.

Allport, G. W. (1954). *The nature of prejudice*. Cambridge, MA: Addison-Wesley.

Allport, G.W. (1966). *ABCs of scapegoating* (5th ed.). New York: Anti-Defamation
League of B'nai B'rith.

Alton-Lee, A. (2003). *Quality teaching for diverse students in schooling: Best
evidence synthesis*. Wellington, New Zealand: Ministry of Education.

American Psychological Association Work Group of the Board of Educational Affairs
(1997, November). *Learner-centered psychological principles: A framework
for school reform and redesign*. Washington, DC: Author.

Amrein, A. L. & Berliner, D. C. (2002). High-stakes testing, uncertainty, and student
learning. *Education Policy Analysis Archives*, 10(18). Retrieved February 14,
2003 from http://epaa.asu.edu/epaa/v10n18/

Amrein, A. L., & Berliner, D. C. (2003). The effects of high-stakes testing on student
motivation and learning. *Educational Leadership, 60*(5), 32–38.

Ansley, F.L. (1997). White supremacy (and what we should do about it). In R.
Delgado & J. Stefancic (Eds.), *Critical white studies: Looking behind the
mirror* (pp. 592–595). Philadelphia: Temple University Press.

Anyon, J. (1997). *Ghetto schooling*. New York: Teachers College Press.

Anyon, J. (2005a). What "counts" as educational policy? Notes toward a new
paradigm. *Harvard Educational Review,75*(1), 65–88.

Anyon, J. (2005b). *Radical possibilities: Public policy, urban education, and a new social movement*. New York: Routledge.

Apple, M.W. (1998). Foreword. In J.L. Kincheloe, S.R. Steinberg, N.M. Rodriguez & R.E. Chennault (Eds.) *White reign: Deploying whiteness in America* (pp. ix–xiii). New York: St Martin's Press.

Applewhite, A., Evans, W. R. III, & Frothingham, A. (1992). *And I quote*. New York: St. Martin's Press.

Archer, L., & Francis, B. (2005a). "They never go off the rails like other ethnic groups": Teachers' constructions of British Chinese pupils' gender identities and approaches to learning, *British Journal of Sociology of Education*, 26(2), 165–182.

Archer, L., & Francis, B. (2005b). Constructions of racism by British Chinese pupils and parents, *Race Ethnicity and Education*, 8(4), 387–407.

Asthana, A. (2006a, March 12). Children of New Labour put schools to the test. *The Observer*.

Asthana, A. (2006b, March 3). Exams cut by third as stress on pupil's soars. *The Observer*.

Au, W. (2004). No child left untested: The NCLB zone. *Rethinking schools*. Accessed at August 4, 2006 http://www.rethinkingschools.org/special_reports/bushplan/nclb191.shtml

Ayers, W. (2004). *Teaching toward freedom: Moral commitment and ethical action in the classroom*. Boston: Beacon Press.

Babbidge, T. (2006, February 10). Anti-CSAP group argues its case. *Rocky Mountain News*, 44A.

Baenen, N. (1988, April). A perspective after five years: Has grade retention passed or failed? Paper presented at the Annual Meeting of the American Educational Research Association, New Orleans, LA.

Baker, C. (2001). *Foundations of bilingual education and bilingualism* (3rd ed.). Buffalo: Multilingual Matters, Ltd.

Baldwin, J. (1985). A talk to teachers. In *The price of the ticket: Collected nonfiction 1948–1985* (pp. 325–332). New York: St. Martin's.

Bandura, A. (1982). Self-efficacy mechanism in human agency. *American Psychologist*, 37(2), 122–147.

Banks, C.A.M. (2005). *Improving multicultural education: Lessons from the intergroup education movement*. New York: Teachers College Press.

Banks, J. A. (1997). *Educating citizens in a multicultural society*. New York: Teachers College Press.

Banks, J. A. (2003). *Teaching strategies for ethnic studies* (7th ed.). Boston: Allyn and Bacon.

Banks, J. A. (2004a). Introduction: Democratic citizenship in multicultural societies. In J. A. Banks (Ed.), *Diversity and citizenship education* (pp. 1–16). San Francisco: Jossey-Bass.

Banks, J. A. (2004b). Multicultural education: Historical development, dimensions, and practice. In J. A. Banks & C. A. M. Banks (Eds.), *Handbook of research on multicultural education* (2nd ed., pp. 3–29). San Francisco: Jossey Bass.

Banks, J. A. (2006). *Race, culture, and education: The selected works of James A. Banks*. London & New York: Routledge.

Banks, J. A., & Banks, C. A. M. (Eds.) (2004). *Handbook of research on multicultural education* (2nd ed.). San Francisco: Jossey Bass.

Banks, J. A., Banks, C. A. M., Cortes, C. E., Merryfield, M. M., Moodley, K. A., Murphy-Shigematsu, S., Osler, A., Park, C., & Parker, W. C. (2005). *Democracy and diversity: Principles and concepts for educating citizens in a global age.* Seattle: University of Washington, Center for Multicultural Education.

Baron, J. B. (1999). *Exploring high and improving reading achievement in Connecticut.* Washington: National Educational Goals Panel.

Bartlett, L., Frederick, M., Gulbrandsen, T., & Murillo, E. (2002). The marketization of education: Public schools for private ends. *Anthropology and Education Quarterly, 33*(1), 5–29.

Bartolomé, L. I., & Trueba, E. T. (2000). Beyond the politics of schools and the rhetoric of fashionable pedagogies: The significance of teacher ideology. In H. T. Trueba & L. I. Bartolomé (Eds.), *Immigrant voices* (pp. 277–292). Lanham, MD: Rowman & Littlefield.

Barton, P. E. (2006). The dropout problem: Losing ground. *Educational Leadership, 63*(5), 14–18.

Bastian, A., Fruchter, N., Gittell, M., Greer, C., & Haskins, K. (1986). *Choosing equality. The case for democratic schooling.* Philadelphia: Temple University Press.

Bell, D. (1992). *Faces at the bottom of the well: The permanence of racism.* New York: Basic Books.

Benedict, R. (1947). *Race: Science and politics* (Rev. edition with *The races of mankind.* by R. Benedict & G. Weltfish). New York: Viking (Original work published 1940)

Benedict, R., & Wetfish, G. (1943). The races of mankind. *Public Affairs Pamphlet No. 85.* New York: Public Affairs Committee.

Benn, T. (1994). *Year of hope: Diaries, papers, letters 1942–1960.* London: Arrow Books.

Benninga, J. S., Berkowitz, M. W., Kuehn, P., & Smith, K. (2006). Character and academics: What good schools do. *Phi Delta Kappan, 87*(6), 448–452.

Berliner, D. C. (2006). Our impoverished view of educational reform. *Teachers College Record, 108*(6), 949–995.

Berne, R. (1995). Educational input and outcome inequities in New York State. In R. Berne & L. O. Picus (Eds.), *Outcome equity in education* (pp. 191–223). Thousand Oaks, CA: Corwin Press.

Bhatti, G. (2004). Good, bad and normal teachers: The experiences of South Asian children. In G. Ladson-Billings & D. Gillborn (Eds.), *The RoutledgeFalmer reader in multicultural education.* New York: RoutledgeFalmer.

Bigelow, B., & Peterson, B., Eds. (2002). *Rethinking globalization.* Milwaukee, WI: Rethinking Schools Press.

Black, D. E. (February 6, 2006). Newton Parents urges school accountability. *TownOnLine.* Retrieved February 13, 2006 at http://www2.townonline.com

Blair, M. (2001). *Why pick on me? School exclusion and black youth.* Stoke-on-Trent: Trentham.

Blair, T. (1999, October 8). Speech to labour party conference. Bournemouth. England.

Bleifeld, M. (1939). A biology unit dealing with racial attitudes. *The American*

Biology Teacher, 2(1), 7–9.

Bleifeld, M., Goldstein, H., Nestler, H.A., Robinson, R., Rock, J.G., Sygoda, D., Weinberg, S., & Nagler, H. (1939). Outline of a teaching unit on mankind. *The Teaching Biologist,* 27–44.

Bloom, A.C. (1989). *The closing of the American mind.* New York: Simon & Shuster.

Boaler, J. (2006). Promoting respectful learning. *Educational Leadership, 63*(5), 74–78.

Boas, F. (1910). The real racial problem. *The Crisis,* 1 (2), 22–25.

Bobbitt, P. (2002). *The shield of Achilles: War peace and the course of history.* London and New York: Penguin Books.

Borman, G. D. (2002/2003). How can Title I improve achievement? *Educational Leadership 60* (4), 49–53.

Borman, G. D., & Overman, L. T. (2004). Academic resilience in mathematics among poor and minority students. *Elementary School Journal, 104,* 177–195.

Boykin, A.W. (2000). The talent development model of schooling: Placing students at promise for academic success. *Journal of Education for Students Placed At Risk,* 5(1&2), 3–25.

Brandt, R. S. (1998). *Powerful learning.* Arlington, VA: Association for Supervision and Curriculum Development.

Bransford, J. D., Brown, A. L., & Cocking, R. R. (Eds.). (1999). *How people learn: Brain, mind, experience, and school.* Washington, DC: National Academy Press.

Braswell, J. S., Lutkus, A. D., Grigg, W. S., Santapau, S. L., Tay-Lim, B.S.-H., & Johnson, M. S. (2001). *The nation's report card: Mathematics 2000.* Washington, DC: National Center for Education Statistics.

Broder, D. S. (2002, 7 April). Education reform controversy lingers. *Washington Post.* Accessed at http://www.washingtonpost.com/wp-dyn/articles/A7345-2002Apr6.html.

Brown, C. (2006, March 24). Contractor who lent Labour £1 million quits over sleaze fears. *The Independent.*

Brown, P., & Lauder H. (2006). Globalization, knowledge, and the myth of the magnet economy. *Globalization, Societies and Education, 4* (1), 25–57.

Bush, G.W. (2003). Transcript of a speech celebrating the first anniversary of No Child Left Behind. Accessed January 23, 2006 at www.whitehouse.gov/news/releases/2003/01/20030108-4.html

Bush, M.E.L. (2004). Race, ethnicity and whiteness. *Sage Race Relations Abstracts,* 29(3–4), 5–48.

Cacioppo, J. T., Hawkley, L. C., Rickett, E. M., & Masi, C. M. (2005). Sociality, spirituality, and meaning making: Chicago health, aging, and social relations study. *Review of General Psychology, 9*(2), 143–155.

Carmichael, S., & Hamilton, C.V. (1967). *Black power: The politics of liberation in America.* London: Penguin.

Carnegie Council on Adolescent Development. (1989). *Turning points: Preparing American youth for the 21st century.* Washington, DC: Task Force on Education of Young Adolescents.

Case, P., Case, S., & Catling, S. (2000). Please show you're working: A critical assessment of the impact of OFSTED inspection on primary teachers, *British Journal of Sociology of Education*, 21(4), 605–621.

Cashmore, E., & Jennings, J. (Eds.)(2001). *Racism: Essential readings.* London: Sage Publications.

Centre for Public Services (CPS). (2003). *Mortgaging our children's future.* Sheffield: Author.

Chubb, J. & Moe, T. (1990). *Politics, markets and American schools.* Washington DC: Brookings Institution.

Coalition of Self-Learning. (2003). Life-long learning. *Learning Cooperatives Quarterly,* 2(1), 1–2. Available at http://www.creatinglearningcommunities. org/resources/lifelonglearning.htm

Cochran-Smith, M. (2004). Stayers, leavers, lovers, and dreamers: Insights about teacher retention. *Journal of Teacher Education* 55(5), 387–392.

Coleman, J. (1966). *Equality of educational opportunity.* Washington, DC: US Government Printing Office.

Combs, A. W. (1986). What makes a good helper? A person-centered approach. *Person-Centered Review,* 1(1), 51–61.

Combs, A. W. (1991). *The schools we need: New assumptions for educational reform.* Lanham, MD: University Press of America, Inc.

Combs, A. W., Miser, A. B., & Whitaker, K. S. (1999). *On becoming a school leader: A person-centered challenge.* Alexandria, VA: Association for Supervision and Curriculum Development.

Commission for Racial Equality. (1992). *Set to fail? Setting and banding in secondary schools.* London: Commission for Racial Equality.

Conley, D. (1999). *Being black-living in the red: Race, wealth and social policy.* Berkeley, CA: University of California Press.

Connecticut State Department of Education. (1990). Impact of Education Enhancement Act. *Research Bulletin,* 1.

Connolly, P. (1998). *Racism, gender identities and young children: Social relations in a multi-ethnic, inner-city primary school.* London: Routledge.

Conservative Party. (2006, September 1). Cameron demands setting in all schools. Press Release. London: Conservative Party

Corbett, D., Wilson, B., & Williams, B. (2005). No choice but success. *Educational Leadership,* 62(6), 8–12.

Council of Great City Schools (2005). *Beating the odds.* Washington, DC: Author.

Covello Archives (1943). BFHS Papers. Unpublished materials. (MSS 40, Covello 60/13).

Covello, L. (1936). A high school and its immigrant community: A challenge and an opportunity. *Journal of Educational Sociology* 9(2), 331–346.

Covello, L. (1939a). Language as a factor in integration and assimilation. *The Modern Language Journal,* 23(5), 323–333.

Covello, L. (1939b). Paper presented at Intercultural conference. New York City.

Covello, L. (1942). *Report on Benjamin Franklin High School.* Unpublished report. (MSS 40, Covello 34/11)

Covello, L. (1945). Letter to BFHS parents. Unpublished material. (MSS 40, Covello 54/8)

Covello, L., & D'Agostino, G. (1958). *The heart is the teacher.* New York:

McGraw-Hill.

Covington, M. V., & Teel, K. M. (1996). *Overcoming student failure: Changing motives and incentives for learning*. Washington, DC: American Psychological Association.

Csikszentmihalyi, M. (1996). *Creativity*. New York: Harper Collins.

C-Span (Sponsor). (2001). *U.S. Senate debate on NCLB*. Video and transcript available upon request. Washington, DC.

CTB/McGraw-Hill. (2001). *Kentucky standard setting technical report*. Monterey, CA: Author.

Darling-Hammond, L. (1989). Accountability for professional practice. *Teachers College Record, 91*(1), 59–80.

Darling-Hammond, L. (1991). The implications of testing policy for quality and equality. *Phi Delta Kappan*, 220–225.

Darling-Hammond, L. (1992). Educational indicators and enlightened policy. *Educational Policy, 6* (3), 235–265.

Darling-Hammond, L. (1997). *The right to learn: A blueprint for creating schools that work*. San Francisco: Jossey-Bass.

Darling-Hammond, L. (2000). Teacher quality and student achievement. *Educational Policy Analysis Archive, 8* (1), Retrieved March 20, 2004, from http://epaa.asu.edu/epaa/v8n1.

Darling-Hammond, L. (2002). Research and rhetoric on teacher certification: A response to "Teacher Certification Reconsidered." *Education Policy Analysis Archives, 10*(36). Retrieved June 1, 2004 from http://epaa.asu.edu/epaa/v10n36.html

Darling-Hammond, L., Ancess, J., & Falk, B. (1995). *Authentic assessment in action*. New York: Teachers College Press.

Darling-Hammond, L., Holtzman, D. J., Gatlin, S. J., & Heilig, J. V. (2005, 12 October). Does teacher preparation matter? Evidence about teacher certification, Teach for America, and teacher effectiveness. *Education Policy Analysis Archives, 13*(42). Accessed at http://epaa.asu.edu/epaa/v13n42/

Darling-Hammond, L., & Ifill-Lynch, O. (2006). If they'd only do their work! *Educational Leadership, 63*(5), 8–13.

Davis, H. A. (2005). Exploring the contexts of relationship quality between middle school students and teachers. *Elementary School Journal*.

Deakin Crick, R., & McCombs, B. L. (in press). The assessment of learner-centered practices surveys (ALCPs): An English case study. Submitted to the *Research and Evaluation Journal*.

DeBray, E., Parson, G. & Avila, S. (2003). Internal alignment and external pressure: High school responses in four state contexts. In M.Carnoy, R. Elmore, & L. S. Siskin (Eds.), *The new accountability: High schools and high-stakes testing*. New York, NY: Taylor and Francis Books, Inc.

Delgado Bernal, D. (2002). Critical race theory, LatCrit theory, and critical raced-gendered epistemologies: Recognizing students of color as holders and creators of knowledge. *Qualitative Inquiry, (8) 1*, 105–126.

Delgado, R. (2003). Crossroads and blind alleys: A critical examination of recent writing about race. *Texas Law Review, 82*, 121–152.

Delgado, R. & Stefancic, J. (Eds.)(2000). *Critical race theory: The cutting edge* (2nd ed.). Philadelphia: Temple University Press.

Department for Education & Employment (1997). *Excellence in schools.* Cm 3681. London: Author.

Department for Education & Employment. (1999). *Excellence in cities.* London: Author.

Department for Education & Skills. (2001). *Schools: Achieving success.* Cmd5230 London: The Stationary Office.

Department for Education & Skills. (2002). *Statistics of education: Permanent exclusions from maintained schools in England.* London: Author.

Department for Education & Skills. (2004). *Five-year strategy for children and learners.* Cm 6272. London: Author.

Department for Education & Skills (DfES)(2005a). *Youth cohort study: The activities and experiences of 16 year olds: England and Wales 2004.* London: Author.

Department for Education & Skills (DfES)(2005b). *Higher standards, better schools for all: More choice for parents and pupils.* Cm 6677. London: Author..

Department for Education & Skills (DfES)(2005c). *Ethnicity and education: The evidence on minority ethnic pupils.* London: Author..

Department for Education & Skills (DfES)(2005d). *Minority ethnic pupils make further progress at GCSE.* London: Author..

Department for Education & Skills (DfES) (2006a). *Trust school prospectus.* London: Author..

Department for Education & Skills (DfES) (2006b). *14–19 Education and skills implementation plan.* London: Author.

Deschenes, S., Cuban, L., & Tyack, D. (2001). Mismatch: Historical perspectives on schools and students who don't fit them. *Teachers College Record, 103* (4), 525–547.

Desimone, L. M., Smith, T. M., & Ueno, K. (2006). Are teachers who need sustained, content-focused professional development getting it? An administrator's dilemma. *Educational Administration Quarterly, 42*(2), 179–215.

Devarajan, S., & Reinikka, R. (2002). *2004 WDR - Initial ideas about motivation and framework from the director & co-director of the WDR.* Making services work for poor people, 25 July 2002. http://siteresources.worldbank.org/ INTWDR2004/Resources/17976-ReinikkaShantaInitialFramework.pdf

DeVise, D. (1999, Nov. 5). A+ plan prompts teacher exodus in Broward county. *Miami Herald.*

Dewey, J. (1938). *Experience and education.* New York: Macmillan.

Dewey, J. (1944). *Democracy and education.* New York: The Free Press.

Diamond, J. B., & Spillane, J. (2004). High-stakes accountability in urban elementary schools: Challenging or reproducing inequity? *Teachers College Record, 106*(6), 1145–1176.

Diamond, L. (2005, July 28). Testing law baffles parents. *The Atlanta Journal Constitution.*

Dillon, S. (2006, August 27). In schools across U. S., the melting pot overflows. *The New York Times,* vol. CLV [155] (no. 53,684), pp. A7 & 16.

Divide and conquer. (1942). Washington, DC: U.S. Government Printing Office.

Dixson, A.D. & Rousseau, C. K. (2005). And we are still not saved: Critical race theory in education ten years later. *Race ethnicity and education, 8* (1), 7–28.

Doane, A.W., & Bonilla-Silva, E. (Eds.)(2003). *White out: The continuing significance of racism*. New York: Routledge.

Donovan, M S., Bransford, J. D., Pellegrino, J. W. (Eds.). (1999). *How people learn: Bridging research and practice*. Washington, DC: National Academy of Sciences - National Research Council, Department of Education.

DuBois, R.D. (1937). Intercultural education at Benjamin Franklin High School. *High Points* 19.

DuBois, R.D. (1939). *Adventures in intercultural education: A manual for secondary school teachers*. New York: Intercultural Education Workshop.

DuBois W. E. B. (1935/1962). *Black reconstruction in America 1860–1880*. New York: Atheneum. (Original work published 1935)

DuBois, R.D., & Okorodudu, C. (1984). *All this and something more: Pioneering in intercultural education*. Bryn Mawr, Pennsylvania: Dorrance & Company.

Dweck, C. S. (1999). *Self-theories: Their role in motivation, personality and development*. Philadelphia: Taylor and Francis/Psychology Press.

Eads, G. (1990). *Kindergarten retention and alternative kindergarten programs: Report to the Virginia Board of Education*. Richmond, VA, Virginia State Department of Education. (Eric Document Reproduction Service No. ED 320).

EALRs. (2006). *Essential academic learning requirements and grade level expectations*. Washington State Standards. Retrieved October 14, 2006 from http://www.k12.wa.us/CurriculumInstruct/EALR_GLE.aspx

Educate America Inc. (1991). *An idea whose time has come: A national achievement test for high school seniors*. Morristown, NJ: Author.

Education International. (2005, May–July). GATS, Paris, Geneva and you. *TradEducation News* (5). Accessed at http://www.ei-ie.org/en/news/20050603.htm.

Edwards, T., & Tomlinson, S. (2002). *Selection isn't working: Diversity, standards and inequality in secondary education*. London: Central Books.

Edwards, T., & Tomlinson, S. (2006). Selection, diversity and inequality in secondary schools. In Hewlett, M., Pring, R., & Tulloch, M. (Eds.). *Comprehensive education: Evolution, achievements and new directions*. Northampton: The University of Northampton.

Eisner, E. (2005). Back to whole. *Educational Leadership, 63*(1), 14–18.

Elmore, R., & Burney, D. (1999). Investing in teacher learning: Staff development and instructional improvement. In L. Darling-Hammond & G. Sykes (Eds.), *Teaching as the learning profession* (pp. 263–291). San Francisco: Jossey-Bass.

Fantini, M. D. (1986). *Regaining excellence in education*. Columbus, OH: Merrill.

Feistritzer, C. E. (1993). *Report card on American education: A state-by-state analysis, 1972–73 to 1992–93*. Washington, DC: National Center on Education Information.

Ferguson, R. F. (1991). Paying for public education: New evidence on how and why money matters. *Harvard Journal on Legislation, 28*, 465–498.

Fielding, M. (2001). Students as radical agents of change. *Journal of Educational Change, 2*(3), 123–141.

Fielding, M. (2002, April). *Beyond the rhetoric of student voice: New departures or new constraints in the transformation of 21st century schooling?* Paper presented at the annual meeting of the American Educational Research Association, New Orleans.

Figlio, D. N., & Getzler, L. S. (2002). *Accountability, ability, and disability: Gaming the system?* Cambridge, MA: National Bureau of Economic Research.

Figueroa, P. (1991). *Education and the social construction of "race."* London: Routledge.

Figueroa, P. (2004). Multicultural education in the United Kingdom: Historical development and current status. In J.A. Banks & C.A.M. Banks (Eds.) *Handbook of research on multicultural education* (2nd ed., pp. 997–1026). San Francisco: Jossey-Bass.

Fisk, C. W. (1999). *The emergence of bureaucratic entrepreneurship in a state education agency: A case study of Connecticut's education reform initiatives.* Unpublished dissertation, University of Massachusetts- Amherst.

The footprints of the Trojan horse: Methods used by foreign agents within the U.S. (1940). Washington, DC: U.S. Government Printing Office.

Forbes, S. (1999). *Holistic education: An analysis of its intellectual precedents and nature.* Unpublished dissertation, Green College, University of Oxford, Oxford, UK.

Franklin, B. M. (1994). *From "backwardness" to "at-risk." Childhood learning difficulties and the contradictions of school reform.* Albany: SUNY Press.

Franklin, J. H. (1985). *George Washington Williams: A biography.* Chicago: The University of Chicago Press.

Freire, P. (1998). *Pedagogy of freedom, ethics, democracy, and civic courage.* Lanham, MD: Rowman & Littlefield.

Friedman, T. L. (2005). *The world is flat.* New York: Farrar, Strauss and Giroux.

Fuhrman, S., & Lazerson, M. (Eds.) (2005). *The public schools.* New York: Oxford University Press.

Fuller E. J., & Johnson, J. F., Jr. (2001). Can state accountability systems drive improvements in school performance for children of color and children from low-income homes? *Education and Urban Society* 33(3), 260–283.

Futernick, K. (2001). *A district-by-district analysis of the distribution of teachers in California and an overview of the teacher qualification index.* Sacramento: California State University, Sacramento.

Gampert, R., & Opperman, P. (1988, April). Longitudinal study of the 1982–83 "Promotional Gates Students." Paper presented at the annual meeting of the American Educational Research Association, New Orleans.

Gándara, P., Rumberger, R., Maxwell-Jolly, J., & Callahan, R. (2003). English Learners in California Schools: Unequal resources, unequal outcomes. *Education Policy Analysis Archives*, 11(36). Accessed October 8, 2003 from http://epaa.asu.edu/epaa/v11n36/

Gardiner, J. (1997, Nov. 14). Blunkett to continue shaming. *Times Educational Supplement.*

Gay, G. (2000). *Culturally responsive teaching.* New York: Teachers College Press.

Gill, C., Parker, L., Cain, L. & Lynn, M. (2006, April). Critical race reflections on racial desegregation and the public interest: Forgotten perspectives and new challenges. Paper presented at the annual meeting of the American Educational

Research Association, San Francisco, CA.

Gillborn, D. (1990). *"Race," ethnicity and education: Teaching and learning in multi-ethnic schools.* London: Unwin Hyman.

Gillborn, D. (1998). Racism, selection, poverty and parents: New Labour, old problems? *Journal of Education Policy, 13*(6), 717–735.

Gillborn, D. (2001). Racism, policy and the (mis)education of Black children. In R. Majors (Ed.), *Educating our black children: New directions and radical approaches* (pp. 13–27). London: RoutledgeFalmer.

Gillborn, D., & Gipps, C. (1996). *Recent research on the achievements of ethnic minority pupils.* Report for the Office for Standards in Education. London: HMSO.

Gillborn, D., & Youdell, D. (2000). *Rationing education: Policy, practice, reform and equity.* Buckingham: Open University Press.

Giroux, H. A. (1988). *Teachers as intellectuals: Toward a critical pedagogy of learning.* Granby, MA:

Glaser, R. (1963). Instructional technology and the measurement of learning outcomes. *American Psychologist, 18,* 519–521.

Glaser, R., & Klaus, D. J. (1962). Proficiency measurement: Assessing human performance. In R. Gagne (Ed.), *Psychological principles in systems development.* New York: Holt, Rinehart & Winston.

Glaser, R., & Nitko, A. J. (1971). Measurement in learning and instruction. In R. L. Thorndike (Ed.), *Educational measurement* (2nd ed.). Washington, D.C.: American Council on Education.

Glass, G. V. (1978). Standards and criteria. *Journal of Educational Measurement, 15* (4), 237–261.

Glasser, W. (1990). *The quality school: Managing students without coercion.* New York: Harper.

Goals 2000: Educate America Act of 1994, Public Law 103–227.

Goldstein, A. (2004, 24 February). Paige calls NEA a "terrorist" group; Teachers union and Democrats are irate. *Washington Post,* sec. A, p. 19.

Goldthorpe, J. (1997). Problems of meritocracy. In Halsey, A. H., Lauder, H., Brown, P., & Wells, A. S. (Eds.), *Education, culture, economy, and society.* Oxford: Oxford University Press.

Gordon, S. P., & Reese, M. (1997 July). High stakes testing. Worth the price? *Journal of School Leadership, 7,* 345–368.

Gotbaum, B. (2002). *Pushing out at risk students: An analysis of high school discharge figures.* New York: Public School Advocate for the City of New York and Advocates for Children.

Gottfredson, G., & Daiger, D. (1979). *Disruption in 600 schools.* Baltimore: Center for Social Organization of Schools, Johns Hopkins University.

Gould, S. J. (1996). *The mismeasure of man* (Revised & expanded). New York: Norton.

Green, D. R., Trimble, C. S., & Lewis, D. M. (2003). Interpreting the results of three different standard-setting procedures. *Educational Measurement: Issues and Practice, 22* (1), 22–32.

Gresson, A. D. (2004). *America's atonement: Racial pain, recovery rhetoric, and the pedagogy of healing.* New York: Peter Lang.

Guisbond, L., & Neill, M. (2004). Failing our children. No Child Left Behind undermines quality and equity in education. *The Clearing House 78* (1), 12–16.

Gurin, P., & Nagda, B. R. A. (2006). Getting to the what, how, and why of diversity on campus. *Educational Researcher, 35*(1), 20–24.

Gutiérrez, K., Asato, J., Santos, M., & Gotanda, N. (2001). Backlash pedagogy: Language and culture and the politics of reform. In M. Suarez-Orozco (Ed.), *Latinos in the 21st century.* Berkeley: University of California Press.

Haberman, M. (1988). Proposals for recruiting minority teachers: Promising practices and attractive detours. *Journal of Teacher Education* 33(4), 38–44.

Haberman, M. (1991). Pedagogy of poverty versus good teaching. *Phi Delta Kappan,* 73, 290–294.

Hallam, S. (2002). *Ability grouping in schools.* Perspectives on Education Policy, number 13. London: Institute of Education, University of London.

Hallam, S., & Toutounji, I. (1996). *What do we know about the grouping of pupils by ability? A research review.* London: University of London Institute of Education.

Hambleton, R. K. (1980). Test score validity and standard setting methods. In R. A. Berk (Ed.), *Criterion-reference measurement: The state of the art* (pp. 80–123). Baltimore, MD: Johns Hopkins University Press.

Hambleton, R. K., & Rogers, J. H. (1991). Advances in criterion-referenced measurement. In R. K. Hambleton & J. N. Zall (Eds.), *Advances in educational and psychological testing* (pp. 3–44). Boston: Kluwer Academic.

Haney,W. (2000). The myth of the Texas miracle in education. *Education Policy Analysis Archives,* 8(41), Retrieved March 20, 2004, from http://epaa.asu.edu/epaa/v8n41/

Hargreaves, D. H. (2004). *Learning for life: The foundations for lifelong learning.* Bristol, UK: The Policy Press.

Harper, D. (2002, March). *Generation www.Y White Paper 2.* Olympia, WA: Generation Y Organization.

Harris, C. I. (1993). Whiteness as property. *Harvard Law Review,* 106, 1707–1791.

Hartocollis, A. (1999, September 2). Most assigned to summer school will not be promoted. *New York Times.*

Hauser, R.M. (1999). Should we end social promotion? Truth and consequences. CDE Working Papers, Center for Demography and Ecology at the University of Wisconsin–Madison. Available: http://www.ssc.wisc.edu/cde/cdewp/99-06.pdf

Hay McBer, (2000, June). *Research into teacher effectiveness.* Report to the U.K. Department for Education and Employment. London: Author.

Haycock, K. (2001). Closing the achievement gap. *Educational Leadership* 58 (6), 6–11.

Hayward, G. (2004). Foreword: A century of vocationalism. *Oxford Review of Education* 30(1), 3–12.

Henriques, J. (1984), Social psychology and the politics of racism. In J. Henriques, W. Holloway, C. Urwin, C. Venn, & V. Walkerdine (Eds.), *Changing the subject: psychology, social regulation and subjectivity.* London: Methuen.

Hess, A. (1986). Educational triage in an urban school setting. *Metropolitan Education, 2,* 39–52.

Hess, F. M. (2004). Inclusive ambiguity: Multicultural conflict in an era of accountability. *Educational Policy 18* (1), 95–115.

Hess, F. M. (2006). *Tough love for schools.* Washington, D.C.: American Enterprise Institute for Public Policy Research.

Hess, G. A., Ells, E., Prindle, C., Liffman, P., & Kaplan, B. (1987). Where's room 185? How schools can reduce their dropout problem. *Education and Urban Society, 19*(3), 330–355.

Heubert, J. P., & Hauser, R. M. (Eds.). (1999). *High stakes: Testing for tracking, promotion, and graduation.* Washington, DC: National Academy Press.

Hill, H. C., Rowan, B., & Loewenberg Ball, D. (2005). Effects of teachers' mathematical knowledge for teaching on student achievement. *American Educational Research Journal, 42*(2), 371–406.

Hirsch, E.D., Jr. (1996). *The schools we need and why we don't have them.* New York: Doubleday.

Hoffman, J. V., Assaf, L., & Paris, S. G. (2001). High stakes testing in reading: Today in Texas, tomorrow? *The Reading Teacher 54*(5), 482–492.

Hogan, D. (1996, Fall). 'To better our condition': Educational credentialing and 'the silent compulsion of economic relations' in the United States, 1830 to the present. *History of Education Quarterly, 36,* 243–270.

Holland, P. (2002). Measuring progress in student achievement: Changes in scores and score gaps over time. *Report of the Ad Hoc Committee on Confirming Test Results.* Washington, DC: National Assessment Governing Board.

Holmes, T., & Matthews, K. (1984). The effects of nonpromotion on elementary and junior high pupils: A meta-analysis. *Review of Educational Research, 54,* 225–236.

hooks, b. (1989). *Talking back: Thinking feminist. thinking black.* Boston, MA: South End Press.

Horng, E. (2005). *Poor working conditions make urban schools hard-to-staff.* University of California All Campus Consortium on Research for Diversity (UC/ACCORD) Policy Briefs. Paper pb-010-0305. Retrieved March 28, 2005 from http://repositories.cdlib.org/ucaccord/pb/pb-010-0305

House of Commons Education and Skills Committee. (2003). *Secondary education: Diversity of provision.* London: The Stationary Office.

House, E.R. (1999). Race and policy, *Education Policy Analysis Archives,* 7(16),1–14. Accessed 9 February 2005: http://epaa.asu.edu/epaa/v7n16.html

Howard, P.S.S. (2004). White privilege: For or against? A discussion of ostensibly antiracist discourses in critical whiteness studies. *Race, Gender & Class, 11*(4), 63–79.

Howard, T. (2003). Who receives the short end of the shortage? Implications of the U.S. teacher shortage on urban schools. *Journal of Curriculum and Supervision, 18*(2), 142–160.

Hursh, D. (2005). The growth of high-stakes testing in the USA: Accountability, markets and the decline in educational equality. *British Educational Research Journal 31*(5), 605–624.

Ignatiev, N. (1995). *How the Irish became White.* New York: Routledge.

Ignatiev, N. (1997). *The point is not to interpret whiteness but to abolish it.* Talk given at the conference 'The Making and Unmaking of Whiteness', University of California, Berkeley, 11–13 April 1997. Accessed at www.postfun.com/racetraitor

Illinois Fair Schools Coalition. (1985). *Holding students back: An expensive reform that doesn't work.* Chicago: Author.

Improving America's Schools Act of 1994, Public Law 103-382.

Ingersoll, R.M. (1999). The problem of underqualified teachers in American secondary schools. *Educational Researcher, 28*(2), 26–37.

Ingersoll, R. (2001). Teacher turnover, teacher shortages: An organizational analysis. *American Educational Research Journal, 38*(3), 499–534.

Ingersoll, R. (2002). The teacher shortage: A case of wrong diagnosis and wrong prescription. *NAASP Bulletin 86*(631), 16–31.

Ingersoll, R. (2003). *Who controls teachers' work: Power and accountability in America's schools.* Cambridge, MA: Harvard University Press.

Ingersoll, R. (2004). Four myths about America's teacher quality problem. In M. Smylie & D. Miretzky (Eds.), *Developing the teacher workforce: The 103rd yearbook of the National Society for the Study of Education* (pp. 1–33). Chicago: University of Chicago Press.

Intercultural Development Research Association. (1996, October). *Texas school survey project: A summary of findings.* San Antonio, TX: Intercultural Development Research Association.

Jacobson, M. F. (1998). *Whiteness of a different color: European immigrants and the alchemy of race.* Cambridge: Harvard University Press.

Jaeger, R. M. (1989). Certification of student competence. In R. L. Linn (Ed.), *Educational measurement* (3rd ed., pp. 485–514). New York: Macmillan.

Jaeger, R. M., Cole, J., Irwin, D. M., & Pratto, D. J. (1980). *An interactive structure judgment process for setting passing scores on competency tests applied to the North Carolina high school competency tests in reading and mathematics.* Greensboro, NC: Center for Education Research and Evaluation, University of North Carolina at Greensboro.

Jaeger, R. M. & Mills, C. (2001). An integrated judgment procedure for setting standards on complex, large-scale assessments. In G. J. Cizek (Ed.), *Setting performance standards: Concepts, methods, and perspectives* (pp. 313–318). Mahwah, NJ: Lawrence Erlbaum.

Jencks, C. (1972). *Inequality.* New York: Allen Lane.

Jimerson, S.R., Anderson, G.E., & Whipple, A.D. (2002). Winning the battle and losing the war: Examining the relationship between grade retention and dropping out of high school. *Psychology in the Schools, 39*(4), 441–457.

Johanek, M. C. (1995). *The public purposes of public education: The evolution of community- centered schooling at Benjamin Franklin High School, 1934–1944.* Unpublished doctoral dissertation, Teachers College Columbia University, New York.

Jones, K. (2004). A balanced school accountability model: An alternative to high-stakes testing. *Phi Delta Kappan Online.* Retrieved February 13, 2006 from http://www.pdkintl.org/kappan/

Just for Kids (2003). *Texas get results.* Austin, TX: Author.

Kanfer, R., & McCombs, B. L. (2000). Motivation. In H. F. O'Neil, Jr., & S. Tobias (Eds.), *Handbook on training* (pp. 85–108). New York: Macmillan.

Kentucky Department of Education. (2001). *Standard setting: Synthesis of three procedures—procedures and findings*. Frankfort, KY: Kentucky Department of Education. Available at www.kde.state.ky.us

Kim, J. S., & Sunderman, G. L. (2005). Measuring academic proficiency under the No Child Left Behind Act: Implications for educational equity. *Educational Researcher, 34*(8), 3–13.

Klein, S. P., Hamilton, L. S., McCaffrey, D. F., & Stetcher, B. M. (2000). *What do test scores in Texas tell us?* Santa Monica: Rand.

Koffler, S. L. (1980). A comparison of approaches for setting standards. *Journal of Educational Measurement, 17,* 167–178.

Koretz, D. (1988). Arriving in Lake Wobegon: Are standardized tests exaggerating achievement and distorting instruction? *American Educator, 12*(2), 8–15, 46–56.

Koretz, D., & Barron, S. I. (1998). *The validity of gains on the Kentucky Instructional Results Information System*. Santa Monica, CA: Rand.

Koretz, D., Linn, R. L., Dunbar, S. B., & Shepard, L. A. (1991, April). The effects of high-stakes testing: Preliminary evidence about generalization across tests. In R. L. Linn (Ed.), The effects of high stakes testing. Symposium presented at the annual meetings of the American Educational Research Association and the National Council on Measurement in Education, Chicago.

Kornhaber, M. L. (2004). Assessment, standards, equity. In J. A. Banks & C. A. M. Banks (Eds.), *Handbook of research on multicultural education* (2nd ed., pp. 91–109). San Francisco: Jossey-Bass.

Kozol, J. (2005). *The shame of the nation: The restoration of apartheid schooling in America*. New York: Crown.

Kuehn, L. (1998). Globalization and the control of teachers' work. Paper presented at the annual meeting of the American Educational Research Association, Montreal.

Labaree, D. F. (1984). Setting the standard: Alternative policies for student promotion. *Harvard Educational Review, 54*(1), 67–87.

Labour Party (1997). *New Labour: Because Britain deserves better*. London: Author.

Ladson Billings, G. (1994). *The dreamkeepers: Successful teachers of African American Children*. San Francisco, CA: Jossey-Bass.

Ladson-Billings, G., & Tate, W.F. (1995). Toward a critical race theory of education. *Teachers College Record, 97*(1), 47–68.

Lambert, N., & McCombs, B. L. (Eds.) (1998). *How students learn: Reforming schools through learner-centered education*. Washington, DC: American Psychological Association.

Lankford, H., Loeb, S., & Wyckoff, J. (2002). Teacher sorting and the plight of urban schools: A descriptive analysis. *Educational Evaluation and Policy Analysis, 24*(1), 37–62.

Lawton D. (2005). *Education and the labour party*. London: RoutledgeFalmer

Lee, C. D. (2001). Is October Brown Chinese? A cultural modeling activity system for underachieving students. *American Educational Research Journal, 38,*

97–142.

Lee, J. (2006). *Tracking achievement gaps and assessing the impact of NCLB on the gaps: An in-depth look into national and state reading and math outcome trends.* Cambridge, MA: The Civil Rights Project at Harvard University.

Leonardo, Z. (2004). The color of supremacy: Beyond the discourse of "white privilege." *Educational Philosophy and Theory,* 36(2), 137–152.

Lewis, D. M., Green, D. R., Mitzel, H. C., Baum, K., & Patz, R. J. (1998). *The Bookmark standard setting procedure:Methodology and recent implementations.* Paper presented at the annual meeting of the National Council on Measurement, San Diego, CA.

Liddle, R. (2005). "It's not race that keeps black boys back." *Sunday Times,* 13 March. Retrieved March 30, 2005 from http://www.timesonline.co.uk/article/0,,2088-1522930,00.html

Lightfoot, S. L. (1988). *Balm in Gilead: Journey of a healer.* Reading, MA: Addison-Wesley.

Linn, R. L. (1994). Criterion-referenced measurement: A valuable perspective clouded by surplus meaning. *Educational Measurement: Issues and Practice,* 13 (4), 12–14.

Linn, R. L. (2000). Assessments and accountability. *Educational Researcher,* 29(2), 4–16.

Linn, R. L. (2003a). Accountability: Responsibility and reasonable expectations. *Educational Researcher,* 32(7), 3–13.

Linn, R. L. (2003b, September 1). Performance standards: Utility for different uses of assessments. *Education Policy Analysis Archives,* 11(31). Available at http://epaa.asu.edu

Linn, R. L. (2005). Conflicting demands of No Child Left Behind and state systems: Mixed messages about school performance. *Educational Policy Analysis Archives, 13(33).* Available at http://epaa.asu.edu

Linn, R. L., Graue, M. E., & Sanders, N. M. (1990). Comparing state and district test results to national norms: The validity of claims that "everyone is above average." *Educational Measurement: Issues and Practice,* 9, 5–14.

Lipman, P. (2004). *High stakes education. Inequality, globalization, and urban school reform.* New York: RoutledgeFalmer.

Lipsky, M. (1980). *Street-level bureaucracy.* New York: Russell Sage Foundation.

Livingston, S. A. & Zieky, M. J. (1982). *Passing scores: A manual for setting standards of performance on educational and occupational tests.* Princeton, NJ: Educational Testing Service.

Losen, D., & Orfield, G. (Eds.). (2002). *Racial inequity in special education.* Cambridge, MA: Harvard Education Publishing Group.

Louie, V. (2005). Immigrant newcomer populations, ESEA, and the pipeline to college: Current considerations and future lines of inquiry. In L. Parker (Ed.), *Review of Research in Education* (pp. 69–106). Washington, DC: American Educational Research Association.

Lugg, C. (1996). *For God and country: American political conservatism and public education.* New York: Peter Lang.

Lynch, J. (1986). *Multicultural education: Principles and practice.* London: Routledge and Kegan Paul.

Lynn, M. (1999). Toward a critical race pedagogy: A research note. *Urban Education, 33*, 606–626.

Lyons, K.B. (2004). Specialized recruitment: An examination of the motivations and expectations of pre-service urban educators. Paper presented at the annual meeting of the American Educational Research Association, San Diego, CA.

Mac an Ghaill, M. (1988). *Young, gifted and black: Student teacher relations in the schooling of black youth*. Milton Keynes: Open University Press.

MacPhail-Wilcox, B., & King, R. A. (1986). Resource allocation studies: Implications for school improvement and school finance research. *Journal of Education Finance, 11*, 416–432.

Macpherson, W. (1999). *The Stephen Lawrence inquiry*. Cm 4262-I. London: The Stationery Office.

Madaus, G., & Clarke, M. (2001). The adverse impact of high-stakes testing on minority students: Evidence from one hundred years of test data. In G. Orfield & M. L. Kornhaber (Eds.), *Raising standards or raising barriers: Inequality and high-stakes testing in public education* (pp. 85–106). New York: Century Foundation Press.

Major, J. (1997). *Britain—The best place in the world*. Text of a Speech to the Commonwealth Institute, January 18. London: Conservative Central Office.

Mansell, W., & Clark, E. (2003). Juniors spend half their time on the three Rs, *Times Educational Supplement*, June 6, p. 2.

March, T. (2006). The new www: Whatever, whenever, wherever. *Educational Leadership 63*(4), 14–19.

Marquand, D. (2004). *The decline of the public*. Cambridge: Polity Press.

Martin, R. A. (2002, April). *Alternatives in Education: An exploration of learner-centered, progressive, and holistic education*. Paper presented at the annual Meeting of the American Educational Research Association, New Orleans.

Mason, D. (2000). *Race and ethnicity in modern Britain*. Oxford: Oxford University Press.

Mathews, J. (2004, January 20). Turning strife into success. *Washington Post*.

McCombs, B. L. (2000). Reducing the achievement gap. *Society, 37*(5), 29–36.

McCombs, B. L. (2001). Self-regulated learning and academic achievement: A phenomenological view. In B. J. Zimmerman & D. H. Schunk (Eds.), *Self-regulated learning and academic achievement: Theoretical perspectives* (pp. 67–123) (2nd ed.). Mahwah, NJ: Lawrence Erlbaum Associates.

McCombs, B. L. (2003). Providing a framework for the redesign of K–12 education in the context of current educational reform issues. *Theory Into Practice, 42*(2), 93–101.

McCombs, B. L. (2004). The Learner-Centered Psychological Principles: A framework for balancing a focus on academic achievement with a focus on social and emotional learning needs. In J. E. Zins, R. P. Weissberg, M. C. Wang, & H. J. Walberg (Eds.), *Building academic success on social and emotional learning: What does the research say?* (pp. 23–39). New York: Teachers College Press.

McCombs, B. L., & Lauer, P. A. (1997). Development and validation of the Learner-Centered Battery: Self-Assessment tools for teacher reflection and professional development. *The Professional Educator 20*(1), 1–21.

McCombs, B. L., & Miller, L. (2006). *Learner-centered classroom practices and assessments*. Thousand Oaks, CA: Corwin Press.

McCombs, B. L., Perry, K. E., & Daniels, D. H. (2006, in review). Understanding children's and teachers' perceptions of learner centered practices: Implications for early schooling. *Elementary School Journal*.

McCombs, B. L., & Pierce, J. W. (1999). *College level assessment of learner-centered practices (ALCP): Instructor and student surveys*. Denver, CO: University of Denver Research Institute.

McCombs, B. L., & Quiat, M. A. (2002). What makes a comprehensive school reform model learner-centered? *Urban Education, 37*(4), 476–496.

McCombs, B. L., & Whisler, J. S. (1997). *The learner-centered classroom and school: Strategies for increasing student motivation and achievement*. San Francisco: Jossey-Bass.

McCombs, B. L., & Vakili, D. (2005). A learner-centered framework for e-learning. *Teachers College Record, 107*(8), 1582–1600.

McCreight, C. (2000). *Teacher attrition, shortage, and strategies for retention*. Washington, DC: National Institute of Education.

McKenzie, K. B. (2003). The unintended consequences of accountability: A response to Skrla *et al*. In L. Skrla & J.J. Scheurich (Eds.). *Educational equity and accountability: Paradigms, policies, and politics* (pp. 251–266). New York: RoutlegeFalmer.

McKenzie, K. B., & Lozano, R. (2006). *Teachers' zone of self-efficacy: Who gets taught, who doesn't get taught, and, more importantly, why?* Paper presented at the annual convention of the University Council for Educational Administration, San Antonio, TX.

McKenzie, K. B., Skrla, L., & Scheurich, J. J. (2006). Preparing instructional leaders for social justice. *Journal of School Leadership, 16*(2), 158–170.

McNeil, L. M. (2000). *Contradictions of school reform: Educational costs of standardized testing*. New York: Routledge.

McQuillan, P. J. (2005). Possibilities and pitfalls: A comparative analysis of student empowerment. *American Educational Research Journal, 42*(4), 639–670.

Meece, J. L., Herman, P., & McCombs, B. L. (2003). Relations of learner-centered teaching practices to adolescents' achievement goals. *International Journal of Educational Research, 39*(4–5), 457–475.

Mehrens, W. A., & Cizek, G. J. (2001). Standard setting and the public good: Benefits accrued and anticipated. In G. J. Cizek (Ed.), *Setting performance standards: Concepts, methods, and perspectives* (pp. 477–485). Mahwah, NJ: Lawrence Erlbaum Associates.

Meier, D. (2002). *In schools we trust*. Boston: Beacon Press.

Meier, D., & Wood, G. H. (Eds.). (2004). *Many children left behind: How the no child left behind act is damaging our children and our schools*. Boston: Beacon Press.

Meisels, S. (1992, June). Doing harm by doing good: Iatrogenic effects of early childhood enrollment and promotion policies. *Early Childhood Research Quarterly, 7*(2), 155–174.

Millar, F. (2004, March 15). Guidance is not going to make school admissions fairer. *The Guardian (Education)*, p. 4.

Mills, C.W. (2003). White supremacy as sociopolitical system: A philosophical perspective. In A.W. Doane & E. Bonilla-Silva (Eds.), *White out: The continuing significance of racism* (pp. 35–48). New York: Routledge.

Min, P.G. (2004). Social science research on Asian Americans. In J.A. Banks & C.A.M. Banks (Eds.), *Handbook of research on multicultural education.* (2nd ed., pp. 332–348). San Francisco: Jossey-Bass.

Miner, B. (2005/2006). Questioning scripted curricula. *Rethinking Schools Online,* 20 (2). Retrieved August 22, 2006, from http://www.rethinkingschools.org/archive/20_02/scri202.shtml

Ministry of Education. (1945). *The nation's schools.* London: HMSO.

Mirza, H.S. (1992). *Young, female and black.* London: Routledge.

Mirza, H.S. (1999). Institutional racism and education: Myths and realities. Paper presentation for Black History Month Seminar Series; Tackling Institutional Racism, Middlesex University, October.

Miron, G. (2001). *What's public about charter schools?* Kalamazoo, Michigan: The Evaluation Centre, Western Michigan University.

Mitzel, H. C., Lewis, D. M., Patz, R. J., & Green, D. R. (2001). The Bookmark procedure: Psychological perspectives. In G. J Cizek (Ed.), *Setting performance standards: Concepts, methods and perspectives* (pp. 249–281). Mahwah, NJ: Lawrence Erlbaum.

Moon, T. R., Callahan, C. M., & Tomlinson, C. A. (2003, April 28). Effects of state testing programs on elementary schools with high concentrations of student poverty—Good news or bad news? *Current Issues in Education, 6*(8).

Morley, L., & Rassoul, N. (1999). *School effectiveness: Fracturing the discourse.* London, Falmer.

Moses, M. S., & Chang, M. J. (2006). Toward a deeper understanding of the diversity rationale. *Educational Researcher, 35*(1), 6–11.

Muir, K. (1990). *Eyes on the prize.* A paper submitted to James A. Banks as a Partial requirement for the course, Educ 423, Educating diverse students. Seattle: University of Washington.

Mulcahy, D. E. (2006, January 9). The continuing quest for equal schools: An essay review. *Education Review, 9*(2). Retrieved February 15, 2006 from http://edrev.asu.edu/essaus/v9n2/.

Mullard, C. (1982). Multiracial education in Britain: From assimilation to cultural pluralism. In J. Tierney (Ed.), *Race, migration and schooling* (pp. 120–133). London: Holt, Rinehart & Winston.

Nader, R. (n.d.). *Equal access to education.* Retrieved January 15, 2006 from http://www.votenader.org/issues/index.php?cid=36

National Audit Office. (2006). *Improving poorly performing schools in England.* London: Author.

National Center for Education Statistics. (1997a). *Digest of education statistics, 1997.* Washington, DC: U.S. Department of Education.

National Center for Education Statistics. (1997b). *NAEP 1996 mathematics report card for the nation and the states.* Washington, DC: U.S. Department of Education.

National Commission on Excellence and Education (1983). *A nation at risk: The imperative for educational reform.* Washington, DC: U. S. Government Printing Office.

National Commission on Teaching and America's Future. (1996). *What matters most: Teaching for America's future.* Washington, DC: Author.

National Commission on Teaching and America's Future. (2003). *No dream denied: A pledge to America's children.* Washington, DC: Author.

National Educational Goals Panel. (1993). *Report of the Goals 3 and 4 Technical Planning Group on the Review of Education Standards.* Washington, DC: Author.

National Education Goals Panel. (1999). *Reading achievement state by state, 1999.* Washington, DC: U.S. Government Printing Office.

National Institute of Education. (1977). *Violent schools/Safe schools: The safe school study report to congress.* Washington, DC: Author.

National School Board Association. (2006). School board members bring NSBA advocacy agenda to Congress. *School board news* [on-line]. Accessed March 19, 2006, from: http://www.nsba.org/site/doc_sbn.asp?TRACKID=&VID=55&CID=682&DID=37875

National Study Group for the Affirmative Development of Academic Ability (2004). *All students reaching the top: Strategies for closing academic achievement gaps.* Naperville, IL: Learning Point Associates.

Natriello, G. (1996). Diverting attention from conditions in American schools. *Educational Researcher, 25*(8), 7–9.

Nehaul, K. (1996). *The schooling of children of Caribbean heritage.* Stoke-on-Trent: Trentham.

Neill, M. (2003). The dangers of testing. *Educational Leadership, 60*(5), 43–46.

Newmann, F., Smith, B., Allensworth, E., & Bryk, A. (2001). Instructional program coherence: What it is and why it should guide school improvement policy. *Educational Evaluation and Policy Analysis, 23*(4), 297–321.

Nieto, S. (2003). *What keeps teachers going?* New York: Teachers College Press.

No Child Left Behind Act of 2001, Pub. Law No. 107.110.

Noddings, N. (2005). What does it mean to educate the whole child? *Educational Leadership, 63*(1), 8–13.

Oakes, J. (1989). What educational indicators?: The case of assessing the school context. *Educational Evaluation and Policy Analysis, 11*, 182.

Oakes, J., Blasi, G. & Rogers, J. (2004). Accountability for adequate and equitable opportunities to learn. In K. Sirtonik (Ed.), *Holding accountability accountable: What ought to matter in public education.* New York: Teachers College Press.

Oakes, J., & Lipton, M. (1990). *Making the best of schools: A handbook for parents, teachers, and policymakers.* New Haven, CT: Yale University Press.

Oakes, J., Stuart Wells, A., Jones, M., & Datnow, A. (1997). Detracking: The social construction of ability, cultural politics, and resistance to reform. *Teachers College Record, 98* (3), 491–510.

O'Connor, M., Hales E., Davies J., & Tomlinson S. (1999). *Hackney Downs: The school that dared to fight.* London: Cassell.

O'Day, J. (2002). Complexity, accountability, and school improvement. *Harvard Educational Review, 72*(3), 293–329.

O'Day, J. A., & Smith, M. S. (1993). Systemic school reform and educational opportunity. In S. Fuhrman (Ed.), *Designing coherent education policy: Improving the system.* San Francisco: Jossey-Bass.

Office for Standards in Education. (2001). *Improving attendance and behaviour in secondary schools*. HMI 242. London: Author.

Office for Standards in Education (Ofsted)(2004). *National academy for gifted and talented youth: summer schools 2003*. HMI 2073. London: Author.

Olson, L. (2005). Defying predictions, state trends prove mixed on schools making NCLB targets, *Education Week, 25*(2), September 7, pp. 1, 26–27.

Orfield, G., & Ashkinaze, C. (1991). *The closing door: Conservative policy and Black opportunity*. Chicago: University of Chicago Press.

Orfield, G., & Gordon, N. (2001). *Schools more separate: Consequences of a decade of resegregation*. Retrieved March 20, 2004, from http://www.law.harvard.edu/civilrights/publications/pressseg.html

Orfield, G., & Kornhaber, M. L. (Eds.). (2001). *Raising standards or raising barriers? Inequality and high-stakes testing in public education*. New York: Century Foundation Press.

Osler, A., & Morrison, A. (2000). *Inspecting schools for race equality: OFSTED's strengths and weaknesses*. Stoke-on-Trent: Trentham.

Ostrowski, P. (1987, November). *Twice in one grade: A false solution. A review of the pedagogical practice of grade retention in elementary schools: What do we know? Should the practice continue?* (Eric Document Reproduction No. ED300119)

Palmaffy, T. (1998). The gold star state: How Texas jumped to the head of the class in elementary-school achievement. *Policy Review* 88, 30–38.

Parker, L., Deyhle, D., & Villenas, S. (Eds.). (1999). *Race is...race isn't: Critical race theory and qualitative studies in education*. Boulder, Colorado: Westview Press.

Parsons, C., Godfrey, R., Annan, G., Cornwall, J., Dussart, M., Hepburn, S., Howlett, K., & Wennerstrom, V. (2004). *Minority Ethnic Exclusions and the Race Relations (Amendment) Act 2000*. Research Report 616. London: Department for Education & Skills.

Patterson, W. (2003). Breaking out of our boxes. *Phi Delta Kappan, 84*(8), 569–574.

Pear, R. (2004, 24 February). Education chief calls union "terrorist," then recants. *New York Times*, p. A20.

Perie, M., Grigg, W., & Dion, G. (2005). *The nation's report card: Mathematics 2005* (NCES 2006–453). U.S. Department of Education, National Center for Education Statistics. Washington, DC: U.S. Government Printing Office.

Perie, M., Grigg, W., & Donahue, P. (2005). *The nation's report card: Reading 2005* (NCES 2006-451). U.S. Department of Education, National Center for Education Statistics. Washington, DC: U.S. Government Printing Office.

Perkins, J. (2004). *Confessions of an economic hit man*. San Francisco: Berrett Koehler Publishers.

Perlstein, D. (2004). *Justice, justice: School politics and the eclipse of liberalism*. New York: Peter Lang.

Perrone, V. (1998). *Teacher with a heart*. New York: Teachers College Press.

Perry, K. E., & Weinstein, R. S. (1998). The social context of early schooling and children's school adjustment. *Educational Psychologist, 33*(4), 177–194.

Pettigrew, T., F. (1998). Intergroup contact theory. *Annual Review of Psychology,*

49, 65–85.

Phillips, M. (1997). What makes schools effective? A comparison of the relationships of communitarian climate and academic climate to mathematics achievement and attendance during middle school. *American Educational Research Journal, 34*, 543–578.

Pipes, T. (2002). *Beneath the surface: Middle school students and diversity.* Unpublished Master's thesis, California State University Monterey Bay.

Pollard, K. M., & O'Hare, W. P. (1999). *America's racial and ethnic minorities. Population reference bulletin, 54*(3), 1–48. Washington, DC: Population Reference Bureau.

Pollock, M. (2001). How the questions we ask most about race in education is the very question we most suppress. *Educational Researcher, 30*(9), 2–12.

Popham, W. J. & Husek, T. R. (1969). Implications of criterion-referenced measures. *Journal of Educational Measurement, 6*, 1–9.

Prensky, M. (2006). Listen to the natives. *Educational Leadership, 63*(4), 8–13.

Presseisen, B. Z. (1985). *Unlearned lessons: Current and past reforms for school improvement.* Philadelphia: Falmer Press.

Pugach, M.C. (1995). Twice victims: The struggle to educate children in urban schools and the reform of special education and chapter 1. In M.C. Wang & M.C. Reynolds (Eds.), *Making a difference for students at risk: Trends and alternatives* (pp. 27–60). Thousand Oaks, CA: Corwin.

Price, J., Schwabacher, S., & Chittenden, T. (1992). *Report on the multiple forms of evidence study.* New York: Fund for New York City Public Education.

Puiggros, A. (repost, 28.02.2004). World Bank education policy: Market liberalism meets ideological conservatism. *NACLA Report on the Americas,* May-June 1995. Retrieved from: http://www.indymedia.org.uk/en/regions/cambridge/2004/02/286118.html

Purkey, S. C., & Smith M. S. (1983). Effective schools: A review. *Elementary School Journal* 83 (4), 427–452.

Ranson, S. (1984). Towards a tertiary tripartism: New codes of social control and the 17+. In P. Broadfoot (Ed.), *Selection, Certification and Control.* London: Methuen.

Ravitch, D. (1990). Diversity and democracy: Multicultural education in America. *American Educator, 14*(1), 16–20, 46–68.

Ravitch, D. (1995). *National standards in American education: A citizen's guide.* Washington, DC: Bookings.

Register Editorial Board. (February 12, 2006). Adopt steps to transform Iowa schools. DesMoinesRegister.com Editorials. Retrieved February 13, 2006 from http://desmoinesregister.com

Reed-Danahay, D. (2005). *Locating Bourdieu.* Bloomington, Indiana: Indiana University Press.

Reese, C. M., Miller, K. E., Mazzeo, J., & Dossey, J. A. (1997). *NAEP 1996 report card for the nation and the states.* Washington, DC: National Center for Education Statistics.

Reiffers, R. (1996). *Accomplishing Europe through education and training.* Brussels: European Commission.

Relin, L. (1937). We take the lead. *Faculty Bulletin.* New York: BFHS.

Resnick, L. (1987). *Education and learning to think.* Washington, DC: National Academy Press.

Rice, J. K. (2003). *Teacher quality: Understanding the effectiveness of teacher attributes.* Economic Policy Institute.

Rich, D. (2005). What educators need to explain to the public. *Phi Delta Kappan,* 87(2),154–158.

Richardson, B. (Ed.). (2006). *Tell it like it is: How schools fail black children.* Stoke-on-Trent: Trentham Books.

Riester, A. F., Pursch, V., & Skrla, L. (2002). Principals for social justice: Leaders of school success for children from low-income students. *Journal of School Leadership.* 12, 281–304.

Rizvi, F. (1993). Critical introduction. In B. Troyna (Ed.), *Racism and education* (pp. 1–17). Buckingham: Open University Press.

Robertson, S., & Dale, R. (2003, 12 June). *Changing geographies of power in education: The politics of rescaling and its contradictions.* A paper presented to the Joint BERA/BAICE Conference on Globalisation, Culture and Education.

Rodberg, S. (2001, 2 July). The CIO without the CIA: Inside the AFL-CIO's Solidarity Center. *American Prospect* (Online edition). Accessed at http://www.prospect.org/print/V12/12/rodberg-s.html

Roderick, M., Bryk, A. S., Jacob, B. A., Easton, J. Q., & Allensworth, E. (1999). *Ending social promotion: Results from the first two years.* Chicago: Consortium on Chicago School Research.

Roderick, M., Jacob, B. A., & Bryk, A. S. (2002). The impact of high-stakes testing in Chicago on student achievement in promotional gate grades. *Educational Evaluation and Policy Analysis,* 24 (4), 333–357.

Roderick, M., Nagaoka, J., Bacon, J., & Easton, J. (2000). *Update: Ending social promotion: Passing, retention, and achievement trends among promoted and retained students, 1995–1999.* Chicago: Consortium on Chicago School Research.

Rodriguez, G. (2002). *Building effective arts programs that reflect and include our community.* Unpublished master's thesis, California State University Monterey Bay.

Rogers, J., & Oakes, J. (2005). John Dewey speaks to *Brown*: Research, democratic social movement strategies, and the struggle for education on equal terms, *Teachers College Record, 107* (9): 2178–2203.

Roithmayr, D. (2004). Tracking left: A radical critique of Grutter. *Constitutional Commentary, 21,* 1–13.

The root of civic culture. (2006, February 14). *The Sacramento Bee,* p. B6.

Rorrer, A. K., & Skrla, L. (2005). Leaders as policy mediators. *Theory Into Practice,* 44(1), 53–62.

Rosaldo, R. (1999). Cultural citizenship, inequality, and multiculturalism. In R. D. Torres, L. F. Mirón, & J. X. Inda (Eds), *Race, identity and citizenship* (pp. 253–261). Malden, MA: Blackwell Publishers.

Rosenhall, L. (2006, July 26). Another court test for exit exam. State Court of Appeal weighs fairness for English learners. *The Sacramento Bee,* p. A3.

Rowan, B., Correnti, R., & Miller, R. J. (2002). *What large-scale, survey research tells us about teacher effect on student achievement.* CPRE Research Report

Series RR-051. University of Pennsylvania, Consortium for Policy Research in Education.

Rowan, B., & Miskel, C. G. (1999). Institutional theory and the study of educational organizations. In J. Murphy & K. S. Louis (Eds.), *Handbook of research on educational administration* (2nd ed., pp. 359–383). San Francisco: Jossey-Bass.

Rubalcava, M. (2005). Let kids come first. *Educational Leadership, 62*(8), 70–72.

Rumberger, R.W., & Larson, K.A. (1998). Student mobility and the increased risk of high school dropout. *American Journal of Education, 107*(1), 1–35.

Russell, A. (2004). Pillars of wisdom. *The Age: Fairfax Digital.* Retrieved on 8/2/2004 from http://www.theage.com.au/articles/2004

Rutherford, B. (2001). Cultural and linguistic diversity and Title I: What do we know? Where do we go? In G.D. Borman, S.C. Stringfield, & R.E. Slavin (Eds.), *Title I: Compensatory education at the crossroads* (pp. 137–170). Mahwah, NJ: Lawrence Erlbaum Associates.

Rutter, M. (1983). School effects on pupil progress: Research findings and policy implications. *Journal of Child Development* 54: 1–29.

Ryan, K. E. (2002). Assessment validation in the context of high-stakes assessment. *Educational Measurement: Issues and Practice, 21*, 7–15.

Ryan, J.E. (2004). The perverse incentives of the No Child Left Behind Act. *New York University Law Review, 79*, 932–989.

Secada, W. G. (1989). Educational equity versus equality of education: An alternative conception. In W. G. Secada (Ed.), *Equity in education* (pp. 68–88). New York: Falmer Press.

Safer, D. (1986). The stress of secondary school for vulnerable students. *Journal of Youth and Adolescence, 15*(5), 405–417.

Saltman, K.J. (2005). *The Edison schools: Corporate schooling and the assault on public education.* New York: Routledge.

Sanders, W. L., & Rivers, J. C. (1996). *Cumulative and residual effects of teachers on future student academic achievement.* Knoxville: University of Tennessee Value-Added Research and Development Center.

Santayana, G. (1905). *Life of reason.* New York: C. Scribner's Sons.

Scheurich, J.J. (1998). Highly successfully and loving, public elementary schools populated mainly by low-SES children of color: Core beliefs and cultural characteristics. *Urban Education, 33* (4), 451–491.

Scheurich, J.J., Skrla, L., & Johnson, J. F. (2000). Thinking carefully about equity and accountability. *Phi Delta Kappan, 82*(4), 293–299.

Schlesinger, A. M., Jr. (1991). *The disuniting of America: Reflections on a multicultural society.* Knoxville, TN: Whittle Direct Books.

Schmitz, B., Butler, J. E., Guy-Sheftall, B., & Rosenfelt, D. (2004). Women's studies and curriculum transformation in the United States. In J. A. Banks & C. A. M. Banks (Eds.), *Handbook of research on multicultural education* (2nd ed., pp. 882–905). San Francisco: Jossey-Bass.

Sennett, R. (2006). *The culture of the new capitalism.* New Haven and London: Yale University Press.

Seligman, M. E. P., & Csikszentmihalyi, M. (2000). Positive psychology: An introduction. *American Psychologist, 55*(1), 5–14.

Sewell, T. (1997). *Black masculinities and schooling: How black boys survive modern schooling*. Stoke-on-Trent, Trentham.

Shanker, A. (1997). Educational reform and basic standards [Electronic version]. *Forum for applied research and public policy, 12*, 78–83. (Wilson Education Full Text, Accession Number: 199728803176013)

Shaw, M. (2004, October 24). Put local children first. *Times Educational Supplement*.

Shepard, L., & Smith, M. L. (1986). Synthesis of research on school readiness and kindergarten retention. *Educational Leadership, 44*(3), 86.

Shepard, L., & Smith, M. L. (1988). Flunking kindergarten: Escalating curriculum leaves many behind. *American Educator, 12*(2), 34–38.

Simon, H. (1983). *Reason in human affairs*. Stanford: Stanford University Press.

Sheets, R.H. (2000). Advancing the field or taking center stage: The white movement in multicultural education. *Educational Researcher, 29*(9), 15–21.

Shepard, L. A. (1980). Technical issues in minimum competency testing. In D. C. Berliner (Ed.), *Review of research in education*: Vol. 8 (pp. 30–82). Washington, DC: American Educational Research Association.

Shepard, L. A. (1984). Setting performance standards. In R. A. Berk (Ed.), *A guide to criterion-referenced test construction* (pp. 169–198). Baltimore, MD: Johns Hopkins University Press.

Skrla, L. (2001). Accountability, equity, and complexity. *Educational Researcher, 30*(4), 15–21.

Skrla, L. (2003). Productive campus leadership responses to accountability: Principals as policy mediators. In W. Hoy & C. Miskel (Eds.), *Theory and research in educational administration* (pp. 27–50). Greenwich, CT: JAI Press.

Skrla, L., & Scheurich, J. J. (Eds.). (2003). *Educational equity and accountability: Paradigms, policies, and politics*. New York: RoutledgeFalmer.

Sleeter, C.E. (1993). How white teachers construct race. Reprinted in G. Ladson-Billings & D. Gillborn (Eds.), *The RoutledgeFalmer reader in multicultural education* (pp. 163–178). New York: RoutledgeFalmer.

Sleeter, C. E. (2005). *Un-standardizing curriculum: Multicultural teaching in the standards-based classroom*. New York: Teachers College Press.

Sleeter, C. E., & Stillman, J. (2005). Standardizing knowledge in a multicultural society. *Curriculum Inquiry, 35* (1), 27–46.

Smith, D. J. & Tomlinson, S. (1989). *The school effect: A study of multiracial comprehensives*. London: The Policy Studies Institute.

Smith, F. (1986). *High school admission and the improvement of schooling*. New York: New York City Board of Education.

Smith, M.L., & Shepard, L.A. (1987). What doesn't work: Explaining policies of retention in the early grades. *Phi Delta Kappan, 69*(2), 129–134.

Smithers, R., & Yafai, F. (2004, Dec. 31). Old-fashioned, out of time: Clarke dismisses Princely view of education. *Times Educational Supplement*.

Snyder, J. (1999). *New Haven Unified School District: A teaching quality system for excellence and equity*. New York: Teachers College Columbia University.

Social Trends. (2003). *Number 33*. Office for National Statistics. London: The Stationary Office.

Solórzano, D. (1998). Critical race theory, racial and gender microaggressions, and the experiences of Chicana and Chicano scholars. *International Journal of Qualitative Studies in Education, 11,* 121–136.

Spellings, M. (2005). Interview. *Harvard Educational Review, 75* (4), 364–382.

Stecher, B. M., Barron, S., Kaganoff, T., & Goodwin, J. (1998). *The effects of standards-based assessment on classroom practices: Results of the 1996–97 RAND Survey of Kentucky Teachers of Mathematics and Writing* (CSE Technical Report 482). Los Angeles: Center for Research on Evaluation, Standards, and Student Testing.

Stein, S.J. (2004). *The culture of education policy.* New York: Teachers College Press.

Stephan, W. G. (1999). *Reducing prejudice and stereotyping in schools.* New York: Teachers College Press.

Steven, S. (1999). Don't they know we're no longer a racist society? *The Mail on Sunday,* 28 February, p. 35.

Stillman, J. (2005). *Taking back the standards: Toward a theory of critical professional practice for specially trained teachers.* Unpublished doctoral dissertation, University of California, Los Angeles.

Stotsky, S. (1998). *Analysis of Texas reading tests, grades 4, 8, and 10, 1995–1998 Report prepared for the Tax Research Association.* Retrieved March 20, 2004, from http://www.educationnews.org/analysis_of_the_texas_reading_te.htm.

Stotsky, S. (1999). *Losing our language: How multicultural classroom instruction is undermining our children's ability to read, write, and reason.* New York: The Free Press.

Strauss, R.P., & Sawyer, E.A. (1986). Some new evidence on teacher and student competencies. *Economics of Education Review, 5*(1), 41–48.

Sukhnandan, L., & Lee, B. (1998). *Streaming, setting and grouping by ability.* Slough, UK: National Foundation for Educational Research.

Summers, J. J., Beretvas, S. N., Svinicki, M. D., & Gorin, J. S. (2005). Evaluating collaborative learning and community. *Journal of Experimental Education, 73*(3), 165–188.

Symcox, L. (2002). *Whose history? The struggle for national standards in American classrooms.* New York: Teachers College Press.

Takaki, R. (1993). *A different mirror: A history of multicultural America.* New York: Little, Brown.

Tanner, L. (1997). *Dewey's laboratory school: Lessons for today.* New York: Teachers College Press.

Tate, W. (1997). Critical race theory and education: History, theory, and implications. *Review of Research in Education, 22,* 191–243.

Teaching Tolerance (producer). (1992). *Shadow of hate* [videocassette]. Montgomery, Alabama: Southern Poverty Law Center.

Tharp, R. G., Estrada, P., Dalton, S. S. & Yamauchi, L. A. (2000). *Teaching transformed.* Boulder, CO: Westview.

Thatcher, M. (1993). *The Downing Street years.* New York: HarperCollins.

Thernstrom, A., & Thernstrom, S. (2003). *No excuses: Closing the racial gap in learning.* New York: Simon & Schuster.

Thomas, J. Y., & Brady, K. P. (2005). The elementary and secondary education act at 40: Equity, accountability, and the evolving federal role in public education.

In L. Parker (Ed.), *Review of Research in Education* (pp. 51–68). Washington, DC: American Educational Research Association.

Thomas, P. (2004). Can we afford the numbers games that rule our schools? *Greenville news* [on-line]. Accessed March 19, 2006 from http://greenvilleonline.com/news/opinion/2004/07/24/2004072435701.htm

Thompson, S. (2001). The authentic standards movement and its evil twin. *Phi Delta Kappan* 82 (5), 358–362.

Thrupp, M., & Willmott, R. (2003). *Education management in managerialist times: Beyond the textual apologists.* Philadelphia: Open University Press.

Tomasevski, K. (2003). *Education denied.* London and New York: Zed Books.

Tomlinson, J. (1999). *Globalization and culture.* Chicago: University of Chicago Press.

Tomlinson, S. (1977). Race and education in Britain 1960–77: An overview of the literature. *Sage Race Relations Abstracts, 2*(4), 3–33.

Tomlinson, S. (1997a). Sociological perspectives on failing schools. *International Journal of Sociology of Education* 11 (3), 261–77.

Tomlinson, S. (1997b). *Education 14–19: Critical perspectives.* London: Athlone Press.

Tomlinson, S. (2005). *Education in a post-welfare society* (2nd Ed.). New York: Open University Press.

Tozer, S. E., Violas, P. C., & Senese, G. (2002). *School and society: Historical and contemporary perspectives* (4th ed.). New York: McGraw-Hill.

Tyack, D. (1974). *The one best system.* Cambridge, MA: Harvard University Press.

Tyack, D., & Cuban, L. (1995). *Tinkering toward utopia.* Cambridge, MA: Harvard University Press.

Urban, W. J. (2000). *Gender, race, and the National Education Association.* New York: RoutledgeFalmer.

U.S. Department of Education (n.d.). *NCLB.* Retrieved February 14, 2006 from http://www.ed.gov/nclb/landing.jhtml?src=ln

U.S. Department of Education. (2001). No child left behind. Retrieved September 18, 2003 at http://www.ed.gov/nclb/overview/intro/execsumm.html

U.S. Department of Education. (2004). *Elementary & secondary education: No child left behind: a desktop reference.* Washington, D.C.: U.S. Department of Education. Retrieved: 25 April 2004 from http://www.ed.gov/admins/lead/account/nclbreference/page_pg4.html?exp=0

Valencia, R.R., Valenzuela, A., Sloan, K., & Foley, D.E. (2001). Let's treat the cause, not the symptoms: Equity and accountability in Texas revisited. *Phi Delta Kappan, 83*(4), 318–321, 326.

Valenzuela, A. (Ed.) (2005). *Leaving children behind.* Albany, NY: SUNY Press.

Vanhuysse, P. (2006). Bees and foxes, spiders and hedgehogs. *Education Review, 9*(1). Retrieved February 15, 2006 from http://edrev.asu.edu/essaus/v9n1/

van Leeuwen, F. (2001, July 25). *Speeches at the third Education International World Congress.* Accessed at http://www.ei-ie.org/congress2001/index.htm.

Villalpando, O. (2003). Self-segregation or self-preservation? A critical race theory and Latina/o critical theory analysis of findings from a longitudinal study of Chicana/o college students. *International Journal of Qualitative Studies in Education, 16*(5), 619–646.

Vinovskis, M. A. (1999). *The road to Chartlottesville: The 1989 education summit.* Washington, DC: National Education Goals Panel. Available at http://govinfo. library.unt.edu/negp/reports/negp30.pdf

Walker, E., & Madhere, S. (1987). Multiple retentions: Some consequences for the cognitive and affective maturation of minority elementary students. *Urban Education, 22,* 85–89.

Wang, J. & Odell, S. J. (2002). Mentored learning to teach according to standards-based reform: A critical review. *Review of Educational Research, 72*(3), 481–546.

Wang, M.C., Reynolds, M.C., & Walberg, H.J. (1995). Inner-city students at the margins. In M.C. Wang & M.C. Reynolds (Eds.), *Making a difference for students at risk: Trends and alternatives* (pp. 1–26). Thousand Oaks, CA: Corwin.

Wasserman, J. (1999, September 2). 21,000 kids left back: Record number to repeat; social promotion ends. *New York Daily News.*

Waxman, H.C., Pardon, Y.N., & Arnold, K.M. (2001). Effective instructional practices for students placed at risk of academic failure. In G.D. Borman, S.C. Stringfield, & R.E. Slavin (Eds.), *Title I: Compensatory education at the crossroads* (pp. 137–170). Mahwah, NJ: Lawrence Erlbaum Associates.

Weber, M. (1947). *Theory of social and economic organizations.* New York: Free Press.

Webster's Third New International Dictionary. Unabridged. Springfield, MA: Merriam-Webster, Inc.

Wehlage, G., Rutter, R., Smith, G., Lesko, N., & Fernandez, R. (1989). *Reducing the risk: Schools as communities of support.* New York: Falmer Press.

Weiner, L. (1993). *Preparing teachers for urban schools.* New York: Teachers College Press.

Weiner, L. (1998, Summer). Albert Shanker's legacy. *Contemporary Education, 69,* 196–201.

Weiner, L. (2005, Winter). Neoliberalism, teacher unionism, and the future of public education. *New Politics, 10,* 101–112. Available at http://www.wpunj.edu/~newpol/issue38/Weiner38.htm

Weiner, L. (2006, Winter). The (people's) summit of the Americas. *New Politics, 10,* 118–123. Available at http://www.newpol.org

Weiner, L. (2006). *Urban teaching: The essentials* (Rev. ed.). New York: Teachers College Press.

Wenglinsky, H. (1997). *How educational expenditures improve student performance and how they don't.* Princeton: Educational Testing Service, Policy Information Center.

West, A. (2006). *Admission to secondary schools in London.* London: London School of Economics. www.lse/ac/uk/collections/CER/research/htm

West, A., & Hind, A. (2003). *Secondary school admission in England: Exploring the extent of overt and covert selection.* London: London School of Economics.

White, J. (in press). Teachers who care are more effective: A meta-analysis of learner-centered relationships. *Review of Educational Research.*

Wielkiewicz, R. M., & Stelzner, S P. (2005). An ecological perspective on leadership theory, research, and practice. *Review of General Psychology, 9*(4), 326–341.

Wiliam, D., & Bartholomew, H. (2001). *The influence of ability-grouping practices on student achievement in mathematics.* Paper presented at the annual meeting of the British Educational Research Association, University of Leeds, September.

Willis, P. (2003). Foot soldiers of modernity: The dialectics of cultural consumption and the 21st-century school. *Harvard Educational Review, 73,* 390–415.

Wraga, W. G. (2006). The heightened significance of *Brown v. Board of Education* in our time. *Phi Delta Kappan, 87*(6), 425–428.

Wong, K.K. & Meyer, S.J. (2001). Title I schoolwide programs as an alternative to categorical practices: An organizational analysis of surveys from the prospects study. In G.D. Borman, S.C. Stringfield, & R.E. Slavin (Eds.), *Title I: Compensatory education at the crossroads* (pp. 137–170). Mahwah, NJ: Lawrence Erlbaum Associates.

Woodruff, P. (2005). *First democracy: The challenge of an ancient idea.* New York: Oxford University Press.

Woodson, C. G. (1921). *The history of the Negro church.* Washington, DC: The Associated Publishers.

World Bank. (2003, September). *World development report 2004: Making services work for poor people.* Accessed at http://econ.worldbank.org/wdr/wdr2004/text-30023

Wright, C. (1987). Black students—white teachers. In B. Troyna (Ed.). *Racial inequality in education* (pp. 109–126). London: Tavistock.

Wright, C. (1992). *Race relations in the primary school.* London: David Fulton.

Wright, C., Weekes, D., & McGlaughlin, A. (2000). *'Race', class and gender in exclusion from school.* London: Falmer.

Yonezawa, S., Wells, A. S., & Serna, I. (2002). Choosing tracks: "Freedom of choice" in detracking schools. *American Educational Research Journal, 39,* 37–67.

Yosso, T.J. (2005). *Critical race counterstories along the Chicana/Chicano educational pipeline.* New York: Routledge.

Young, M. (1958). *The rise of the meritocracy.* London: Penguin.

Youdell, D. (2000). *Schooling identities: An ethnography of the constitution of pupil identities.* Unpublished Ph.D. Thesis, Institute of Education, University of London.

Youdell, D. (2003). Identity traps or how black students fail: The interactions between biographical, sub-cultural, and learner identities. *British Journal of Sociology of Education, 24*(1), 3–20.

Zieky, M. J. (1995). A historical perspective on setting standards. In *Proceedings of the Joint Conference on Standard Setting for Large-Scale Assessments in Statistics* (pp. 1–38). Washington, DC: National Assessment Governing Board and National Center for Education Statistics.

Zimmerman, J. (2002). *Whose America? Culture wars in the public schools.* Cambridge: Harvard University Press.

About the Editor and the Contributors

Christine E. Sleeter is Professor Emerita in the College of Professional Studies at California State University, Monterey Bay, and was recently Visiting Professor at Victoria University in New Zealand. Her research focuses on anti-racist multicultural education and teacher education. She is currently serving as vice president of Division K (Teaching and Teacher Education) of the American Educational Research Association. Dr. Sleeter has received several awards for her work including the California State University Monterey Bay President's Medal, the National Association for Multicultural Education Research Award, and the AERA Committee on the Role and Status of Minorities in Education Distinguished Scholar Award. She is the author of about 100 articles and book chapters, and several books, including *Un-Standardizing Curriculum*, and *Culture, Difference and Power*.

Cherry A. McGee Banks is Professor of Education and Interim Director of the Education Program at the University of Washington, Bothell. In 1997, she received the Distinguished Teaching Award from the University of Washington, Bothell, and in 2000 she was named a Worthington Distinguished Professor. Her current research focuses on intergroup education and the role that public school educators play in linking schools to communities. Professor Banks has contributed to such journals as the *Phi Delta Kappan, Social Studies and the Young Learner, Educational Policy*, and *Theory Into Practice*. She is associate editor of the *Handbook of Research on Multicultural Education*, cocditor of *Multicultural Education: Issues and Perspectives* and co-author of *Teaching Strategies for the Social Studies*. She currently chairs the AERA Editorial Book Board.

James A. Banks is Kerry and Linda Killinger Professor of Diversity Studies and Director of the Center for Multicultural Education at the University of Washington, Seattle. He is a past president of the American Educational Research Association and the National Council for the Social Studies. He was a Spencer Fellow at the Center for Advanced Study in the Behavioral Sciences at Stanford during the 2005–2006 academic year. Professor Banks is a specialist in multicultural education and in social studies education. He has written more than 100 articles and written or edited books in these fields. His books include *Cultural Diversity and Education: Foundations, Curriculum and Teaching; Diversity and Citizenship Education: Global Perspectives*; and *Race, Culture, and Education: The Selected Works of James A. Banks*. Professor Banks is the editor of the *Handbook of Research on Multicultural Education*.

Linda Darling-Hammond is the Charles E. Ducommun Professor of Education at Stanford University, where she has launched the Stanford Educational Leadership

Institute and the School Redesign Network. Prior to Stanford, she was William F. Russell Professor in the Foundations of Education at Teachers College, Columbia University. She is a past president of the American Educational Research Association, and was founding Executive Director of the National Commission for Teaching and America's Future, the blue ribbon panel whose 1996 report, *What Matters Most: Teaching for America's Future*, catalyzed major policy changes across the United States to improve the quality of teacher education and teaching. Her research, teaching, and policy work focus on teaching quality, school reform, and educational equity. *The Right to Learn* received the American Educational Research Association's Outstanding Book Award for 1998, and *Teaching as the Learning Profession*, co-edited with Gary Sykes, received the National Staff Development Council's Outstanding Book Award for 2000.

David Gillborn is Professor of Education, Head of the School of Educational Foundations & Policy Studies, and Associate Director of the Centre for Critical Education Policy Studies at the Institute of Education, University of London. He is active in antiracist politics and frequently contributes to public debates on race inequity in education. Professor Gillborn edits the international refereed journal *Race, Ethnicity, and Education* and pursues a range of research interests in the field of inequity and social policy. His study, *Rationing Education* (co-authored with Deborah Youdell), was acclaimed as "best book in the field of educational studies" by the Standing Conference on Studies in Education/Society for Educational Studies.

Jori N. Hall is a doctoral student in the Department of Educational Policy Studies in the College of Education at the University of Illinois at Urbana-Champaign. Her research focuses on the implications of educational accountability policies and practices.

Robert L. Linn is Distinguished Professor Emeritus of Education at the University of Colorado at Boulder and former Co-Director of the National Center for Research on Evaluation, Standards, and Student Testing. He has published over 225 journal articles and chapters in books dealing with theoretical and applied issues in educational measurement. He served as editor of the third edition of *Educational Measurement* and as editor of the *Journal of Educational Measurement*. Awards for his contributions include the ETS Award for Distinguished Service to Measurement, the E.L Thorndike Award, the E.F. Lindquist Award, the National Council on Measurement in Education Career Award, and the American Educational Research Association Award for Distinguished Contributions to Educational Research. He is past president of the American Educational Research Association, past president of the National Council on Measurement in Education, past president of the Evaluation and Measurement Division of the American Psychological Association, and past vice-president for Division D (Measurement and Research Methodology) of AERA.

Barbara L. McCombs is a Senior Research Scientist at the University of Denver Research Institute in Colorado where she directs the Human Motivation, Learning and Development Center. She currently serves as Vice President of Division C (Learning and Instruction) of the American Educational Research Association. Her current research is directed at new models of teaching and learning, including transformational teacher development approaches and the use of technology as a primary tool for empowering youth. She is the primary author of the *Learner-Centered Psychological Principles*, disseminated by the American Psychological Association. Learner-centered models of teaching and learning are being used in numerous national and international schools and colleges.

Kathryn Bell McKenzie is Assistant Professor in the Department of Educational Administration and Human Resource Development at Texas A&M University. Dr. McKenzie received her Ph.D. in Educational Administration from The University of Texas in Austin. Her research foci include equity and social justice in schools, school leadership, qualitative methodology, and critical white studies. During her more than 20 years in public education, Dr. McKenzie was a classroom teacher, curriculum specialist, assistant principal, and principal. Her work has appeared in numerous journals, including *Educational Administration Quarterly, Educational Theory,* and the *Journal of School Leadership.*

Laurence Parker is Professor in the Department of Educational Policy Studies in the College of Education at the University of Illinois at Urbana-Champaign. His area of interest is critical race theory and educational policy issues. His articles appear in journals such as *Education Theory, Urban Review,* and *Journal of School Leadership.* His co-edited books include *Race Is. . .Race Isn't: Critical Race Theory and Qualitative Studies in Education* and *Interrogating Racism in Qualitative Research Methodology, Counterpoints.*

James Joseph Scheurich is a Professor and the Head of the Department of Educational Administration and Human Resource Development at Texas A&M University. His research interests include race and racism, equity in education, accountability, Foucault, and qualitative research methodologies. He is the author/co-author of five books, including *Anti-Racist Scholarship: An Advocacy*; and over 30 articles. He has served on several committees in University Council for Educational Administration, including the Executive Committee, and AERA, including the AERA Publications Committee and the AERA Presidential Nominating Committee.

Linda Skrla is Professor of Educational Administration and Associate Dean for Research in the College of Education and Human Development at Texas A&M University. She holds a Ph.D. from the University of Texas at Austin and has extensive experience as a public school teacher and administrator. Her research focuses on equity issues in school leadership and policy, including accountability, highly successful school districts, and women superintendents. Her work has appeared in numerous journals, and she has co-authored or co-edited four books, including, most recently, Accountability and Equity: Policies, Paradigms, and Politics.

Jamy Stillman is Assistant Professor of Education at Barnard College, Columbia University. Her research and teaching focus on the educational experiences of language minority students, particularly in the area of language and literacy. She also explores intersections between educational policy, K–12 language arts instruction, and multicultural teacher education.

Sally Tomlinson is Emeritus Professor of Education Policy at Goldsmiths College, London University and a Senior Research Fellow in the Department of Educational Studies, University of Oxford, England. She has taught, researched and published for over 25 years in the areas of educational policy, race and education, and special education. Her most recent book is *Education in a Post-Welfare Society*. Her critique of recent government policy on race and education, "Race, Ethnicity and Education Under New Labour" in the *Oxford Review of Education*, was among the five top downloaded journal articles internationally in 2005-06.

Lois Weiner is a Professor of Elementary and Secondary Education at New Jersey City University where she coordinates a graduate program in teaching and learning in urban schools. She is the author of *Preparing Teachers for Urban Schools: Lessons from Thirty Years of School Reform* and *Urban Teaching: The Essentials*. She serves as a member of the editorial board of *New Politics* and is co-editing a book on neoliberalism's assault on teaching and teachers unions.

Index